In the Trenches

In the Trenches

Those Who Were There

Edited by
Rachel Bilton

Pen & Sword
MILITARY

First published in Great Britain in 2016 by
PEN & SWORD MILITARY
an imprint of
Pen & Sword Books Ltd
47 Church Street
Barnsley
South Yorkshire
S70 2AS

Copyright © Rachel Bilton, 2016

ISBN 978-1-47386-713-0

The right of Rachel Bilton to be identified as the author of this work has been asserted by her in accordance with the Copyright, Designs and Patents Act 1988.

A CIP catalogue record for this book is available from the British Library.

All rights reserved. No part of this book may be reproduced or transmitted in any form or by any means, electronic or mechanical including photocopying, recording or by any information storage and retrieval system, without permission from the Publisher in writing.

Typeset by Concept, Huddersfield, West Yorkshire, HD4 5JL.
Printed and bound in England by CPI Group (UK) Ltd, Croydon CR0 4YY.

Pen & Sword Books Ltd incorporates the imprints of Pen & Sword Archaeology, Atlas, Aviation, Battleground, Discovery, Family History, History, Maritime, Military, Naval, Politics, Railways, Select, Social History, Transport, True Crime, and Claymore Press, Frontline Books, Leo Cooper, Praetorian Press, Remember When, Seaforth Publishing and Wharncliffe.

For a complete list of Pen & Sword titles please contact
PEN & SWORD BOOKS LIMITED
47 Church Street, Barnsley, South Yorkshire, S70 2AS, England
E-mail: enquiries@pen-and-sword.co.uk
Website: www.pen-and-sword.co.uk

CONTENTS

List of Plates vi
The Authors viii
  1. General for a Day *by A.P.G. Vivian* 1
  2. A Human Document *by Harold Ashton* 19
  3. A First Visit to the Trenches *by Wilfrid Ewart* 23
  4. The First Gas Attack *by Antony R. Hossack* 28
  5. I Charge! *by Captain A.O. Pollard, VC, MC, DCM* 32
  6. With the Foreign Legion in Gallipoli *by Ex-Sergeant A.R. Cooper* 37
  7. Festubert – 1915 *by Mark Severn* 47
  8. The Battle of Kut *by W.J. Blackledge* 58
  9. A Personal Record *by R.H. Mottram* 66
10. Storm Over Albert *by Guy Chapman* 113
11. A City of the Dead *by Charles Douie* 119
12. At Passchendaele *by Ex-Private X* 127
13. At a Sap-Head *by David Phillips* 141
14. A Padre in Salonika *by Henry C. Day* 146
15. In Retreat *by Herbert Read* 160
16. A Battle of Monsters *by F. Mitchell* 179
17. The Advance – 1918 *by Mark Severn* 187
Index 195

LIST OF PLATES

An aerial view of the Passchendaele battlefield: a lunar landscape punctuated with shattered trees and the remains of German fortified constructions.

An earlier view of the same Passchendaele battlefield before craters filled the land.

German artillerists manoeuvring a large artillery piece during the Spring Offensive of 1918.

German stormtroops during the Kaiserchlacht of Spring 1918.

Troops resting in the remains of a shattered village.

Prisoners in March 1918. The Germans left them to make their own way back.

British troops with tanks moving up to the front in late Spring.

British artillery in 1914 during the mobile phase.

Captured German troops.

Turkish troops attacking British positions on Gallipoli.

British troops sheltering behind an above ground trench made of sandbags filled with soil.

German troops are in a temporary position that allows them to see above the parapet.

French African troops waiting to go 'over the bags' in 1915 during the Gallipoli campaign.

French troops in Gallipoli.

A French officer giving orders to French African troops before moving up to attack positions.

General Townsend, the officer in charge at Kut, with his staff.

A British soldier resting at a dugout somewhere on the Somme in 1916.

A tank moving to the front to support the attack.

A photograph showing the devastation caused by artillery on the Somme.

British troops resting after an attack somewhere on the Western Front.

The 'Leaning Virgin' at Albert.

German troops being sent back to PoW cages during a British offensive.

A German spotter plane above a British tank, partially obscured by smoke from shelling in the area.

A German tank.

The unpopular German A7V.

German troops fill a train in an attempt to return home.

British cavalry in Salonika.

Turkish troops entering the trench system in Gallipoli.

Badly wounded British soldiers guarded by German troops during the Festubert battle.

General Townshend in a car with a personal escort.

The Cloth Hall and the Cathedral, Ypres.

THE AUTHORS

Alfred Percival George Vivian (General For a Day). Vivian enlisted to the army when he was just 14 years old. He had served for seven years when the war broke out and was a Lance Corporal in the Fourth Battalion of the Middlesex Regiment. Vivian was a first class shot but because he was in charge of the stretcher section of eight men, he was not able to use his abilities. Eventually he managed to change position and became a fighting soldier. Later in the war he was commissioned into the Royal Fusiliers, later transferring to the RAF. He survived the war and wrote about his early experiences.

Harold Ashton (A Human Document). During the early months of the war Ashton, a war correspondent for *The Daily News*, toured northern France in search of news from the front lines or failing that, interesting human-interest stories regarding the war. In 1914 he published a book of his experiences, *First from the Front* from which this extract is taken. This was followed in 1916 by *Private Pinkerton, Millionaire*. Ashton was the son of a grocer in Spaldwick.

Wilfrid Ewart (A First Visit to the Trenches). First World War novelist and essayist Wilfrid Herbert Gore Ewart (1892–1922) was born on May 19, 1892. His father, Herbert Brisbane Ewart, came from a noted military family and served as comptroller to the widow of a Russian nobleman. His mother, Lady Mary 'Molly' Ewart, was of aristocratic birth, the youngest daughter of the third Earl of Arran. He was blind in one eye and had poor eyesight in the other.

Despite his bad eyesight and general poor health, Ewart joined the army in the summer of 1914. He obtained a commission, serving as a captain in the Scots Guards. During his wartime service Ewart wrote articles, sometimes pseudonymously, about the Scots Guards and combat. After the war, he published a novel, *The Way of Revelation: A Novel of Five Years* (1921), which drew on his wartime experiences. *The Way of Revelation* became a bestseller and was highly praised even at a time when readers were becoming weary of war memoirs and novels.

Having survived the First World War, Ewart met a tragic early death. Near midnight on December 31, 1922, Ewart stepped out onto his hotel balcony to observe the New Year's festivities. He was killed by a stray bullet fired by a reveller celebrating below.

Captain A.O. Pollard VC, MC, DCM (I Charge!) – Alfred Oliver Pollard was born on 4th May 1893 in Wallington, Surrey. Originally, Pollard was a clerk at an insurance company when he volunteered for service in August 1914. Despite being badly wounded twice, he returned to his unit after his recovery, showing extreme bravery. He was given the most number of awards as a solider in his unit during the war because of his immense courage, including the Victoria Cross. He later became an author of mystery and crime books.

Ex-Sergeant A.R. Cooper (With the Foreign Legion in Gallipoli). Cooper had a colourful life. Born in Baghdad in 1899 he was kidnapped at the age of 6 months by Bedouins and spent a year in the desert with them. By the age of 10 he had been rescued from wolves in Turkey, escaped an ambush by Kurdish bandits and had been shot during the Young Turks uprising. He joined the French Foreign Legion in 1914 at the age of 15 after an adventurous few years at sea. He enlisted at Algiers under the name of Cornélis Jean de Bruin and was sent to Fort St Thérèse at Oran and thence to Sidi Bel Abbès, the headquarters of the legion in Algeria. After over twelve years service he was discharged. During the Second World War he spied for Britain. He died in Britain at the age of 89.

W.J. Blackledge (The Battle of Kut). Blackledge served with the 2nd Dorsets. He wrote *The Legion of Marching Madmen* about his experiences in Mesopotamia. Born in Bolton in 1886 he was a clogger before the war. After the war he became a journalist and wrote a number of books. He died in 1948.

Ralph Hale Mottram (A Personal Record). Mottram, born 30 October 1883, was an English writer; known as a novelist, particularly for the *Spanish Farm* trilogy, for which he won the 1924 Hawthornden Prize, and as a war poet of the First World War. Mottram went from being a bank clerk in Norwich before the war to becoming lord mayor there in 1953. He enlisted in the Norfolk Regiment but was soon commissioned and sent to Flanders. Thanks to his ability to speak French he became a liaison officer behind the front line dealing with complaints about damage caused by British troops. He died on 16 April 1971.

Guy Chapman (Storm over Albert). Chapman was born in 1889 and died in 1972. He attended Christ Church at Oxford University and the LSE. During the Battle of Arras he suffered mustard gas poisoning, but recovered and returned to the western front where he served until the end of the war. He was an author, historian, professor, and editor.

Charles Douie (A City of the Dead). Douie was posted to the 1st Dorsets towards the end of 1915 when he reached the age of 19, though before reporting to them he spent a short time with an entrenching battalion. After service on the Somme and in Flanders he was detached from his battalion and was in Italy when the war finished.

Ex-Private X (Passchendaele). Ex-Private X (A.M. Burrage) was born in 1889 and died in 1956. He was a writer from a young age, following in the footsteps of his father and uncle, publishing his first story when he was only 15 years old. He was famous for his short fiction published in magazines. Burrage became a member of the Artists Rifles (28th Battalion, London Regiment) in 1917 and served until April 1918 when he was invalided with trench foot. Ex-Private X was a very fortunate man: he not only served and survived the war but managed to record his personal experiences as a private soldier, which he later published.

David Phillips (At a Sap-head). Private David Phillips enlisted on 14 September 1914. He served in England and France with the 23rd County of London Regiment. Graded C3 in 1917 he was transferred to Brigade of Guards Section, Army Pay Corps.

Henry C. Day (A Padre in Salonika). Father Henry Day was a Jesuit who had been public school educated, served as a chaplain with an elite cavalry regiment and its associated units. He wrote two books about his experiences during the war.

CHAPTER ONE

GENERAL FOR A DAY

By A.P.G. Vivian

The shelling of our position continued throughout the day, punctuated by lulls of short duration, which were very thankfully received.

The enemy infantry could only be seen by the aid of powerful glasses, and then only spasmodically, as they moved about the position they had taken up about 2,000 yards from our front. They had evidently too much respect for our powers with our rifles to venture until the artillery had blown us away and enabled them to advance at a cheaper price; consequently we did not have much to occupy our minds except to look after the wounded who, whenever opportunity offered, were taken to the rear.

We had been told, when first occupying this line, that we were to hold on to it, at all costs, until two o'clock in the afternoon. It had now passed four, and still we lingered. Certain signs were now manifest, however, which conveyed to me the impression that the overdue move was about to be executed.

At this interesting juncture I heard the particular shell, bearing my name upon it, making directly for me, its thrill cry of ecstasy as it spotted me standing out clearly from among the ordinary racket of the others.

With a last joyful shriek, it burst with wild abandon right over me, and I subsided gracefully, paying tribute to its might.

I opened my eyes slowly and gazed up into a gloriously blue sky, and then wondered suddenly who was being so spiteful as to subject my head to a brutal kicking.

I wearily thrust up my hand to act as a buffer between my sore head and those vicious blows, and then learnt that they were being directed from the inside of my head.

I withdrew my hand and stared at the crimson mess adhering to it incomprehensively for a moment, and then came remembrance.

I attempted to struggle up, but was forced by an attack of vertigo to subside. The shattering explosions of bursting shells had died away, and the air was strangely calm and still.

Again I essayed to rise, this time with more success, and gazed stupidly around.

A dejected, forlorn, khaki-clad figure stood close by me, leaning against the torn side of the trench, his head bowed down and resting on his arms, apparently sobbing bitterly.

Feeling my head gingerly, I mechanically noted that with the exception of dozens of forms lying pathetically still in queer attitudes and this man, the position was deserted.

I discovered that upon the back of my head was a deep groove running from just below the crown to the base, which was bleeding freely, accompanied by great stabbing pains. This had been done by a splinter of shell which had struck me down from directly above.

I slowly ran my hands over the other parts of my anatomy and was relieved to learn, as far as I could discover, that this constituted my sole injury. I therefore extracted my field dressing and clumsily bandaged it as well as I could manage.

I then approached the man who appeared to be the only other occupant alive, and who continued to emit what I took to be deep sobs of grief, and leant my hand encouragingly upon his shoulder.

No acknowledgement was vouchsafed until I had repeated this movement several times. Finally he raised his head, presenting a face ghastly in its paleness and painful expression, and sobbed out a desire to know what was required.

It did not take me long to learn that he was not sobbing of grief, but for breath, having been struck in the lungs.

He gaspingly informed me that he had shared that shell with me, which came just as the battalion retired. He had collapsed for a moment, and the others, obviously believing both him and I dead, had left us where we lay. I now groped my way along the trench and inspected the other occupants, and the fact that I did not find another living survivor confirmed my impression that the wounded had been carried away.

Returning to the badly stricken one I tried to soothe his pain, but my efforts were hopeless.

I remembered that a church a little to our rear had been converted into a dressing post, and with a faint hope that the doctor in charge and his staff would still be found there I assisted my companion from the trench, and directed his faltering footsteps towards this place.

Great was my joy and relief to find that it had not been abandoned.

We stepped inside and glanced around. Every inch of available space was occupied by badly wounded men, who lay on heaps of straw which had been provided to make them as comfortable as the circumstances would permit.

Busily engaged among the victims of the attack was a young officer of the Royal Army Medical Corps. Surrounded by the paraphernalia of his profession, coat removed and shirt sleeves rolled up, he swiftly, with an air of efficiency, went about his work, assisted by one medical orderly.

On our appearance this orderly came over to us and examined my companion gravely. He turned away, reappearing almost immediately with a bundle of straw which he spread on the porch and with my assistance the new patient was lowered on to this improvised bed.

The doctor was advised of this serious additional casualty, and immediately he came over and subjected him to a thorough examination. In the meantime the orderly cleansed the wound in my head and applied suitable dressings which afforded me huge relief.

Standing at the entrance of the porch, I took stock of my surroundings.

The church had been struck several times by shells, and this in spite of the fact that a huge Red Cross flag had been prominently displayed. It still hung fluttering bravely, although half the steeple to which it was affixed had been ruthlessly blown away.

Looking out over the direction of our old position, a movement in the distance caught my eye, and I saw hordes of enemy infantry, about three-quarters of a mile away, advancing in the direction of the village.

Feverishly I rushed into the improvised hospital and warned the doctor of this development. Without pausing for a moment from his work, he said: 'That does not concern me in the least, my work is here with these men. As they cannot get away the same applies to me. Don't worry about me, I shall be quite all right.'

'Then I shall try and get clear, sir!' I said. To which he replied:

'Go by all means, you can do nothing here. Good luck.'

Hurrying outside, taking advantage of all cover, I made tracks in the opposite direction to this approaching wave.

I went on unmolested for about a mile until I came to a cutting. Here a doleful sight presented itself to my gaze and arrested my progress.

The centre of the picture was held by the ruins of four guns of our Royal Field Artillery. They had caught the effects of the avalanche fully, being completely shattered, while the mutilated bodies of their faithful servants lay around, mute evidence that they had nobly executed their duty.

Two men of this battery appeared to be the sole survivors. One sat on a smashed gun trail his head bowed into his hands, moaning softly, while his comrade busied himself by collecting the identity discs of his late colleagues.

Other signs of life in the cutting were provided by three privates of my own regiment, one driver of the Army Service Corps, whose wagon had been blown practically from under him, one private of the Royal Scots, and one of the Royal Irish Regiment.

I threw myself down among these men and gloomily watched the gunner complete the sad work he had engaged himself in.

We presently all joined in an exchange of mutual conversation, until I suddenly remembered that the clouds of Germans I had seen a short time before were likely to be upon us at any moment.

I rapidly communicated my fears to the others, and I climbed to the edge of the cutting to ascertain the amount of the enemy progress. I was mortified to find that they were a scant 300-yards distance, and sliding down to my new companions without ceremony I imparted to them the disturbing knowledge I had gleaned by my brief view.

With one accord we hotfooted it away.

We rushed along under the cover of a bank until, arriving at the end, we found a small wood and dived into its shelter just as the advancing German troops defiled into the cutting we had so recently and timely evacuated.

They saw us and opened fire, to which we replied with a defiant burst before turning and scrambling, hell for leather, into the deepest part of that wood, and we continued going until exhaustion bade us stop.

We now held an impromptu conference to discuss our unenvious and perilous situation. They all looked to me as the senior ranking member of the party to decide upon our future course of action.

I was sorely exercised as to the best procedure to adopt, having no maps or any idea of the lay of the country, and only a very vague notion of the general direction of the retirement of our army. I decided that our best chance of getting away and keeping away was to lay a straight course as near as possible as the crow flies in a direct line away from the direction of the enemy's advance, taking all obstacles in our stride.

I submitted this resolution to the others, who gave it their entire approval, and having all expressed a determination to do everything in our power to resist and avoid capture we commenced what was to prove a most unusual and interesting adventure.

I was filled with pride at the brave command that had been vested in me, and felt like the whole of the Napoleons rolled into one.

Was I not the commander of a force composed not only of three different regiments, but also artillery, and a supply column as represented by our friend of the Army Service Corps.

My thoughts were pleasantly interrupted by a 'Faith, giniril, 'tis a whowl brigade your havin' here,' the disturber being our Irish friend.

'Aye! a Phantom Brigade,' contributed the Scot.

This last remark possessed a flavour pleasantly savouring of the mysterious, and so tickled everybody that we there and then elected unto ourselves this nomenclature, which made us all feel important and jolly.

Crossing fields and fences, hills and dales, we passed leisurely on our way at first, with many an anxious glance towards our rear, but gradually abandoning this watchfulness as we proceeded without interference.

Occasionally we would stumble upon a building, which we would subject to a minute search in the hope of finding something to satisfy our hunger, for we were all pretty well starving, and depended entirely on the country for our sustenance.

We, up to this time, met with no success in this line, as all the houses we struck had been abandoned and emptied of their contents.

Darkness falling, found us still blithely toiling along without interruption, except a slight incident which, at the time threatened to deprive us of our 'commissariat department'.

We were negotiating a large field in the complete darkness, spread out in line, when we were startled by the sounds of a loud splash and a despairing yell, followed by a terrible commotion and an awe-inspiring smell coming from the left of our line.

Rushing to the scene of the disturbance, we discovered the whole of our Army Service Corps floundering about in a slimy pool. With encouraging exhortations and advice to save the women and children first, the supply column was rescued from the watery and decidedly unpleasant grave into which he had unfortunately fallen.

Stationing him well to windward, we continued our advance until, on coming out of the field, we struck a road upon which stood a promising-looking building.

On examination, this proved to be a deserted estaminet which we entered silently with about the same expectations of discovering anything useful to us, in view of our former experiences, as a burglar would entertain on breaking open a gas-meter in Aberdeen.

We spread ourselves all over it, and commenced a thorough examination by the light of matches. Our first discovery was half a dozen half-consumed candles, which we found in the kitchen. Lighting these, we prosecuted our hunt for food. Some bread was next unearthed, which, judging from its condition, had been baked in prehistoric days, and had been preserved as a family heirloom.

A whoop of joy and triumph drew us back into the room that would normally have served as the bar.

Here we found a couple of the boys dancing around a barrel half filled with French beer that they had found under the counter. Without wasting any time we tapped that barrel and were just enjoying our third or fourth taster when we were almost scared stiff by the sounds of riot proceeding from some point outside the building.

Terrified cacklings, mixed with the sounds of falling and scrambled bodies, punctuated by hoarse and excited shouts of encouragement and finally victory, rent the still night air.

Two boisterous, dishevelled-looking apparitions, bursting into the room bearing the corpses of a couple of hens, amply explained the cause of this unseemly commotion.

They had directed their energies to the exploration of the outbuildings, and had surprised and captured these wretched birds.

Possessed of the material promise of a good feast, we decided to remain in the estaminet and do the thing handsomely.

Carefully screening the windows, we built a fire, and procured a couple of saucepans, into which we popped the birds and the stale bread.

We then sat around the fire as happy as sandboys, quaffing flagons of ale, and eyeing with eager anticipation the simmering pots, while waiting for the fowl to cook.

Hardship, suffering and danger were totally forgotten, and we lived only for the present as we gathered around, exchanging good-humoured banter, telling yarns, and occasionally breaking into song. We even became so foolish as to venture the opinion that War was not so bad after all.

One of the artillerymen created a humorous diversion by appearing from a cellar-like chamber wearing an old apron he had found, and a huge beard and moustache constructed from the stuffing of an old arm-chair.

Dangling a napkin over his arm he displayed proudly a bottle, three parts full of cognac, that he had unearthed, and assumed the airs and duties of a 'fully licensed man'.

The food being voted cooked and ready for consumption (this opinion being arrived at mainly because the water was boiling), we drew around a table to enjoy the banquet.

What a fine sight for starving men. We gloated over a table containing unlimited supplies of beer, some cognac, two chickens and plenty of 'soup'.

The birds, having been rudely severed into nine more or less equal portions, were handed around, and the only sounds heard for the next few minutes were the vigorous champing of jaws.

I had always laboured under the impression that 'spring chickens' were of the tenderest variety but, judging by the effort I found it necessary to make to dispose of those chicks, I formed the conclusion that, in their case, the spring part of the business had been so overdone that it had left no space available for the chicken. However, our determined onslaughts did eventually overcome them, and now, being replete, I suggested a little exercise in aid of our digestion.

Securing every receptacle capable of holding liquid, and filling them with the precious beer, the erstwhile publican regretfully resigned his self-imposed duties, and we went forth into the night, leaving the estaminet behind us, only because we recognised the impossibility of taking it along with us.

On becoming accustomed to the gloom, we oriented ourselves with regard to our direction, and continued our pilgrimage without anything happening to mar our pleasant reminiscences, until just after midnight.

At this time we were jogging along almost half asleep when we were scared into alertness by the unmistakable sounds of a body of armed men marching across the front of the direction in which we were proceeding. We were then moving along on the outskirts of a forest, and, on hearing these alarming sounds, threw ourselves flat as noiselessly as possible. Shortly afterwards a body of about 200 enemy infantry passed before us, emerging unexpectantly from the forest, along a road that cut clear through it. They passed within 50 yards of the spot wherein we lay with bated breath, and passed out of sight.

I began to fear that we would be compelled to pay for the little indulgence we had permitted ourselves at the house behind us, with the loss of our liberty, or worse.

The scare given us by the unexpected appearance of this body of the enemy, caused us to press on with greater vigour, and with additional precautions against surprises of this nature.

Dawn found us flitting like shadows through this same forest. One man out on each flank and another leading about 20 yards ahead, while the remainder of us followed him in single file.

I trudged along, wondering what fate this new day, the 27th August, held in store for us.

Mercifully the veil was drawn close, but was even at this moment on the verge of being lifted, to disclose the first of a series of shocks and surprises of a nature both pleasant and the reverse.

The leading man, reaching the side of a road passing through the forest across the line of our direction, signalled to us to halt while he scanned the road to ascertain if it was clear. Apparently satisfied that it was, he was about to emerge from cover when we saw him start at something that had impinged on his vision, and that froze him into immobility for a moment. Turning swiftly, he came towards us with a rush, and told us that there were a body of men, mounted on cycles, coming along the road in our direction.

We all crept forward and carefully scrutinised these cyclists, and soon acquired the knowledge that they were no friends of ours.

One man rode ahead, and about 50 yards in the rear followed ten others, and, as far as we could tell, they were entirely unsupported by other enemy troops.

We hastily conferred together, weighing the pros and cons of the policy of aggression against that of allowing sleeping dogs to lie. Decision was brought to our divided councils by a remark made by one of the artillery section.

He stated emphatically that, as far as he was concerned, he would as lief die as to continue to live amid the agony he was enduring from his feet, which were protesting mightily against the unusual amount of abuse put upon them by all this marching.

The idea of continuing our travels mounted on bicycles was certainly an attractive one, so without more ado, we selected positions for our intended ambuscade of the enemy.

We had the advantage of surprise in delivering our attack, which amply outweighed the enemy's slight superiority in numbers.

We decided that it was necessary to let the leading man pass us unmolested, and we waited, lying in the thick underbush that grew within a few yards of the side of the road, with palpitating hearts and stifled breath, and fingers itchingly playing with the triggers of our ready rifles, for the arrival of the fateful moment that would decide the issue.

Only a moment, a moment that seemed a period of hours, could have passed, when a creaking announced the advent of cyclist number one.

With tingling apprehension we observed him cast a glance on and over our place of concealment, but, happily for us, entirely unsuspicious of our presence, he continued forging ahead.

The main body appeared immediately after, shouting carefree remarks to one another with the accompaniment of much laughter.

With a hideous crash we slipped into action, rudely curtailing their badinage and jokes, and causing the entire force to collapse, a tangled mass of machines and men, on to the road.

For an instant the pile stilled, and then heaved convulsively again, as six survivors of that volley, most of them wounded, crawled to the opposite side of the road, and valiantly returned our fire.

Their efforts availed them nothing, for we had them at an overwhelming disadvantage, being so well concealed that they could only hazard a guess at our position from the sound of our rifle fire, while they lay fully exposed to us.

A scant few minutes, then the arm of the sole survivor shot up in token of surrender.

We immediately concentrated our attention to our flank, where the first cyclist was busy trying to rake us from that direction. On the outbreak of the firing he had gallantly returned to the scene of action to render all possible aid to his comrades. Seeing the annihilation of his troop, and realising that to continue his resistance was useless, he quickly followed the example set by his compatriot and surrendered.

We carefully left our positions and approached the unfortunate victims, making a careful and comprehensive survey of the road in each direction, without seeing anything to cause us undue alarm.

We gathered together our prisoners, fastened them together with straps taken from their equipment, and sat them back to back in the ditch beside the road.

We then attentively examined the fruits of our victory, which we had gained without suffering a scratch, so complete had been our surprise.

The bicycles were efficient-looking machines, heavy and strongly made, and we each selected one, with the exception of our Irishman, who we discovered, to our consternation, did not know how to ride.

However, each cycle was equipped with a serviceable-looking carrier behind, and we decided to take turns in giving him a lift, and in this manner solved this unexpected difficulty.

All being ready, I gave the order to mount and away, as it obviously would have been an exhibition of extremely bad tactics to have remained longer than necessary in the quarter in which we had so well advertised our presence.

We started off, taking the same direction in which the German patrol was travelling before our interruption, and I became considerably concerned by a worrying little question that cropped up: 'Were they going or coming?'

No satisfactory answer seemed forthcoming to the anxious query, and I began to weigh the possibilities that the possession of the bicycles would do us more harm than service, and had almost made up my mind to discard them, and to proceed along our original line on foot, when my anxiety was relieved by the discovery of an intersecting road that led away at right angles, in the very direction I deemed it advisable to pursue.

We changed our course and took this turning, and could see that the road led as straight as a ruled line through the forest, until, at a distance of about half a mile away, it emerged into open country beyond. We pedalled hastily down this avenue, casting fearful glances into the forest looming forbiddingly on either side of us, as we proceeded, expecting momentarily to hear from their depths the peal of fire which would, in turn, end our misguided careers.

On reaching the end of the road unscathed, an occurrence that evoked our hearty expressions of mutual congratulation, we halted, and before exposing ourselves in the open, made a close and careful reconnaissance of the country for signs of the foe.

Finding the beauty of the landscape unmarred by any such nasty sights, we remounted and continued to sail easily along. This mode of procession certainly had 'foot-slogging' beaten to nowhere, ensuring a nice, speedy, comfortable means of travel, and we felicitated each other upon the sound common sense displayed in engaging in the action that had been the means of securing these iron steeds to us.

Moving quickly and happily, we reached the summit of a hill, and finding that from this eminence we commanded a clear view of the surrounding country for at least a mile in every direction, we again subjected every inch to a very careful scrutiny, with a negative result that gave us much satisfaction.

Freed from any danger of sudden surprise and attack, I decided to call a halt for a much-needed rest. This decision was greeted with the utmost enthusiasm.

We now found leisure to devote more attention to our captures.

Each one had a bulky leather satchel strapped to the crossbar of the frame, which we removed and sat down to examine.

I opened mine and looked in, and the contents projected into my vision by this action caused me to gasp in amazed surprise, for it was almost filled with articles of silver.

Delving into the bag, I removed dozens of solid silver knives, forks and spoons, and also two beautifully-chased silver mugs, but the things that really appealed to me more than any other I found at the very bottom.

A bottle of wine, a large hunk of bread, some butter, and a tin of potted meat.

The air was full of exclamations of wonder, as the others pawed over the articles found in the bags that had fallen to their lot. Watches, bracelets, and silverware of every description, lay strewn all over the grass where we sat. Those Huns had collected the entire contents of some unfortunate silversmith's shop.

As my companions caught sight of the real treasures yielded by my bag they promptly forgot the silverware, and concentrated on the interior of their bags in a frenzied hope of making a discovery of equal importance to mine in the form of food, with great success, to everybody's comfort.

We regaled ourselves upon this abundance of good food and drink, until we had sated our appetites, and, after drawing lots to select a sentry, we settled down to enjoy an hour's nap. We were awakened by our look-out at the end of the hour, and, with the country still bathed in tranquillity, we hopped on to our steeds and pushed away along the trail that would, we fondly hoped, eventually lead us to safety.

The fact that we had not caught up to our own army perturbed me mightily, for we had been travelling constantly for the last twenty-four hours with scarcely a stop, and we must have covered, with the aid of both our bicycles and our feet, between 25 and 30 miles of ground.

I could not understand this phenomenon at the time, but was considerably amused, and more or less amazed at our extraordinary good fortune in evading capture, on learning later the reason for our failure to make contact.

We had marched on a line that proceeded diagonally so faithfully that it had kept us the whole time mid-way between our retreating army and the advancing German forces.

We had covered about 5 miles since last halting, and were half-way up the slope of a small hill, when we were surprised by the thunderous sounds of charging horses' feet coming behind us.

A glance around filled us with consternation, as we beheld a band of at least thirty Uhlans charging down, with wild hoops, upon us.

We leapt from our machines, and sprang for the only possible positions of temporary safety, automatically. This was the top of a bank about 10 feet high that bounded the road upon one side at this point. They came so near getting us that my rifle was, for a moment, imprisoned, as the point of a lance went between the sling and the barrel, pinning it to the side of the incline as I drew myself clear over the top of the embankment.

Dashing past us, impelled by the momentum of their vicious onslaught, they presented to us the splendid target of their backs, an opportunity of which we took such good advantage that their ardour became suddenly checked.

Dismounting from their chargers, they proceeded to continue their attack upon us on foot, some of them climbing out on the bank higher up above us, and subjecting us to a worrying fire, whilst others engaged us from the road below.

We soon learned, with great dismay, that another portion of this enemy party had worked down the road and had mounted the bank below us, and had opened a harassing fire upon us.

We were, by these tactics, practically surrounded, and any attempt at escape rendered impossible.

We had been extremely lucky so far, but we all entertained the feeling that such good fortune could not possibly last, and was bound to end sometime. Now it had arrived, for we had not an earthly chance against the odds facing us.

Grimly we fought on in desperation, expecting every moment to see the end of the farce.

Four of our party were struck, fortunately not seriously enough to place them *hors de combat*, and we started to bid each other a fond farewell.

At my side, which was near the edge of the top of the bank, I became aware of a scrambling, and turned to see the heads of half a dozen of the enemy mounting over the top. Shouting for assistance, I desperately engaged this new menace with the bayonet. Three or four others sprang to my succour, and we madly stabbed and thrust in an effort to keep our fate at bay.

When all hope had fled, more sounds of charging horses became audible above the clash of arms, and with a mad cheer a troop of British cavalry swept into view, scattering our attackers like chaff.

Nearly fainting with exhaustion and excitement, we did our best to assist our rescuers in their task of subjugating the enemy, with such success that he was put to flight, leaving us victorious on the field.

Our cavalrymen returning with seven unwounded prisoners, we hastened to pay our respects and gratitude for their timely deliverance of us from our very awkward predicament.

Our saviours were a lancer patrol consisting of twenty-odd men under the command of a sergeant.

We examined the battlefield, on which we found lying six enemy dead and eight wounded.

The sergeant imparted to us the good news that we were quite close to our own army, which lay on a course at right angles to the one we had been pursuing.

It was then that I learned that we had been travelling parallel between the two armies.

Receiving concise directions as to the route to be followed to reach our objective, we left the troop, happy and relieved in the knowledge that we were in contact with our forces at last, and with a prayer of thanksgiving for the successful issue from the attempt the enemy had made to nip our gay careers in the bud.

We repaired to our bicycles, and on rescuing them from the spot on which they had been hurriedly thrown, we found that they had all, more or less, suffered damage by being trampled upon. This ill-usage had put three of them out of commission.

We managed quite well, and, carefully following the instruction we had received to guide us on our route, we careered along, four of the machines being doubly burdened, until our progress was arrested by a river.

The bridge that had once afforded the means of crossing had been blown clean away. We could not gauge the depth of the river, so our Army Service Corps detail volunteered to strip and try it out. He was very fond of water, that chap.

Undressing, he dived in, and we soon learnt that, at its deepest, it was no more than 5 feet.

With one accord, on acquiring this information, we followed his example and stripped.

First we gathered our clothing into bundles, and, holding them well out of the water upon our heads, ferried them across to the other side. Returning, we performed like offices for our arms, equipment and bicycles.

The feel of water, after being strangers to it so long, was glorious, and as soon as we had moved everything over, we could not resist the temptation to turn back and revel in the refreshing caress of that river.

We dived and splashed and romped about, and enjoyed ourselves like a lot of kids, entirely without care or thought of danger.

Utilising a rolled-up puttee as a ball, we indulged in a strenuous game of water polo for some time.

Eventually, tiring of this sport, we scrambled out and resumed our clothing.

The bandage about my head had now come off, and I was amazed at the rapid rate of progress toward recovery the wound was making. With the assistance of one of my comrades it was rebound, and we all carried on up the hill, running from the river, until we arrived at the crest, about 300 yards distance from the scene of our aquatic exploits.

Arriving at this eyrie, we glanced out over the farther side, where we saw the welcome spectacle of the British Army apparently very busy preparing positions of defence 500 or 600 yards away.

Now that we were well within sight of our long-sought goal, we decided that there was no immediate need to join them, or it would be far better to remain where we were until they had finished digging, so that there would be no danger of us running into that kind of thing.

Service in a freelance army was much more acceptable than the other, we unanimously agreed; and we decided that, as we were now perfectly secure, we would preserve our independence a while longer, and rest where we were.

There we lay, like storm-battered sea-dogs resting in the calm and safety of the harbour.

We freely discussed the War in all the phases we had experienced, and concluded that although there were occasional bright spots, they were few and far between, and the horrors rendered the very small amount of glory very insignificant by comparison. As one of the London lads put it: 'The blokes what makes such a shout about the glory to be found in War must have got their ideas in the Salvation Army.'

One of our number, foraging about, now captured a hedgehog, which he brought back to the circle with him. Here, with a very business-like air, he produced his knife and killed it. I was rather surprised at this brutal and wanton action, and I asked him why he had done it.

'Ter eat, o' course,' he replied, smacking his lips and evincing signs of anticipation of gastronomic pleasure.

The body of the little beast was enclosed in a ball of clay. A fire was kindled and the ball placed in it and covered over. The remainder sat around watching these proceedings with great interest, not unmixed with repulsion at the thought of anybody eating such a thing.

Presently, the ball having cracked open through the effects of the heat, our gourmet removed it, and, breaking it in half, exposed to our view the steaming carcass of the hedgehog, devoid of all its bristles, which had been left imprisoned in the clay.

The result was a tasty-looking and pleasant smelling morsel.

He handed this product of his culinary prowess around, permitting each of us to take one small pinch by way of a taster, and, as he put it, to teach us to refrain from sneering at the knowledge possessed by our betters.

It proved extremely succulent and delicious, and we sat around him, enviously watching him with watering mouths, like a crowd of expectant hounds, as he consumed the remainder with aggravating noises of profound enjoyment and satisfaction.

A startled tirade by our Irishman jerked us out of the state of somnolence into which we had drifted.

'Be the holy saints, the blackguards we've just been after killing are not dead at all, for there comes ivery wan uv them.'

Following the direction of his outstretched finger, we saw, with great concern, numerous bodies of enemy infantry approaching the river from the other side.

We had foolishly imagined them to be many miles away, and now here they were again almost on top of us. That supplied the reason for the vigorous defensive preparations being executed by the British troops in our rear; they were expecting these visitors, if we were not.

We remembered that we had the unbridged river between us, so we decided to stay a while and keep observation upon them for as long as possible. Our rear was quite clear, and on our bicycles, on the good road running downhill to the positions behind us, we could rapidly cover the distance intervening between us and safety.

We therefore proceeded to view the movements of these troops with the greatest interest.

Snuggled down out of sight, closely, we saw the vanguard of the enemy reach the side of the river, where they prowled restlessly up and down, obviously looking for some means by which they could cross, throwing glances, fraught with apprehension, in our general direction, although I am certain they were not aware of our nearness.

Finding that no bridges existed in the immediate neighbourhood, they apparently decided to cross in the same manner previously adopted by us. They reluctantly stripped themselves of their clothing, stepped gingerly into the river, and, holding their coverings above their heads, commenced to wade across.

We lay watching this manoeuvre with glistening eyes, rooted to the spot by fascination.

Quite a crowd of German troops had by this time assembled on the opposite bank, and on seeing their advance guard arrive safely across, they commenced to hastily undress and follow suit.

Soon both banks were covered by men in all stages of undress, those on the side nearest us in the process of dressing, and those on the other side busy disrobing, while the river swarmed with naked men wading slowly across.

This opportunity was too good to miss, and proved fatal to our resolutions, based on sound common sense, to lay low and say nothing.

I glanced at the other lads and found them all wearing expressions that undoubtedly pleaded for immediate action, and so I rapped out: 'Let 'em have it!' And we did, putting all our finest workmanship into the burst of rapid fire that we poured into that mob, instilling them with indescribable fear and panic.

Those left standing on our side of the river plunged, just as they were, back into the stream. The men on the other side attempted a retreat, presenting a spectacle that filled our eyes with the tears of laughter. Some floundered helplessly and comically as their trousers, hanging down around their ankles, tripped them as they ran. Others, wearing but their shirts, ran with the tails of these garments streaming out behind them fluttering in the strong breeze created by the speed of their going. Yet others pranced about naked as the day on which they were born.

We gurgled and choked with laughter as we sprayed their bare hides with lead, only ceasing to pour out our deadly hail sufficiently long enough to enable us to clear our eyes of the tears that were blinding them.

Fully clothed reinforcements appeared and engaged us viciously in an attempt to wipe out the indignity that had been inflicted upon the Kaiser's soldiers.

Possessed of the slightest atom of sense, I would have ordered a retirement at this juncture, but, being over-ruled by the influence of a pervading spirit of invincibility, I chose to continue the action, being strengthened in this resolve by the sight of lines of our troops advancing from the positions in rear towards the scene, attracted by the sounds of our engagement.

Passing the word along to await the arrival of these troops, we cheerfully continued our defiance.

I was thrusting a clip of cartridges into the chamber of my rifle when suddenly, for some unaccountable reason, the arm performing this operation attempted to fly away from me. Jerking it back to ascertain the cause, I discovered that a stream of blood was spurting gaily from either side of my right wrist, where it had been shot clean through by a bullet.

Three of the others received slight wounds at about the same instant, and I strongly suspect that it was the work of a machine gun. I therefore issued an order to slip back a bit, and take advantage of the cover to be found a little lower down the ridge.

I foolishly stood up to retreat, and had not gone two paces before I was again struck, in the right heel. Almost at the same moment I heard my second exclusive visitor from the Boche artillery winging its airy way towards me. I heard its progress right up to the moment that it seemed to poise gracefully above me and burst. Several tons seemed to fall on my right shoulder and thrust me clean through the ground.

I returned to consciousness with a feeling that the whole of my right side had been torn away and replaced by a painful and aching void.

I felt slowly about me and found that on the top of my right shoulder existed a torn and gaping hole, while every attempt to draw breath was accompanied by agony untold, and blood frothingly (*sic.*) oozed from my mouth and nostrils.

I guessed that this was the end, for I knew that in addition to the other minor injuries inflicted, they had got me in the lungs.

It was now quite dark and I could see nothing, but my ears caught the sound of retreating troops, which I knew to be British, as I caught scraps of their conversation. They were evidently the troops I had seen coming up to us from the position behind.

I essayed a shout, which only resulted in a frothy burbling and a nerve-tearing pain in my chest.

I fell to musing on the fate of my late merry command of the 'Phantom Brigade', none of whom I have ever seen again to this day, and in conning over our foolishness in neglecting to move to safety when the occasion offered.

An absurd ballad of sentimental rubbish persisted in claiming the attention of my thoughts. I had often heard it produced in the canteen by drunken soldiers in the last stage of maudlin sentimentality, and now its cheerful refrain kept running through my head:

> Just tike the news to muvver
> An' tell 'er that I luv 'er
> Tell 'er not ter wite fer me
> For I'm not a'comin' 'ome.

Finally, driven in desperation by the uninspiring pictures conjured up by this imaginary dirge to frenzied endeavours, I decided that if I was to die it would be far more desirable if that interesting little event should happen whilst I was keeping my mind actively employed on an attempt to reach the main body. There certainly was no sense lying there alone with my morbid thoughts.

Transforming my resolution into action, I started off with set teeth, painfully dragging my agonised body over the rough and pitiless ground.

I seemed to crawl in this manner for ages, every move a damnable torture, slipping often into unconsciousness through exhaustion and loss of blood and the excruciating agony caused by the movements.

Eventually, as the grey light of the 28th August was paling the sky, I arrived, crawling on my hands and knees, which were now hanging ribands, within hailing distance of the objective towards which I had struggled so painfully through the night.

In my anxiety I attempted to draw the attention of the defenders of the position to my presence and plight by delivering a mighty shout. This effort proved too much for my torn lung to stand, and caused me so much agony that I swooned.

I opened my eyes and stared into the heavens, and lay wondering dully at the pains that gnawed at me in every part of my body, and at the awful noise raging in my vicinity.

Gradually recovering, I began to remember the events of the night before, and eventually traced them up to the time I had collapsed at the very threshold of my desire.

I tried several times to rise, but was forced to desist, to relieve the agony in my stiffened wounds.

Finally, however, by a stupendous and agonising effort, I was at last able to draw myself up sufficiently to permit me to glance about.

Behind me on the hill that had witnessed me receive my *conge* the enemy infantry were in force. I could not observe any signs of activity on the part of the occupants of the British position on my immediate front, about which shells were still falling spasmodically, and I was afraid to shout because of the intense suffering it had inflicted upon me in my previous attempt.

Struggling frantically, I wriggled my way forward towards this position, until I finally tumbled over the edge on to some corpses lying in the bottom of the trench.

I had recovered consciousness just a few minutes too late to obtain any succour and relief as it was obvious that this position had been very recently evacuated, and I saw British troops disappearing in the distance at the other side of a small hamlet that stood about 300 yards in the rear.

Dispirited, I almost surrendered myself to the inevitable, but happening to glance along towards my flank, I was considerably encouraged to see one of our guns a short distance away on the other side of a road that ran back into a hamlet very much in action, being served by four or five men.

I gave a last look around the trench I was in which was for the greater part obliterated, and contained a great number of its original bold defenders, now for ever rendered helpless.

The troops that had been holding this position had suffered enormously.

I heaved myself out of that trench and crawled along towards the hamlet, hugging a shallow ditch that ran alongside the road.

Still the lone gun on my right was being frantically worked by those British artillerymen, sending out a shower of shells towards the enemy with a fine show and spirit of unconquerable defiance.

I reached the hamlet, which was deserted, and crawled through it; shells were dropping about it, which filled me now with terror, as I could only progress at a snail's pace on my lacerated hands and knees.

I managed to work through the hamlet, and, arriving out at the opposite side, I found myself confronted by three branching roads. As I knelt there, trying to make up my mind which one to follow, the sun went out, and I passed away for the third time, outraged nature's protest against the awful abuse she was being subjected to.

My next awakening was distinctly rude. I became semiconscious, and lay with my eyes closed, a prey to the most serious misgivings. My body felt as though it was being kicked and stabbed all over.

It suddenly flashed upon me that I was lying surrounded by Germans, who were fiendishly kicking, and bayoneting my poor wrecked body.

'You filthy, bloody swine,' I muttered, 'stop throwing me about, and end it.'

'Hullo, me dear, so you'm not dead then, no, not be long chalks, to my way o' thinkin'.'

Like music from Heaven that West County dialect penetrated my sorely bemused senses and brought my eyes open with a snap.

I gazed up into a pair of steady eyes, twinkling with humour, and encouragement, set in a rugged, homely face, a face that perhaps only a mother would be proud of, but to me by far the sweetest face I'd e'er gazed on, surmounted by a khaki cap bearing a badge that has since held a prominent place in my affections.

Clasped safely in the arms of this benevolent giant, I was being borne along on the limber of a field gun. Hence the sensations of being tossed about, and pain that had assailed me on my return to consciousness.

This proved to be the very gun that had excited my admiration by its devotion to duty at the hamlet outside which I had experienced my last collapse.

My new-found Samaritan helped me into an upright position, and, as I clung to the wildly swaying vehicle, attempted to wash my wounds, using the contents of his water-bottle, and then to bandage them. He succeeded after a fashion, which brought me a great deal of relief.

He then imparted to me the story of my rescue.

The gun, manned by a sergeant and four men, had been in action since daybreak that morning, and they had all sworn to stick where they were until their last shell had been exhausted. In their great endeavour they had been on the verge of capture, or destruction, and the last shots were fired at point-blank range into the ranks of the enemy infantry as they closed upon their prey, creating frightful havoc among them.

Their oath fulfilled, with their last shell gone, in the very face of the enemy they limbered up their gun and galloped furiously away.

Dashing through the village, exposed to a perfect tornado of shot, the leading driver had discovered my bleeding and unconscious form lying across and blocking the road. Finding that it would be impossible to pass without riding over me, he, not being able to bear the thought of committing, to his mind, such an irreverent act, although fully convinced that I was dead, pulled up his horses and shouted out a request for somebody to move me out of the way.

My gunner friend had jumped off the limber and approached me to comply with this request. He discovered, to his surprise, when he lifted me to place me clear, that I was alive. He thereupon bore me in his arms to the gun, and away we all continued, the whole of this incident occurring amid a terrific fire that was being directed upon them by the mortified enemy.

In time we caught up with our troops, and passed through their line.

Immediately we had attained this temporary security, the horses were slowed down to a walk, for which I was extremely grateful, as it relieved my aches and pains enormously, and assisted my wounds to stop bleeding.

We jogged along, the sergeant making frequent inquiries in the hope of ascertaining the whereabouts of the division to which he was attached and of securing further supplies of ammunition.

Eventually a motor ambulance came along and my rescuers hailed it. I transferred myself to it from the gun that had been my haven of refuge, and with deep and grateful thanks I bade these gallant artillerymen farewell.

In the ambulance was an orderly of the Royal Army Medical Corps, who immediately busied himself by giving my wounds some much-needed professional attention. When this was done I was given some beef tea, and, lying more comfortably than I had dreamed would be possible a few hours before, I gave up the dying idea and surrendered myself to sleep.

This was first broken when I was transferred to a train of cattle trucks, fully occupied by hundreds of wounded, who were lying about the bare floor of the wagons.

Every time that the train stopped or started we were subjected to a hellish torture as each truck bumped or crushed into another, causing the air to resound with frightful cries of agony from the poor devils most badly wounded.

We, in our wretched train, arrived at Rouen, and were taken into a temporary hospital, and put immediately to bed, of which I took the fullest advantage by straightway relapsing into slumber, for I had a terrible amount of leeway to pull up in that line.

I next awoke, roused by a voice asking if I would like to go to England, to see a cheerful, smiling doctor standing at the foot of my cot. He directed an orderly to hand me my clothes, and I sprang out of bed with the intention of getting into them, and fell prone and unconscious on to my face.

I next recovered to a gentle, swaying movement that puzzled me greatly for a moment, until I saw a sailor busy doing a kindly act with a bucket and a mop.

We arrived at Southampton, and as I lay on a stretcher on the quayside, crowds thronged around in admiration and pity.

I wanted neither of these. I wanted a good cigarette, and presently I was showered with them. I took one and nearly died, for I had forgotten my lung. My smoking days were over for some time to come.

Later on, when in a train, I had the curiosity to ask somebody whither we were bound, and to my delight he answered: 'Plymouth'.

Arriving at Plymouth on September 3rd, 1914, I had thus seen the world, both heaven and the deepest depths of hell, an experience which had changed for ever my outlook on life in the short space of twenty-eight days. I became an inmate of the first temporary hospital at the Salisbury Road Schools, Plymouth.

One of the most indefatigable workers in the cause of our comfort was Lady Astor, who was affectionately known among us as 'Nancy,' and to whom I now record my thanks.

Having been made comfortable in hospital I became concerned for the welfare of my young brother. I was exceedingly worried about him, and fervently prayed that he had escaped the awful fate that had overtaken so many of my stalwart comrades.

My mind was eased on this score by the receipt of a letter from my parents. From this I learned that he had also arrived safely in England, having been wounded a few days after I had received my *conge* and that he was in a fair way towards recovery.

I conclude this story, holding fond thoughts of that gallant body of adventurers it was my high honour to command as Lance-Corporal, Acting Brigadier-General, entirely unofficially and decidedly unpaid – 'The Phantom Brigade' – and, finally, by rising to salute the memory of five gallant and unknown gentlemen of the Royal Field Artillery.

CHAPTER TWO

A HUMAN DOCUMENT

By Harold Ashton

One warm, thirsty afternoon found me wandering aimlessly along the empty, dusty 'High Street' of the small village of Crécy-en-Brie. Most of the houses here, as in other villages round about, were shuttered and desolate. The street was littered with rubbish. Half-starved woebegone cats lay in the sun, sleeping in pitiable attitudes of dejection. Presently an English Tommy, a hefty curly-headed chap, with his forage cap stuck jauntily on the back of his head, came along out of an alley-way carrying a French baby on his broad shoulder – talking British nonsense to the wide-eyed brat.

'Hallo!' said he, 'you're British! Glory Hallelujah! Come to the Green Dragon – that's the English for the bloomin' pub down the street – the only place in this God-forsaken hole where you can get a tiddley; and that nothing but rum. But not so bad!'

He piloted me to the Dragon Vert, and there, squatting on a bench in the little sanded bar-parlour, we found six other khaki fighting men of the Fourth Ammunition Column, Third Section, Royal Field Artillery. They had a camp of spare battery horses out amid the trees at the other end of the village; they had wandered aimlessly across the country from the coast with what they called their 'spare-parts.'

'Rotten business,' said my friend, when he had set the baby down at the Green Dragon's hospitable door, and told it to toddle home. 'Rotten business. All graft and no glory.'

'No fighting?' I asked.

'Lord, yes; any amount. Hot as blazes too. But we had a dam'd sight too much to do in looking after our 'orses to be able to enjoy the scrappin' properly. Our attention was took off the business. Our string of thorobreds – thorobreds, I *don't* think – took colic, and took it bad. And what with looking after their stummicks, pore beggars, and writin' up my diary which I'd promised the missus faithful I'd do, I've had no time for anything else, so to speak.' He unbuttoned the flap of the breast pocket of his tunic and pulled out a penny washing-book.

'If you'd like to cast your optic through it, sir, you're welcome.'

I not only cast my optic through it; I found it a document so human that I craved Driver Thatcher's permission to copy it out.

'There ain't time, sir. There's stacks and stacks of it – Gawd knows the time it took me to write it all out. But I'll read it to you, if you like, so as you can get the hang of it. I've got to go and water the 'orses in half an hour ...'

So he read it out, word for word, with all the pride of authorship shining in his honest, smudgy face. Here it is. I would not alter a line or word of it for worlds. It tells, with sublime nonchalance, of the worries and troubles of Driver Thatcher, Royal Field Artillery, during that tantalising time when his string of spare-parts took the colic. That was all he cared about.

Hell was thundering about his ears, shells were screaming, death riding riot. Driver Thatcher brushes all that away with impatience. How to stop that dam'd colic ... that's the thing that matters.

> Troops moving toward France. Well, we started off from Hendon ..., to entrain at Park Royal, and we got to Southampton about two o'clock next morning. Got horses on board all right, though the friskiest of them kicked a lot ... Got to Havre safe. Good passage and quick. My little lot camped in a village outside the town. Nice little house us four had, but the back premises was rather stinky. They mostly are in this country. Food good – rabbit and potatoes and plenty of beer, not our English sort, but the colour of cyder. Us four enjoyed ourselves with the family, and had a good time, and left ten o'clock next day well filled up.
>
> Our objective was a place called Compiègne, on the Ouse. We marched off from Ham Somme about seven o'clock on the 25th; left three dead horses lying on the road. We got through all right, watering our horses on the way from pumps and taps at private houses. The people were awful kind, giving us quantities of pears, and filling our water-bottles with beer.
>
> That was all right. Our welcome was splendid everywhere. The people in the houses came out and cheered and gave us plain chocolate, fruit, and beer, and several other items.
>
> At Compiègne we got into touch with the Germans. Very hot work. All our guns in action all round, and the people of the villages flocking in a pannick towards Paris. It made us feel downhearted what we saw here.
>
> We marched from Compiègne about eleven o'clock on the 30th, which was Sunday. Our way was through a pretty little village, where the people tore down the heavy laden branches of the damson trees and sent us off munching the fruit and very cheerful. The way was hard. Terrible steep hills, which knocked our older and weaker horses. Collick (colic) broke out among them, too, and that was bad. We lost a good many and had to leave them dead or dying alongside of the road.
>
> We got within six hours of Paris when the Germans surprised us and drove us back. We skooted quick and dodged them in the dark until one o'clock in the morning, when we lay on the roadside, men and horses together, fagged out. Slept until 5.00am and then marched on again, still retreating. Hot as hell it was. Nothing to eat or drink. Plenty of tea, but nothing to boil it with. At last we got some dry biscuits and some tins of marmalade. Bill Thomson,

whose teeth were bad, went near mad with toothache after the jam. But toothache is better than starvation, anyway ...

We marched through Ralentir and Pierreponds. ...

[*Note*: Though Mr Thatcher is very careful to note down names and dates, it is not to be wondered that he occasionally makes little slips, due more, perhaps, to ignorance of the puzzling French language than anything else. 'Ralentir', which he mentions here is, of course, no town at all; signposts bearing that word are to be met with along most of the main roads. 'Ralentir' is a warning to motorists that there is danger ahead. It means, literally, 'go slow.']

Food on the way – apples and water. Now we make our way through the woods toward the ferry. No dead horses, thank God, to-day. I hope we have checked that – collick, but my horse fell into a ditch going through the wood and could not get out for over an hour. I couldn't go for help, because the Germans had got the range of the place and their shells were ripping overhead like blazes.

Poor old Dick (the horse), he was that fagged out by the long march. At last I got him out and went on, and by luck managed to pick up my pals.

The woods were 23 miles long. We thought we should never get out – they seemed everlasting. It was night and moonshine when we at last got to Satiness Satuern (?).

We are all stoney broke, having had no money since we left Southampton, which seems years and years.

At 4.00am next morning we got to Reary and right into the middle of it, with our tired horses and us tireder still – nothing to eat and dry as bones. The Germans were lambing in at us with their artillery, and poor old Dick got blowed up. I thank God I wasn't on him just then...

Half the horses of L Battery, Royal Artillery, got smashed, and we had to bung in our poor old tired ones to fill up. Only a few gunners were left, but they stood by firing on still and singing 'Onwards, Christian Soldgiers (*sic*.).' Then the Germans charged, and our gunners did a bunk, but not before they had drove spikes into the guns so as to make them useless to the enemy. They said they guessed they would get them back in a day or two, and if they did they could repair them easy enough. The Germans don't know these tricks, and we can do them down any time.

September 1. The battle still going on very fierce ... (No more is said about the fight, for 'collick' among the horses has again broken out, and our gallant driver is much more troubled at that, and the job he has in stopping it, than the actual fighting.)

September 2. More fighting and worser than ever. I don't believe we shall ever get to Paris ... Now we come to Montagny, and lighting all the time. Rabbitts (*sic*.) and apples to eat gallore, but still no money, and no good if we had, because we carn't spend it. We've got nothing to smoke, so we are not 'alf happy, I don't think! We have also captured a lot of German horses, mostly officers' chargers, which have galloped into our lines. I supposes the officers are corpses. I stopped one, and found a yellow packet of French cigars in one of the saddlebags. It wasn't half all right, I tell you.

September 3. We progressed this day 4 miles in twelve hours. Took the wrong road, and had to crawl about the woods on our stummoks (*sic.*) like snakes to dodge the German snipers. We had one rifle between four of us, and took it in turns to have goes. We shot one blighter and took another prisoner. They was both half-starved and covered with soars. Then the rifle jammed and we had nothing to defend ourselves with.

At last we found the main body again. They wanted more horses, and we were just bringing them up and putting them to the guns when a German areyplane (*sic.*) came over us and flue (*sic.*) round pretty low. The troops tried to fetch him down, and some bullets went through the wings, but then he got too high. We were still letting go at him from the low trees where we was laying when we suddenly found out his game. He got up higher and dropped a bomb in the middle of us, but it exploded very weak and nobody was hurt.

Next day we started on a night march, and got to Lagny Thorigny, and camped outside the town, where the people fed us on rabbits again. I said I was sick of rabbits, and me and Bill Thompson walked acrost (*sic.*) to a farm-house and borrowed three chickens, which we cooked. It was fine. They wasn't tuff as you might expect, because Bill knowed the dodge. If you kill a chicken and cook it straight away before it is cold, it is as tender as anythink. Bill knows a lot of dodges like that, and he is a useful chap to be with on the march. At Lagny Thorigny we heard good news and found that the guns of the L Battery had been taken back from the Germans by the Thirty-second Brigade Royal Field Artillery.

Outside Lagny there was more fierce fighting – 20 miles of it – and the Germans were shot down like birds. We got in another hot corner, and managed to get out just in time, after mending the L Battery guns, which had been spiked by our chaps two minutes before the Germans collared them. We had just left our camp and some wagons there, when the German shells fell into it and blew it all to bits.

September 3 (continued). Firing is still going on, but it is not so fierce, though scouts have come in and told us there are 10,000 Germans round us this day. To-night I got two ounces of Navy Cut. It was prime.

September 4. We marched from camp at 5.30pm and kept on marching until three in the morning...

September 8. We are marching on farther away from Paris. We shall never get there, I guess. And no more will the Germans if me and Bill knows anythink.

September 11. Marching to Crécy. Passing hundreds of bodies lying about like rotten sheep. We are behind the main army now, but can hear the guns going.

September 12. In the village of Crécy. Plenty of food and houses to sleep in. Here we have got to stay until further orders. Collick still very bad. But, the rum at the publick (*sic.*) house very good. I hope it will last our time.'

Here, for the time, I will leave Driver Thatcher, of the Royal Field Artillery, and Bill Thompson, that crafty borrower of chickens, and the rest of these careless Wanderers of war, who love their horses beyond all things, and do not care a jot for screaming shell and battering shrapnel so long as their 'spare-parts' are snug and safe and well out of the way of the racket.

We shake hands on the well-worn doorstep of the Green Dragon; Mr Thatcher carefully buttons the flap of his pocket over his precious washing-book.

'Cheer-o!' says he.

CHAPTER THREE

A FIRST VISIT TO THE TRENCHES

By Wilfrid Ewart

The morning of February 23rd, 1915, breaks cold and misty. Picture to yourself my billet, a dilapidated farmhouse by the roadside, which seems to be in the centre of a wide plain. Everything is very dirty – that is the first impression. The farm buildings, as always in this country, are grouped around a square courtyard with a midden in the centre – a midden that reeks of damp manure. Everywhere mud, slush and water, ankle deep. In the farmhouse itself two rooms are habitable – the one a kitchen containing a table, a number of boxes (used as chairs) and a cooking fire, usually struggling for existence on the hearth; the other, a rather smaller apartment with a brick floor, which is lived and slept in by the two company officers. One must confess it is a cheerless room. There is barely space for a table and a couple of broken chairs. The window, which looks out across the road to a vista of plough land, willows, and flat, dreary fields, has lost several of its panes, which are made good by rather inadequate sheets of brown paper. The walls are peeling from chilling dampness. There is no room for a fire here. To get and keep warm one has to stay in the kitchen, where with the servants one crouches round the struggling flame.

In barns and outhouses, whose interstices and gaps are numerous, the men are billeted. Behind the farm is a very water-logged orchard which is used as a parade ground. So deep, clinging and sticky is the mud that everywhere one has the greatest difficulty in moving about.

Such are the Brigade reserve billets, a little over a mile behind the trenches, which are occupied for four days. The Battalion, having come out of the firing-line two nights before, is due to go in again two nights hence, after which it returns to what are known as Divisional or 'rest' billets some 2.5 miles farther back.

After a breakfast consisting of porridge, bacon and poached eggs, bread, butter and marmalade, we go out on parade. To an eye accustomed to the niceties of King's Guard and soldiering in London, the men appear war-worn, variegated and ragged. What else is to be expected? Their khaki, clean and free from mud though it is, has turned many different shades of colour, so has the equipment. The caps are in many cases different, some men wearing woollen sleeping caps, others the regulation head-gear. These were the days before steel-helmets, and regulation caps were not always easy to obtain. But, considering the vicissitudes to which their clothing is subjected, the men (of whom it is always expected that they shall spend their time in reserve billets chiefly in cleaning up) turn out most creditably.

Not a sound breaks the stillness of this misty winter's morning save the singing of larks and the sharp words of command of the platoon sergeants, drilling their men. But for something lacking in the appearance of the countryside one might easily imagine oneself in England. What a contrast to previous conceptions of 'a mile behind the front', where one had imagined the guns to be always booming and the clatter of machine guns and rifle-fire to be incessant! But this morning, except when an aeroplane sails lazily overhead, there is no sound. Perhaps the absence of visible life is the nameless something which appears to be lacking in this utterly featureless countryside: not a human being in sight save an occasional soldier walking along the road; not a bird or animal save the rising larks, and a distant string of artillery horses.

In the early afternoon there is an inspection of the newly arrived draft by the Brigadier-General. After the inspection, which takes place in a field behind Battalion Headquarters, the Brigadier makes a short speech in which the vital importance of discipline in trench warfare is impressed upon the men and they are exhorted to follow in the footsteps of their forebears, the heroes of the Retreat from Mons, the Aisne, and the First Battle of Ypres.

That evening, I learn, is to provide my first experience of the trenches. I am detailed for a working party.

* * *

It is time to start on the first trip to the trenches. Nor, with the sombre winter's evening falling, is the prospect a particularly inviting one, despite a natural curiosity and the excitement born of long anticipation. There lies before us a 2-mile walk, a long night's work and, for the newly-joined ensign, a number of unique experiences.

It is four o'clock. We parade in the road – it is said a German machine gun sprays the first crossing – and set off. Soon we take to the fields. The men have spades and rifles to carry, and it is not long before we struggle knee-deep in mud and fall over strands of barbed wire and into holes. Having drawn extra tools from a shattered barn, we take to crawling.

'Zip!' There is no mistaking the sound; the first bullet I have heard in the war whistles overhead with a peculiar clear-cut twang. One feels interested rather than frightened, for obviously the sergeant and the men take bullets as a matter of course. We are in the machine gun zone. The sergeant says: 'You had better double along. Keep down here, sir.' Bright moonlight makes these 300 yards of exposed ground as clear as day.

A little farther on an engineer officer is waiting to point out the work to be done. Two sections of trench have to be linked up by a third which is to run over the crest of a small hill. After getting the men strung out in a long irregular line and setting the NCOs their appointed task, I make my way along a rough breastwork which has been built up as a temporary protection. The English front-line trench is on the forward face of the little hill. Here I find an old machine gun emplacement in which occasionally to sit down and rest, whence may be obtained a view of the working party on one side and across to the German lines on the other. No Man's Land spreads in between.

Many a night subsequently was I to look out over a similar scene, but never did the details of the picture impress themselves so vividly on my mind as upon that first visit to the trenches. And suddenly out of the long silence there came the obscure reminders, the swift stirrings of war: the faint clink of spades away down in the trench where the men are working, stertorous masculine breathings, a muttered exclamation, an occasional curse. Sometimes a stray bullet whistles out of the darkness and goes singing on its way; sometimes a party of soldiers, heavily burdened, tramps by, crouching low. Often – about the middle of the night – a machine gun speaks with its metallic 'clack-clack', or the sharp crack of a rifle comes from near at hand, or somewhere afar off a great gun booms sullenly. Then silence, and one listens intently. Always there is a feeling of tenseness and expectancy. Only the 'click-clack' of our picks and shovels at work and 80 yards away the answering 'thud-thud' of the German wiring parties driving in their stakes!

Then, rising and creeping to the parapet of the little fort, I peer over, my head and body partly concealed by the sandbags. The ground slopes sharply away to the confused region of moonlight and shadows. At first the eyes cannot probe this dusky space. Yet after a few minutes you make men out – flitting here and there, fetching, carrying, digging, working like demons, bent figures silhouetted in the moonlight. They look rather like Cossacks from famous pictures of 1812. And occasionally the non-commissioned officers can be heard cursing those grey soldiers of the Fatherland. There is a partial truce between us. By night everybody works at that part of the line; by day everybody fights desultorily.

And, looking out for the first time across that country so dark and shadowy, so pregnant with fate for us all, the strange baffling mystery of it confronts one. Now and again the crack of a rifle breaks the stillness, and at intervals there comes to the ear the infernal 'clack-clack' of a machine gun, than which there is no sound more sinister in war. 'Twas on such a clear moonlit night, when a fresh wind blew to the nostrils the first scents of spring, that a man working in the midst of his fellows fell silently to the ground – dripping blood – nor ever spoke again. That is the impenetrable problem, the everlasting mystery of it; experience can go no further. The interminable lines of watching men stretching away into the dim distance towards the battlefield of Ypres, where the guns boom and the machine guns chatter all night long – the interminable lines of watching men quenching their fears (of each other) as best they may, awaiting their chance to kill, to wound – for why? For what? 'For some idea but dimly understood?' The same blood, indeed, the same God, the same humanity, the same mentality, the same love of life, the same dread of death – one could not hate them, one could only wonder – and pity.

And as I watched that night, there came to my ears the sound of a man singing. Do you know the curious quality of a man's voice heard at a distance? Strangely the voice rose and fell on the wings of the night; it was joined by others, and the Germans began to sing 'The Watch on the Rhine' and the Austrian National Hymn. This, as I learned later, happened every Sunday evening. On an off-night they would have been 'strafed,' but now all was still. And often afterwards there would come from the enemy trenches – generally, as I subsequently learned, to screen some particularly important work they were engaged upon – strains of wild, windy music, like the sighing of pine forests, such songs as the Southern Germans love. And every now and then there came, too, the sound of a mouth-organ, cheap and bizarre, to remind one of a *cafe chantant* in Paris, or – why I know not – of the hot midday in some London street.

Soon after midnight our task is finished, and we trudge back to billets beneath the waning moon, towards a darkness in which there is as yet no hint of dawn.

CHAPTER FOUR

THE FIRST GAS ATTACK

By Antony R. Hossack

It was Thursday evening, April 22nd, 1915. In a meadow off the Poperinghe-Ypres road, the men of the Queen Victoria Rifles were taking their ease. We had just fought our first big action in the fight for Hill 60. We had had a gruelling time, and had left many of our comrades on its slopes. We survivors were utterly spent and weary; but we felt in good heart, for only an hour ago we had been personally congratulated by Sir John French, also the Army Commander, General Smith-Dorrien.

Now some of us were stretched out asleep on the grass, others making preparations for a much-needed toilet. Our cooks were preparing a meal, and on our right a squad of Sappers were busily erecting huts, in which we were to sleep. Alas! we never used them. As the sun was beginning to sink, this peaceful atmosphere was shattered by the noise of heavy shell-fire coming from the north-west, which increased every minute in volume, while a mile away on our right a 42-cm burst in the heart of the stricken city of Ypres.

As we gazed in the direction of the bombardment, where our line joined the French, 6 miles away, we could see in the failing light the flash of shrapnel with here and there the light of a rocket. But more curious than anything was a low cloud of yellow-grey smoke or vapour, and, underlying everything, a dull, confused murmuring.

Suddenly, down the road from the Yser Canal came a galloping team of horses, the riders goading on their mounts in a frenzied way; then another and another, till the road became a seething mass, with a pall of dust over all.

Plainly something terrible was happening. What was it? Officers, and Staff Officers, too, stood gazing at the scene, awestruck and dumbfounded; for in the northerly breeze there came a pungent, nauseating smell that tickled the throat and made our eyes smart. The horses and men were still pouring down the road, two or three men on a horse, I saw, while over the fields streamed mobs of infantry, the dusky warriors of French Africa; away went their rifles, equipment, even their tunics, that they might run the faster. One man came stumbling through our lines. An officer of ours held him up with levelled revolver. 'What's the matter, you bloody lot of cowards?' says he. The Zouave was frothing at the mouth, his eyes started from their sockets, and he fell writhing at the officer's feet. 'Fall in!' Ah! We expected that cry; and soon we moved across the fields in the direction of the line for about a mile. The battalion is formed into line, and we dig ourselves in.

It is quite dark now, and water is being brought round, and we hear how the Germans have, by the use of poison gas, driven a French army corps out of the line, creating a huge gap which the Canadians have closed *pro tem*. A cheer goes up at this bald statement, though little we knew at what a cost those gallant souls were holding on.

About midnight we withdrew from our temporary trenches and marched about for the rest of the night, till at dawn we were permitted to snatch what sleep we could under a hedge. About the middle of the morning we were on the move again, to the north, and were soon swinging along through Vlamertinghe. About 2 miles out of that town we halted in a field. By this time we had joined up with the remainder of our Brigade, the 13th, and, after a meal had been served, we were ordered to dump our packs and fall in by companies. Here our Company Commander, Captain Flemming, addressed us. 'We are,' he said, 'tired and weary men who would like to rest; however, there are men more weary than we who need our help. We may not have to do much; we may have to do a great deal. Whatever happens, fight like hell. I shall at any rate.' A few moments more – then off we go again towards that incessant bombardment, which seemed to come closer every minute.

The Scottish Borderers led the Brigade, followed by the Royal West Kents, then ourselves – all with bayonets fixed, for we were told to be prepared to meet the Germans anywhere on the road.

We were now in the area of the ill-fated French Colonials. Ambulances were everywhere, and the village of Brielen, through which we passed, was choked with wounded and gassed men. We were very mystified about this gas, and had no protection whatever against it.

Shortly after passing through Brielen we turned to the left down a road which led to the Canal, along the south side of which ran a steep spoil bank, and, as the head of our battalion reached this, we halted. We could see nothing of what went on on the other side, but knew by the rattle of musketry that there was something doing. So there was, for when we finally crossed the pontoon we found that the Jocks had met the Germans on the north bank and had bundled them helter-skelter up the slope to Pilckem. This saved us any dirty work for that day, so we spent the rest of it till midnight in carrying supplies and ammunition to the Jocks and Kents, and afterwards lay in reserve on the Canal bank. It froze hard that night, and after the sweating fatigue of carrying boxes of SAA all night we were literally aching with cold.

All night there seemed to be a spasmodic bombardment all round the Salient.

Next morning about 12 o'clock the Adjutant, Captain Culme-Seymour, was chatting to Captain Flemming a few paces away from where I was lying, when up rushed a breathless despatch rider and handed him a message, which he read aloud to Flemming. I caught three words, 'Things are critical.' In about five minutes the Colonel had the battalion on the move. We moved off in double file by companies, our company leading; as we did so a big shell burst in the midst of 'D' Company, making a fearful mess. We moved on quickly, like a gigantic serpent, with short halts now and then. As we skirted Ypres there was a roar of swift-moving thunder and a 17-inch shell, which seemed to be falling on top of us, burst a quarter of a mile away, covering us with dirt.

Over meadows and fields green with young crops which would never be harvested, past cows peacefully grazing that had had their last milking, we went, passing curiously unperturbed peasants, who watched us from the farms and cottages.

As we crossed the Roulers road a lone cavalryman came galloping down it, hatless and rolling in his saddle as though drunk. Some wag throws a ribald jest at him. He turns his ashy face towards us, and his saddle it seems is a mess of blood. Above us a Taube appears and, hovering over us, lets fall a cascade of glittering silver-like petals. A few moments more and shells begin to fall about us in quantities, and gaps begin to appear in our snake-like line.

We pass a field battery; it is not firing, as it has nothing to fire, and its commander sits weeping on the tail of one of his useless guns. We quicken our pace, but the shelling gets heavier. It seems to be raining shrapnel. Captain Flemming falls, but struggles to his feet and waves us on with encouraging words. We double across a field, and in a few moments come on to the road again. Here was action indeed, for barely had we reached the road and started to work our way towards St Julien, than we found ourselves amongst a crowd of Canadians of all regiments jumbled up anyhow, and apparently fighting a desperate rearguard action. They nearly all appeared to be wounded and were firing as hard as they could. A machine gun played down the road. Then comes an order: 'Dig in on the roadside.' We all scrambled into the ditch, which, like all Flanders ditches, was full of black, liquid mud, and started to work with entrenching tools – a hopeless job. A woman was bringing jugs of water from a cottage a few yards away; evidently she had just completed her week's washing, for a line of garments fluttered in the garden.

'Dig! Dig for your lives!' shouts an officer. But, dig! How can we? 'Tis balers we need.

A detonation like thunder, and I inhale the filthy fumes of a 5.9 as I cringe against the muddy bank. The German heavies have got the road taped to an inch. Their last shell has pitched on our two MG teams, sheltering in the ditch on the other side of the road. They disappear, and all we can hear are groans so terrible they will haunt me for ever. Kennison, their officer, stares dazed, looking at a mass of blood and earth. Another crash, and the woman and her cottage and water jars vanish and her pitiful washing hangs in a mocking way from her sagging clothes line. A bunch of telephone wires falls about us. To my bemused brain this is a catastrophe in itself, and I curse a Canadian Sapper beside me for not attempting to mend them. He eyes me vacantly, for he is dead. More and more of these huge shells, two of them right in our midst. Shrieks of agony and groans all round me. I am splashed with blood. Surely I am hit, for my head feels as though a battering-ram has struck it. But no, I appear not to be, though all about me are bits of men and ghastly mixtures of khaki and blood.

The road becomes a perfect shambles. For perhaps half a minute a panic ensues, and we start to retire down the road. But not for long. Colonel Shipley stands in the centre of the road, blood streaming down his face. The gallant Flemming lies at his feet, and the Adjutant, Culme-Seymour, stands in a gateway calmly lighting a cigarette.

'Steady, my lads,' says the Colonel. 'Steady, the Vics! Remember the regiment.' The panic is ended.

'This way,' says Seymour. 'Follow me through this gate here.' As we dash through the gate, I catch a glimpse of our MO working in an empty gun-pit like a butcher in his shop. Many were the lives he saved that day.

Once through the gate we charge madly across a field of young corn. Shrapnel and machine gun bullets are cracking and hissing everywhere. Ahead of us is a large farm, and advancing upon it at almost right angles to ourselves is a dense mass of German infantry.

We are carrying four extra bandoliers of ammunition as well as the rest of our equipment. Shall I ever get there? My limbs ache with fatigue, and my legs are like lead. But the inspiring figure of Seymour urges us on, yet even he cannot prevent the thinning of our line or the gaps being torn in it by the German field gunners, whom we can now plainly see.

At last we reach the farm, and we follow Culme-Seymour round to its farther side. The roar of enemy machine guns rises to a crazy shrieking, but we are past caring about them, and with a sob of relief we fall into the farm's encircling trench. Not too soon, either, for that grey mass is only a few hundred yards off, and 'Rapid fire! Let 'em have it, boys!' and don't we just! At last a target, and one that we cannot miss. The Germans fall in scores, and their batteries limber up and away. At last we have our revenge for the discomfort of the afternoon. But the enemy re-form and come on again, and we allow them to come a bit nearer, which they do. We fire till our rifles are almost too hot to hold, and the few survivors of our mad quarter of an hour stagger back. The attack has failed, and we have held them, and thank God that we have, for, as our next order tells us, 'This line must be held at all costs. Our next is the English Channel.' And hold it we did, through several more big attacks, though the enemy set fire to the farm and nearly roasted us, though our numbers dwindled and we were foodless and sleepless, till, thirty-six hours later, we were relieved in a misty dawn, and crept back through burning Ypres for a few hours' respite.

CHAPTER FIVE

I CHARGE!

By Captain A.O. Pollard, VC, MC, DCM

The 15th June, 1915, was a broiling hot summer's day. There was scarcely a breath of wind as we set off on the 8-mile march which would take us to our 'jumping-off' position. The Poperinghe-Ypres road was, as usual, crowded with traffic; troops in large and small parties, some in full equipment, some in light fatigue dress; limbers drawn by horses, limbers drawn by mules; endless ammunition columns; siege guns and howitzers; strings of lorries; motor cycle despatch riders; every conceivable branch of the Service was represented going about its business in orderly confusion. Even the cavalry, who, since the inception of trench warfare, were rather out of fashion, had their part in the pageant. They sat their horses with the same erectness as in peace time, but their drab equipment was in sad contrast to the shining breastplates, scarlet cloaks, and nodding plumes with which they entrance the nursemaids in the Mall.

On this occasion they rode with something of an air. When we succeeded in boring a hole through the enemy's defences on the following morning they would come once more into their own. Thundering hoofs and steaming nostrils would race in pursuit of a flying enemy. Sharp steel and quivering lance would clear the way for us to consolidate our victory.

We did not go right into Ypres. We turned off short of Hell Fire Corner across the fields. In one of these a stray shell knocked the Adjutant off his horse, though luckily without killing him. It was only a minor incident, but it warned us that we were under fire; our big adventure had commenced.

A student of psychology would notice a subtle difference between troops marching away from the line for a rest, and the same troops going up the line into action. Leaving the line, when every step means a further distance from bullets, and shells, there is an atmosphere of gaiety; songs are heard, jokes are exchanged, laughter is frequent. Going up, on the other hand, is a very different business. There is an air of seriousness, remarks are answered in monosyllables, men are mostly silent, occupied with their own thoughts. Some laugh and chatter from a sense of bravado, or to prevent their imaginations from becoming too active; others to bolster up the shrinking spirits of their weaker comrades. Only a few are natural.

On this occasion there was a tenseness in the bearing of the Battalion quite different from our normal visits to the trenches. We started off with a swing as if we were going for a route march. Every one walked jauntily, and one could sense the excitement in the air. Gradually this spirit faded, helped no doubt by the heat of the day, and the sweat of marching. The wounding of the Adjutant was like the period at the end of a paragraph. After that first shell scarcely a word was spoken. We were going into something of which we had no experience. No man felt sure he would live through the coming ordeal.

We were halted in a field to await the coming of dusk. Tea was provided from the cookers, which were afterwards taken back to the transport field. I wonder how many watched them go off with envious eyes for the Company cooks and the drivers. I wonder whether any of those returning envied us?

We moved forward in the twilight in single file. Our way lay along a railway line, and we stumbled forward and cursed the sleepers. They were either too far apart or too near; I have never been able to determine which. What I am sure of is that they are damnably awkward things to walk on, especially in full battle order.

At last we reached our position. It consisted of row after row of narrow, shallow trenches, each row being intended to accommodate successive waves of attacking troops. We were herded into ours literally like sardines. There was no room to lie down; the trench was too narrow to sit down in except sideways; if one stood up, one was head and shoulders over the top. Such were the quarters in which we were to pass the night.

Ernest and I and Percy got to work with our entrenching tools and hollowed out a space so that we could crouch in some sort of comfort. It was not worthwhile to put in too much work, as we should only be there for a few hours. As it was, it took us over an hour to get ourselves settled.

Smoking was strictly forbidden in case Fritz spotted the glow of the cigarettes, but of course we smoked. We managed to get a light from an apparatus which I had had sent out from home. It consisted of some sort of cord which was ignited by sparking a flint with a small wheel. Its merit lay in the fact that it glowed without making a flame. We were able to light up in perfect safety.

Sleep was out of the question. Not only was I too uncomfortable but I was far too excited. In a few hours I was to go over the top for the first time. I felt no trace of fear or even nervousness; only an anxiety to get started. The hours seemed interminable. Would the dawn never come?

Fritz started spasmodic shelling in the small hours. Whether he suspected anything or not I cannot say. I do not think he can have done, for a concentrated bombardment of these congested assembly trenches would have meant a massacre. The stuff he was sending over was shrapnel, and he caused some casualties, though not in our trench.

About an hour before zero hour a message came down the line that I was to report to Captain Boyle. Thankfully I climbed out of my cramped lodgement and made my way to Company Headquarters. Captain Boyle had great news for me. Two men were required to accompany the first wave as a connecting link. I was one of the two chosen; the other was a fellow called Springfield, whose father was editor of *London Opinion*.

Springy and I were delighted; I especially so. My ambition was to be realised. I was to take part in a real charge. With luck I might bayonet a Hun.

We reported to Captain Spooner of the 1st Lincolns. The Lincolns were in the British front-line trench, and were consequently very much more comfortable than we were in the assembly trenches. We had scarcely arrived when the barrage commenced.

Bang! Bang! Bang! Bang! Bang! Swish, swish, swish. Crump! Crump! Crump! Crump! Crump! Deafening pandemonium! One had to shout in one's neighbour's ear to make oneself heard at all. I knew the Hun was replying because an occasional shower of dust and earth descended on my head, but the continuous noise of guns and shells rendered my sense of hearing completely inoperative. Guns firing and shells bursting were so intermingled, friend and foe, that there was one endless succession of shattering detonations.

Springy and I stood and waited; Captain Spooner from time to time looked at his watch; the men of the Lincolns fidgeted with their equipment. My pulse raced; the blood pounded through my veins. I looked at Springy and grinned; Springy grinned back. Only a few more minutes.

At last Captain Spooner turned and smiled. His lips formed the words, 'Only a minute to go!' Instantly all was bustle and confusing. Short three-rung ladders were placed against the parapet. A man stood by each one, his foot on the first step, his rifle and bayonet swung over his shoulder.

Captain Spooner raised his hand; then swarmed up the ladder in front of him. I followed close at his heels. Springy was only a second behind me. Right and left along the line men were clambering over the top.

With the memory of the Moulin Rouge fresh in my mind, I fully expected that we should be met with a withering fire as we emerged into the open. I anticipated the crackle of machine guns, the rattle of musketry, the sweeping away of our gallant charge. Except that I never once dreamed or considered that I myself should be hit. Even in this first attack I had the extraordinary feeling of being myself exempt, though not to the same degree as later on when I was an officer. I shall therefore leave the analysis of this peculiar sense until I record the period when it became more pronounced.

Instead of a hail of machine gun and rifle bullets, there was – nothing! Not a sign of life was to be seen anywhere around the enemy position. Overhead the shells still whined and screeched; behind us and in front great spouts of earth went up in bursts. The noise was deafening, but from the menacing line of earth works opposite, not so much as a puff of smoke.

Just ahead of me Captain Spooner ran in a steady jog-trot across No Man's Land. Right and left stretched long lines of troops. All were running forward, their rifles gripped in their hands.

About 400 yards to go! We ran steadily on. Springy and I had lengthened our stride until we were right at Captain Spooner's heels. Still not a movement in the trench we were rapidly approaching.

What should we meet when we got there, I wondered? Perhaps they were reserving their fire until the last moment. Perhaps a hidden machine gun nest would suddenly sweep us away like chaff before the wind. Or it might be that the infantry would rise to meet us with a yell in a counter bayonet charge. I clenched my teeth and gripped my rifle tighter.

Just 10 yards from the trench Springy and I both sprinted. Two minds with but a single thought. We both wanted to be first to engage the enemy. There was no wire to bother us. It had been utterly destroyed by our fierce barrage. We passed Captain Spooner in a flash.

What a shock met my eyes as I mounted the German parapet. The trench was full of men; men with sightless eyes and waxen faces. Each gripped his rifle and leaned against the side of the trench in an attitude of defence, but all were dead. We were attacking a position held by corpses!

For a single moment I could not believe my eyes. I thought it must be some trick of the Hun to fill the trench with dummies the better to lure us into a trap. Then, when at length I realised what I was looking at, I felt suddenly sick with horror. This was unvarnished war; war with the gloves off. There was something ludicrous about that trench of dead men. One wanted to laugh at their comical appearance. There was also something fine; every man in his place with his face towards the enemy. But mostly they aroused a feeling of pity. Death must have come to them so suddenly, without giving them a chance in their own defence. They certainly gave me a very different reception from anything I had anticipated.

The Lincolns swept past and on to the second line. Springy and I turned and ran back to the 'jumping off' trench. Our job was to report that the first German line was clear. Captain Boyle was standing on the parapet talking to Major Ward. I informed them that the Lincolns had gone on, and then, without waiting for the battalion to advance, ran back again to the German position. I suppose, strictly speaking, I should have re-joined my section. But I had received no definite orders to do so, and I wanted to get back to the Lincolns and see some of the fighting. I was still sure there would be a hand-to-hand contest.

There was now considerably more activity from the Huns. Machine guns were intermingling their clatter with the roar of the shells. They were firing from some reserve positions, and I could hear the whine and whistle of the bullets as they passed me or ricocheted overhead.

The German trench I had first entered was situated on the edge of a small wood. This I now passed through to the second trench at the back; then on up to the German communication trench. Here I saw my first live Hun. He was lying half in and half out of a dug-out, pinned down by a beam of wood which prevented him from moving the lower part of his body. All the same he was full of fight. He had a thin face with an aquiline nose on which were perched steel-rimmed glasses. He reminded me forcibly of a German master we had at my preparatory school. In his hand he held an automatic with which he was taking pot shots at whoever passed him. He had killed one man and wounded one, and I arrived just in time to see a Tommy stick him with his bayonet.

I passed right up the communication trench until I found the Lincolns. They were holding what had been the fourth German line, which they were putting in a condition of defence. I made the mistake of reporting to Captain Spooner, who at once ordered me to rejoin my unit. There was no sign of any hand-to-hand fighting anywhere up there. All was peace and quiet. The Hun had cleared out without waiting for the British advance. I concluded the whole thing was over and returned to the wood.

CHAPTER SIX

WITH THE FOREIGN LEGION IN GALLIPOLI

By Ex-Sergeant A.R. Cooper

At Sidi Bel Abbès we were met by a sergeant of the Legion, taken to the barracks and marched in through the great central gate.

On each side of a tree-bordered avenue are the four-storied buildings in which the men live; at the end of the avenue are the offices and beyond (a place very well known to every *Légionnaire*!) the canteen, also the wash-house, stores and other buildings; on the right of the main building is the *Salle d'Honneur*, where all the trophies and flags of the Legion are kept, and beyond that the prison, all enclosed by a high wall.

We arrived at Sidi Bel Abbès on the 14th October, 1914. Everything was in a state of commotion. The 3rd Battalion had just received orders for active service. We recruits were sent right away to the stores to get our kit, rations, rifles and ammunition and then were told to fall in with the rest. A pretty raw and awkward bunch we must have been.

The kit issued to us in those days consisted of képi, which was red with a blue band, blue tunic, red trousers, and a short vest which we called *veste de singe*, an overcoat and the blue woollen belt which it is compulsory to wear over our tunics as a precaution against dysentery. The *couvre nuque* (a shaped piece of white linen to be worn under the képi to protect the neck from the sun) was also issued but, in spite of the fact that in films about the Legion the officers and men are always shown wearing it, day and night, this is not so in reality. It is never worn. The only use to which it is put by Légionnaires is to strain their coffee or even water when it is very muddy! The epaulettes, which are also 'featured' in films and fiction, have not been worn since 1907. The only epaulette a Legion soldier wears is a little blue rosette of felt which he sews on his right shoulder in order to hitch his rifle over it. When we were in the Dardanelles in 1914–15 blue linen trousers called *salopettes* were issued to us to wear over our red ones. During the war, when the French troops got their *bleu horizon*, we were given khaki and since then all the French Colonial troops have worn khaki. The French Government bought up all the American uniforms at the end of the war.

Within a few hours of our arrival at Sidi Bel Abbès the battalion was entrained for Perrigaux. As we got there we heard firing and learned that the Arabs had attacked the town and that we had to push them back into the mountains. This attack on Perrigaux was the last Arab revolt in Algeria.

Our forces consisted of one battalion of the Legion, some French Colonial troops and a few *Tirailleurs*.

We dug a trench. We could see the Arabs only about 200 yards away and knew that there were a lot more that we could not see, among the rocks at the foot of the hills. The rifle that was issued to us in those days was the *fusil gras* which had been in use since 1870. It was monstrously heavy and fired great big bullets [this was later replaced by the Lebel rifle – Ed.]. I had no idea how to use it but I lay down in the trench next to an old soldier and watched what he did. The first shot I fired there was a terrible kick which made my shoulder sore for days! I opened the bolt very carefully and slowly for fear of what would happen so that the ejector did not work and I had to poke the cartridge case out with a pencil!

The soldier next to me laughed and showed me how to use the rifle and after that it was better and I began to enjoy firing it.

After an hour of this we were ordered to fix bayonets and charge. In a charge like this, it is the old soldiers, who have experience of colonial warfare and know how to take cover and watch out for the Arabs, who get through. On that charge nearly all the recruits who came up with me were killed.

I was not at all afraid and to my own surprise I was not even excited. I seemed to feel quite cool; in those days I was unconscious of danger. I did not know what it meant. Everyone was all over the place. I found myself face to face with an Arab and plunged my bayonet into him, but in doing so I turned it so that I could not get it out again and had to leave it in his body. The Arabs do not like facing steel and they began to run away towards the mountains with our troops after them in any sort of order.

I had already been told that for every enemy killed a *Légionnaire* cuts a notch in his rifle and as I went on I got out my knife and started to make a notch on mine. It was very hot and I was dead tired with running over the rough ground and carrying the heavy rifle and kit, and so I sat down on a rock to rest. Suddenly I saw a party of Arabs quite near to me on the right. They closed round me and I realised that I was their prisoner but, not really knowing what that meant, I was not frightened and thought it best to be friendly so I offered them cigarettes. They took them and also took my cartridges away from me, but left me to carry the heavy rifle. I could not understand what they said but something in their faces and gestures alarmed me in an unexpected way, and when one of them started to put his hands on me in a nauseating, caressing way I upped with the butt of the rifle and smashed his head in. That ended all friendly relationship with my captors!

When they got me back to their camp I was handed over to the women. It is the women who do the torturing. On the way up to Perrigaux in the train an old soldier had been telling of his adventures and had talked of having been taken prisoner by the Arabs. I remembered his saying that if this should happen to a man the only thing to do to escape torture was to pretend to be mad as the Arabs, they think that a madman is 'possessed' by a spirit and will not touch him. So I thought I had better do this and I started catching flies where there were none, catching at my own thumb and making any idiotic face and gesture I could think of. When I saw them draw back from me I wanted to laugh, but I managed not to do so.

They put some food near me which I was glad of by then and in the evening they brought me to the Marabou (a sort of holy man or priest) who could speak French and he questioned me about the strength of the battalion. I don't think I even knew, but, anyway, I made up some tremendous number and all the time I was playing the fool to make him believe me mad.

The Arabs evidently did not think much of me as a prisoner for that night they took me down to the plain near where we had been fighting that day and signed to me to go back to our lines. But they had taken my rifle away from me and that bothered me very much. I did not want to go back without it. Already I had been made to understand that it was a terrible offence in the Legion to lose any part of your kit or equipment but also my rifle had that notch in it for my 'first man'. I went on for a few hundred yards towards Perrigaux and then I hid behind a bush and began wondering how on earth I could get my rifle back. The rest of the night I lay out there between the lines.

Early in the morning the Legion started to attack again and a lot of them came right past me. The Arabs were shooting from behind their boulders and bushes and the Arab marksmen are deadly sure. They have any kind of rifle they can get hold of and they do not use the sights, but put two fingers on the barrel when they aim. A Legion soldier fell dead, shot through the head, within a yard of where I was hiding. Then I came out, made sure he was lifeless, picked up his rifle and joined in the attack.

When it was over I went to my Captain and reported. I told him all that had happened. He seemed to find it amusing, as I did when I started to talk about it, and he laughed and said he was pleased with me, that I was a good soldier. I felt very proud of that.

We quelled the Arab revolt in, I think, four or five days and then we went back to Sidi Bel Abbès.

II

When we were back in barracks I got in touch with an old soldier who promised to show me the ropes and put me wise to the ways of the *Légionnaires*. He was a very nice fellow, a bugler from Brittany called Le Gonnec.

When a man joins the French Foreign Legion the first thing he has to learn is the *base de la discipline* – the Legion's code. It is:

La discipline étant la force principale de la Légion il importe que tous supérieurs obtiennent de ses subordonnes une obéissance entière et une soumission de tous les instants, que les ordres soient exécutées instantanément, sans hesitation ni murmure, les autoritées qui les donnent en sont responsable et la reclamation n'est permise a l'inférieur que lorsque qu'il a obéi.

(Discipline being the principal strength of the Legion it is essential that all superiors receive from their subordinates absolute obedience and submission on all occasions. Orders must be executed instantly without hesitation or complaint. The authorities who give them are responsible for them and an inferior is only permitted to make an objection after he has obeyed.)

The second thing a *Légionnaire* must learn is how to get drunk when he has no money to buy wine!

In 1914 there were three battalions and each battalion had four companies (after the war this was changed and every battalion has a 1st, 2nd and 3rd company and a *compagnie mitrailleuse* (or machine gun company)).

My company was the 9th of the 3rd Battalion of the 1st Regiment commanded by Captain Rousseau. He was a splendid officer and understood his men, having been a ranker himself. His old mother used to keep a canteen in Sidi Bel Abbès. Although there were the sergeants and corporals between them and the men, the good officers always studied their men and knew their characters, when to overlook their faults, when to punish, and how to get the best out of them.

A second-class soldier is an ordinary private. First-class soldiers are rare and are not thought anything of as, in order to gain this nebulous distinction, a man must have no punishment, and that is practically impossible for a real *Légionnaire*. The best soldiers in the fighting line spend a great deal of their time in prison when their battalion is in barracks.

I always hated parades and one morning when the sergeant who was drilling us had made us stand to attention and slope arms several dozen times, I began obeying slackly, just bending my knee and not moving my feet apart at the word *repos* and, when he went for me, I threw my rifle down on the ground. For this I was tied to a tree for the rest of the morning, with the woollen belt which, as I have said, we all wore, by orders, over our tunics. Afterwards I was reported to the Captain.

When he asked me why I had behaved like that, I said: 'I am intelligent enough to know how to stand at attention and slope arms after doing it once; I don't need to go on doing it fifty times an hour.'

As a matter of fact, I was rather a favourite with Captain Rousseau. He knew my age, as indeed they all did (unofficially, of course) and he chose to overlook both my 'crime' and my cheek.

He cautioned me that to refuse to obey a command meant court-martial and prison and told me not to do it again. But by his orders I was given a job in the store-room and so escaped those eternal and infernal parades.

In February, 1915, it was posted in orders that any man who wished to do so could volunteer for active service. I think nearly the whole battalion wanted to. I was for rushing off to find the Captain to put my name down then and there. Someone tried to stop me and explained that I must go to the Corporal, who would forward my name to the Sergeant and *he* would give it to the Lieutenant for the Captain.

'Not I!' I called to them, as I went off. 'I'm going straight to God, not to all his Saints first!'

I found Captain Rousseau in the mess-room, saluted and said: 'If you please, sir, will you put my name down for active service?'

'That's all right, de Bruin' – he smiled – 'you're down already!'

III

The 1st Battalion of the *Premier Régiment de Marche d'Orient* was formed, with three companies of *Légionnaires*, at Tiaret, the training centre in West Central Algeria.

From Tiaret we were sent to Oran where we camped in an old Roman arena which is surrounded by a very high wall, the idea being that this would make it difficult for us to break camp and go into the town to drink. As a matter of fact, the authorities are never very optimistic about the success of their expedients in this direction. They know the *Légionnaires* too well. Those of us who were determined to get into the town that night fastened our leather belts together and so managed to scale those noble Roman walls.

Many are the ways in which a Legion soldier will earn drinks or the money to buy them. I used to go into the cafés and entertain people by blowing fire out of my mouth (a trick easily done with petrol), eating the red-hot end of my cigarette (the doctors say it is good for the stomach!) and piercing my cheeks with needles or pins. This does not hurt in the least if you do it quickly enough. The price of these edifying exhibitions was enough wine to keep me happy for the evening.

So well do the authorities know what is going on that they send out patrols to bring the truants back under arrest, sometimes unconscious. But there is no punishment on the eve of going into action.

The morning after we camped at Oran, half the battalion was missing, but *Légionnaires* do not desert when they know they are going to fight and gradually they came in. Some turned up even without hats and other parts of their kit when we were on the quay ready to embark, but the battalion left Oran full strength.

We went on *La France*, which had been a passenger boat plying between Marseilles to Tunis. She had been converted into a troopship. At Malta we had to stay on board and we were disembarked at Alexandria. There we were attached to the *Régiment de Marche d'Afrique*, composed of volunteers from regular French regiments, under General d'Amade. We camped at the back of the Victoria Hospital on English territory. We still did not know our destination.

We had been kept hanging about, on the boat and at Alexandria, for over two months. There was a shortage of cigarettes and wine and there was a faction in the battalion which began to be actively discontented and to discuss whether it would not be a good thing to desert. We were on English territory and the idea was that if we could get away we might join the English forces and see some of the fighting for which we had volunteered. I was young and easily led and anything that sounded like an adventure was in my line so I threw in my lot with about forty men who decided to get away. It was a very abortive effort at desertion and we were caught and brought back to camp under arrest.

Then orders came through that there was to be a review. Whether this was intended to occupy us or impress someone else, I don't know; but on account of it those under arrest were released and put back into the lines. When the review was over we were again put under arrest.

At last we were embarked on the *Bien Hoa*, one of the ships which had relieved Casablanca when the town was captured by the Arabs in 1907.

It was a relief to know that we were on our way somewhere, presumably to the fighting line and, on board, those under arrest were released.

We landed at Mudros on the Island of Lemnos and again camped. We had now been without tobacco for a month and so a right royal welcome was accorded to an old Greek who turned up with a whole cartload of cigarettes. Guided by his native knowledge of the laws of supply and demand and in blissful ignorance of the ways of the Legion and the *Systéme D*, (*Système débrouillage*: the *Légionnaires*' system of helping themselves to what they want) he expected to make his fortune. The price of the tobacco rose, so did the old Greek, who was lifted bodily and dropped splashingly into the harbour. The battalion enjoyed its first smoke for a month.

While we were in camp at Mudros, British troopships kept coming into the harbour and we learnt at last that we were going to the Dardanelles.

IV

On April 28th, 1915, we landed on Gallipoli from the *Petite Savoie*. We were the first French troops to do so. We went ashore on V Beach just beside the *River Clyde*, the ship from which the British had landed with rafts a few days before. The sea was full of dead bodies. The English had cleared the way and our landing was without incident, but very soon the Turks started shelling from Fort Chanak. It was my first experience of shellfire and I did not like it very much.

We started marching straight away. There was no camping; that night we rested on a hilltop. We had no idea where the enemy was. It was pitch dark and raining in torrents. The 12th Company was lost and Captain Rousseau detailed me, with four or five other men, to go out in different directions to find them and lead them back to the Battalion.

I walked for about half an hour through the rain and darkness, stumbling over rocks and dead bodies, and, at last, scrambling up a hill, I saw a dim silhouette at the top. I was glad to see any living human being and went right up to him and spoke in French. With a yell the man dropped his rifle and fled, calling on Allah in Turkish. The best part of it was that I was so startled that I did the same thing; that is, I dropped my rifle and ran. When I was about 100 yards down the hill bullets began to whistle over my head. I stopped and dropped down and then I realised that I must get back and retrieve my rifle at all costs, so I started crawling cautiously up hill. Gradually the firing died down. But when I got near the spot where the sentry had been he was back there, or another man in his place. I lay out there behind a bush all night in the rain. I could just see my rifle lying on the ground. Eventually the sentry moved away. There was utter silence, except for the sound of the rain, and I crept forward an inch at a time until I could reach the rifle. Then I made off down the hill as fast as I knew how and got back to camp just before dawn.

That day we started marching and in the afternoon (the 29th) the real fighting began. We were holding the right of the line farthest from the sea with the British on our left. It was chiefly hand-to-hand bayonet fighting and we were up against what seemed to be an inexhaustible force of Turks. It was terrible to see the way our men were slaughtered. We lost about half the battalion and three-quarters of our officers were killed.

The fighting went on day after day, getting fiercer and fiercer. On May 1st, Captain Rousseau was wounded. He got a bullet through his arm. Although this might not have been very serious for another man, his constitution had been undermined by service in China where he had taken to opium smoking and he died of that wound.

We had now no officers left and the senior sergeant, Léon, was promoted Lieutenant on the field and took charge of what was left of the battalion. He got the *Légion d'Honneur* for his courage and efficiency that day and he deserved it. He was in command of the battalion for just over a month, until he was wounded himself on June 4th. He was a little, wiry man, incredibly brave, and had the respect of all the men who fought under him. Although only an NCO, his tactics were better than those of some of the superior officers, and the casualties were not so heavy while he was in command although the fighting was fiercer than ever. Our officers, although excellent at their own job, which was desert fighting such as the Legion gets against the Arabs, had no practical experience of modern warfare.

On May 4th we got reinforcements and the fighting went on.

The Legion had been very upset because the Flag of the *Régiment de Marche* was given to the 3rd Zouave Regiment to carry. But during the third day's fighting in the Dardanelles the Turks captured it from them. We were determined to get it back and we made a special, unauthorised, attack in order to recover it. We did so, but it was impossible, during the fighting, to get it back to our lines and so it was buried. It was a fortnight before we were able to return for it, then the Flag of the Regiment was unearthed and brought back in triumph by the soldiers of the Legion. Afterwards General d'Amade gave orders that the Legion should carry the Regiment's colours.

We were holding a part of the line about 8km from V Beach, the right wing of the British Expeditionary Force, north of Cap Hellès. I had got used to the shelling by this time and in the intervals between actual attacks I used to get across to the English lines and do a bit of 'scrounging'. We used to make deals over rations … exchanging our supplies for theirs. One of our greatest needs was cigarettes, and after a battle certain of us used to volunteer to creep out and search the dead Turks for tobacco of which they seemed to have plenty. One night I found a nice big packet of tobacco in the coat pocket of a dead Turk. On the way back to our lines I rolled myself a cigarette but at the first puff I was nearly sick. God knows how long that Turk had lain out there but the tobacco had become tainted by his decaying body and was putrid. I rolled about twenty cigarettes and distributed them to the men in my company, who were duly grateful – until they tried to smoke them! Our jokes were a bit on the gruesome side, but then so were the conditions in which we were living and dying.

One of the worst jobs we had was to take a ravine called, officially, Kereves-Deré, but known to us as *Le Ravin de la Mort*. We were on one side of the ravine and the Turks on high ground the other side, commanding the only point at which we could enter it. To occupy it we had to jump down, across a kind of gully, and had orders to do this in single file, then, one by one, we had to run to the end of the place marked out for a trench and start digging. But as each man jumped he was picked off by a Turkish sniper and fell dead or wounded.

This happened ten times; one man after the other was shot down just as he jumped. I was the eleventh man to go. It was not exactly an enlivening job as it looked like certain death. But I had an idea. Instead of jumping I dived – threw myself down and the Turkish bullet whizzed above my body and I picked myself up and ran for the head of the trench, which was sheltered from their line of fire by the overhanging side of the ravine. The man who followed me did the same thing and got past, then the next, but the Turks were on to the trick by then and got him. I started shouting to them.

'Don't all do the same thing ... Some jump, some dive ...' They did so, and most of the rest of them got through and we dug our trench and were able to hold the ravine. I suppose it was for my initiative (and for getting down alive!) that my officer recommended me for a medal, but it never came through ...

While we were holding the ravine I got friendly with an Italian in my company. He had been gun-running in Morocco before he joined the Legion and was an adventurous sort of creature. He was also a very good swimmer and he told me that he was going to get out and swim the Dardanelles to Asia Minor. We were quite near to the water. He knew I spoke Turkish and Greek and I may have told him I had relations in Asia Minor, and he asked me if I would go with him. It sounded a bit hazardous but not more dangerous than sitting in that ravine with the Turks on the high ground above us and I thought I might as well have a shot at it.

So one night we got down to the water, took off our clothes and went in. About 100 yards from the shore we were caught by a terrifically strong current and carried right downstream. I thought we would be swept out to sea, but as a matter of fact we managed to get ashore just near the foot of the peninsula, not far from where we landed originally. And there we were, stark naked, 8km from our company! We made those 8km during the night and got back, our feet torn and bleeding and the spirit of adventure low in us!

I felt rather bad about this attempt to desert which I had really only agreed to on impulse and because we were all pretty fed up with what we had been through, and, to salve my own conscience, I determined to do all I could for the Legion, and afterwards I was always volunteering for any extra or dangerous mission.

V

On May 1st and 2nd, orders came through from General d'Amade to attack the enemy with bayonet although they were over a kilometre from our lines. Of course our losses were appalling. Although the official reason that General d'Amade was relieved of his command shortly afterwards was that he had a nervous breakdown, it was generally believed that his retirement from the Dardanelles was connected with these disastrous bayonet charges, also he was always at loggerheads with General Ian Hamilton and General Braithwaite, Chief of Staff.

On May 5th, I was sent down to Cap Hellès to take over the job of telephone operator at Headquarters. It was there I first met Mr Ashmead Bartlett, the English war correspondent. How it happened was that I saw that he was smoking an English cigarette. We were always short of tobacco at that time, and I followed him about in the hope that he would throw down the end of his cigarette and I could get it. He noticed me and called me up.

'Hallo, youngster, what d'you want?'

I told him what I was after and he gave me a cigarette and started talking to me. He was very interested in the Legion. He told me that he had been with them during the fighting at Casablanca in 1907 and had known General d'Amade there. He asked me about our landing in the Dardanelles on the 28th and I gave him what particulars I could.

Admiral Roger Keyes, General Ian Hamilton, General Braithwaite, Admiral Guàpratte and General d'Amade were having a conference in the next room. We could hear the sound of their raised voices; evidently some pretty heated arguments were in progress. Although Mr Ashmead Bartlett was questioning me I could see that he was, at the same time, trying to hear what was going on. As the generals came out after the conference I thought I heard General Hamilton say to General Braithwaite with brusque emphasis, 'He's no damned good.'

Later in the day Turkish prisoners were brought in and I got into conversation with some of them. General d'Amade walked in and was obviously astonished to hear one of his soldiers talking fluent Turkish. He gave me a look of deepest suspicion and turning to one of his officers, said: 'Have that man relieved at once.'

My work at Headquarters lasted just fourteen hours!

General d'Amade's place was taken, shortly afterwards, by General Gouraud.

It was on May 1st that I was recommended for the *Croix de Guerre* and later had permission to put it up, although I was not officially decorated until December when I got back to Sidi Bel Abbès. This was the first *Croix de Guerre* given in the Legion and it is entered in the *Livré d'Honneur* as such.

In the middle of May I was sent down to the Island of Tenedos with a fatigue party consisting of half a company, to get rations, clothing and so on. The *Askold* was lying there, the only Russian gunboat in the Dardanelles. She was called by the English soldiers 'the packet of Woodbines' because of her row of funnels.

While we were waiting, the ship was shelling, and I was watching the sailors firing when a shell from the Fort Chanak burst and all the gunners were killed or wounded. The gun was untouched. I rushed forward impetuously and started turning the firing-handle as I had seen them do. The ship was turning and of course I did not and could not have turned the gun. In another moment I should have been firing on our own men and allies but luckily I was stopped in time. I expected to get court-martialled for that but I never heard any more about it.

Towards the end of May I was sent with a man called Dixon to Cap Hellès to pilot the Paymaster back to our ranks. Dixon was a Frenchman. He did not speak a word of English although he had joined the Legion as an Englishman. He was the champion 'scrounger' in the battalion. It was with him that I used to crawl out into 'no man's land' at night in search of Turkish tobacco, only Dixon was not particular what it was he could find on the dead Turks and appropriated to his own uses anything he fancied.

On the way back from Cap Hellès a shell from a 6-inch gun burst near us, killing the Paymaster and sending flying the attaché-case in which he was carrying the money for the battalion. Notes were scattered all over the place, 5-franc notes, 10, 20, 50, 100-franc notes ... Dixon went after them. Shells were bursting all round and I took cover.

But Dixon sat down and began calmly to count a pile of notes and shouted to me to come on out if I wanted some money and get it while there was still some to get. At that moment another shell burst and decapitated him; his head was thrown right on to my knees. I felt pretty sick and as soon as I could I got away, made for our lines and reported what had happened. A party was sent out to look for the money. It was stated that the amount the Paymaster was carrying was 10,000 francs (about £400 in those days). All that was recovered was 550 francs. Some of the rest no doubt had found its way into the searchers' pockets and perhaps some poor blighters in the trenches literally had a 'windfall'!

Another imperturbable character in our company was an Austrian. He had joined the Legion as a Swiss. He was an excellent cook, in fact he had been a chef at the Hotel Meurice in Paris. One day he was making soup when a shell killed a *Légionnaire* named Keller. A great piece of his flesh was thrown into the stock pot. The Austrian simply cut it up and cooked it in the soup. Rations were neither plentiful nor palatable and we all ate that soup, which tasted of pork, with a relish. When, afterwards, he told us what he had done, many of the men were sick.

An incident which very nearly caused trouble with our men was connected with an Arab who was in our company. One of the officers, a lieutenant, had spotted him in hiding while we were in action. Afterwards the lieutenant made us form up in single file. He marched down the line with his revolver in his hand and when he came to the Arab he stopped and shot him dead. Then he took his body and flung it down the slope.

The men did not like this because he had waited until after the attack. They thought he ought to have killed him at the time or not at all, and grumbled a good deal.

But nevertheless the spirit of the Legion, especially when we were in action, remained the same.

CHAPTER SEVEN

FESTUBERT – 1915

By Mark Severn

To the men in Flanders, that first long winter of 1914–1915 was the most terrible of all. Their trenches were waterlogged for want of suitable material to build and drain them, their reliefs were few and far between for want of men, their efforts to keep the enemy in check were rendered abortive for want of artillery support. All day long they were shelled with 'whizz-bangs' and 'woolly bears,' 'coal-boxes' and 'Black Marias', but nothing ever went back. The Field Artillery had no ammunition, the heavy artillery had no guns. The poor battered infantry were paying England's usual penalty, one which has a precedent in every war in her history, the penalty of being unprepared.

Meanwhile those at home were straining every nerve to repair that tragic lack. Our four siege batteries at Lydd were trained and ready to the last field dressing. Only one thing was wanting – guns. Other batteries were being formed and mobilised in Coast Defence stations all over the country, waiting to proceed to Lydd as soon as room should be made for them by the departure of the first four. Finally, in February, the long awaited orders were received. Two batteries, armed with 9.2-inch howitzers, were to embark for France immediately, and two, armed with 6-inch howitzers, were to proceed to Portsmouth, there to await the final collection of their stores and guns before sailing.

It now transpired that the real cause of the delay in sending the 6-inch howitzers across was the vexed question of traction and transport. A specially constructed lorry with a four-wheel drive had been devised to pull the gun and carry the gun's crew. Other lorries were to carry the ammunition, and the vast amount of technical stores considered necessary to keep a siege battery continually in action in the field. The experiments with the F.W.D.s, as these special lorries were called, had not yet been completed. They were carried out then and there on the Portsmouth Downs, and this mode of traction proved eminently satisfactory. In countries with good and sufficient roads, such as were fought over on the Western Front, the F.W.D.s were infinitely superior in speed and mobility to the old-fashioned teams of cart horses. The 60-pounders, however, kept to their horses, and occasionally had the doubtful satisfaction of lending them to their tractor-driven brethren in order to help them out of the mud, as after heavy rain the tractors were helpless off the road.

Shadbolt (a very youthful gunner-subaltern) once saw this situation reversed when a 60-pounder got so stuck in a ploughed field on the Somme that it took seven caterpillar-tractors hooked on in tandem to extract it. The caterpillar was an ungainly monster, not unlike a steam roller with caterpillar wheels substituted for rollers which formed the mode of traction for all siege artillery of larger calibre than the 6-inch howitzer (with the exception of those on railway mountings).

All forms of traction for the siege artillery, caterpillars, F.W.D.s and lorries, were in charge of the ASC, who supplied the necessary drivers and effected all the repairs. This arrangement was not an entirely satisfactory one from the point of view of the artillery. It meant that a Battery Commander had no direct control over his own power of movement. It was true that an ASC subaltern was attached to each battery nominally under the orders of the BC, but in practice this did not amount to a great deal. In the line, the lorry park, for obvious reasons, was situated a long way in rear of the battery. Lorries were wanted by all sorts of formations for all kinds of jobs, and it was only in the nature of things that they should sometimes be commandeered by local deities for their own particular ends. Nor was it always easy for the ASC to decide the relative importance of a battery's needs and those of higher formations. But on the whole, they worked wholeheartedly and loyally for the artillery, and the RGA owe them a very deep debt of gratitude.

At last all was ready and our two batteries, complete with lorries, guns, ammunition and enough baggage and impedimenta to do justice to the Queen of Sheba on a state visit to King Solomon, set sail for France. The Germans must have had news of this imposing armament, for the ship containing the guns was but a few hours out from Avonmouth when the dreaded periscope of a submarine was sighted. Undaunted, the subaltern in charge pulled a 6-inch howitzer out of the hold, and proceeded to open fire. Imagine trying to hit an active trout in a pond by lobbing at it with a cricket ball! No shot fell within a quarter of a mile of the submarine, but this strange combat went on for nearly two hours. For some reason, at the end of this period the submarine gave up the chase, and was no more seen.

Three days after landing at Rouen, the two batteries, now formed into a brigade, proceeded by road to Aire. After a further week's delay, orders were received to occupy positions in the line near Festubert.

Moving into a battery position at night within a mile of the front line was always an unpleasant if not necessarily a hazardous undertaking, but on this occasion it was carried out without incident. The long column of lorries and guns, with all lamps doused, crawled up the narrow pavé road from Bethune in the darkness. Presently they saw for the first time that amazing firework display of Very lights which every night from dusk to dawn, from Switzerland to the sea, illuminated the Western front. There was little or no gunfire, but the silence was broken by the occasional rat-tat of a machine gun or the crack of a solitary rifle. The general effect might be compared to that of a life-size picture by Doré of Dante's approach to Inferno. The waving arms of a shattered tree, the derelict remains of a sightless house, appeared and disappeared in the fitful light of the distant flares. These flares were sparks thrown up from the fires of hell, and the crackle of rifle fire was the shrivelling in the furnace of the bones of the damned. At one point the road was blocked by infantry coming out on relief, and a sergeant of the Loamshires, out since Mons, spent an enjoyable two minutes regaling the newcomers with a complete list of the battalion casualties since that date.

The position taken up was in an orchard off the Rue de Chevattes, near Richebourg. There was only room for two guns, so the other two went into action about 50 yards farther down the road. The first two, under Captain Gregory, led an isolated but extremely strenuous existence in the orchard. Gregory was an old mountain gunner, who had seen some active service on the frontier, a small man with a large personality, brimful of energy, and with Spartan ideas about discipline and the proper conduct of a war. He lived in a pair of large rubber thigh boots and went to bed at night under a bivouac on the ground, the rubber boots, with his feet in them, sticking out from under the flap.

The guns were always manned at dawn. From then onwards every man was kept hard at it, sorting ammunition, polishing breech-locks, digging dug-outs, doing gun-drill, quite apart from the actual firing. All meals were eaten off a tin plate, balanced precariously on the knees, and consisted of bully beef and biscuits, varied by ration stew as provided for the troops by a benevolent Government. It was considered extremely unsoldierlike for an officer to supplement these rations with luxuries from home or the local canteen. These views did not, however, appeal to the sybarites Alington and Shadbolt, and they made unavailing efforts to soften the heart of that grim soldier, Gregory, and to induce him to eat his food off a table, take his boots off at night, and share the amenities of the farm cart lined with straw where the two subalterns slept side by side like the Babes in the Wood.

This question of comfort in the line was ever afterwards one to which Shadbolt gave his particular attention. He took the view that as the gunners were nearly always in the line, and seldom, if ever, went out on rest like the infantry, it was up to them to make their permanent home as comfortable as the conditions would allow. A man's efficiency was not improved, but actually impaired, by undergoing unnecessary discomforts. Even Shadbolt, however, could not live up to the high standard of a certain Corps Commander, who in 1917 came to inspect a siege battery in the line near Ypres. After being shown the guns, the dug-outs, the BC post, the telephone exchange, and even the latrines, the Great Man said, 'And now I should like to see the men's dining-room.'

Batteries, of course, were always being moved from one part of the line to another. No sooner had they settled in and got themselves really comfortable than orders came from headquarters for a move, and the whole business of home-making had to be gone through again. Here the garrison gunner had a big pull over other units, as, like the well-known denizen of the garden, he carried his house on his back. When a siege battery moved, the lorries would be packed with chairs, tables, wire beds and other furniture, in addition to the legitimate stores. This was strictly against orders, but the wise Battery Commander always turned a blind eye to this house-moving, provided the golden rule was not broken, comfort without impairment of efficiency.

This is really a corollary to Napoleon's maxim: 'An army marches upon its stomach.'

The above panegyric on comfort and its relation to efficiency in war should not lead the reader to deduce that the heavy artillery was always comfortable. Far from it. This will be made abundantly clear if he has the patience to pursue this history a little further.

Another mountain gunner of the old school was the Colonel of the Brigade. He was entirely without fear, and if he had been allowed his own way would, without doubt, have put all his 6-inch howitzers into the front line trench, there to blow the opposing enemy trench sky-high like a stockade of savages in the jungle. The observation post (OP) at that period was a house on the Rue de Bois, about 400 yards from the German front line. Half the side of the house facing the enemy was intact, the other half was completely blown off, leaving the upper rooms exposed. Shadbolt was on duty one morning observing from the intact side of the house, when the Colonel came up and suggested they might get a better view from the exposed upper room. He accordingly strolled upstairs, followed by the reluctant subaltern, and there remained erect, manoeuvring a telescope in full view of the whole German Army. After five or six minutes, during which Shadbolt felt as if he were standing naked before a firing squad, he wandered tranquilly down again and proceeded on his way. As usually happened on these occasions, the Germans turned belated but accurate shell fire on the spot where the gallant old Colonel had been, so that those who were left behind had to suffer for his indiscretion.

Shortly afterwards the Brigade suffered its first casualty in the loss of the subaltern on duty at this very OP. The Colonel continued on his foolhardy course, utterly regardless of his life or safety, was promoted to Brigadier-General a year later, and then, whilst exposing himself more recklessly than usual, was killed by a wandering bullet.

On May 9th the Brigade took part in the Battle of Festubert. The night before Alington and Shadbolt slept lightly and uneasily in their farm cart. About an hour before dawn they rose in the darkness and crept shivering on to their guns. Except for an occasional rifle shot, the front was deathly quiet, and one could plainly hear men stumbling about and shouting in the neighbouring fields as, by the fitful lantern-light, they prepared their monstrous gods for the coming day.

Suddenly there was a deafening crack, followed by four stabbing flashes of flame. The 18-pounder battery behind had opened fire. As if this were the signal, every battery on the front crashed into a thunderous accompaniment, and the whole earth seemed to shake to the blasting roar of their guns. Shadbolt's first battle had begun. In the half-light behind the gun he watched the mechanical feeding of an insatiable monster by its statuesque slaves, their grey, unshaven faces contorted by the flickering gun-fire into something evil and unearthly. This diabolic illusion was increased by their continual ramming and stoking, their tireless activity, and their silence. Across the orchard the men on Alington's gun were working with the same precise and deadly concentration. Through the trees he could see his friend's long legs moving restlessly to and fro, as he checked the sights and ammunition, and superintended the working of his detachment.

The whole of that bright May day this devil's work went on, and in the evening its first results appeared in the shape of a few shaken-looking prisoners in muddy field grey, who crept in listless batches down the road behind the battery position. The gunners crowded round them demanding 'Souvenir,' the only word common to all the nations at war. Each man returned with a helmet, the old German 'pickle-haube (*sic.*)', a set of buttons, a belt or a haversack. One wondered if these poor prisoners would retain even their clothes by the time they arrived in rear.

The next day Shadbolt was sent forward to observe from a captured German trench. Taking with him his batman, Gunner Langmead, and two signallers, he threaded his way through a maze of battered trenches. Sandbags and dead bodies lay jumbled there in wild confusion, as if some petulant giant, growing tired of play, had thrown down his broken toys in heaps. Finally they arrived in a little trench so choked with dead and so void of all semblance of a parapet, that it had been left unoccupied by our troops. Sandbagging up one corner of this, Shadbolt and the signallers settled down to the day's work, whilst the cherubic-faced batman set off on the inevitable souvenir hunt. He had just left when the enemy began a tremendous bombardment, the exact centre of which seemed to be situated on their isolated and defenceless little post. Shells were bursting with thundering concussions in front and in rear, to the right and to the left and in the air above when the Major rang up from the battery to inquire what was happening, and whether a counter attack was impending. These were points which Shadbolt would gladly have been clear about himself, as he knew that between him and the enemy, a few hundred yards away, there was only one tired company of Coldstream Guards in a hastily thrown up trench. 'You must go and find the infantry OC, ask what's happening and what we can do to help.' This meant 150 yards, mostly over the open. At school Shadbolt had won a cup for the quarter mile, but he beat his own record that day. Arriving panting and splashed with mud, he was informed by a bored sentry that the officers were having lunch about two bays down the trench, and as he rounded the next traverse he caught the words, 'Fruit salad, m'lord?' Apparently quite unmoved by the activities of the enemy, they asked him to lunch, and suggested that, when things had quieted down, he should shoot up a machine gun which was worrying them. Declining the friendly invitation, he only stayed to locate the offending machine gun, and then bolted back to reassure the Major.

A quarter of an hour later, when the bombardment had died down to scattered shelling, in staggered Master Langmead, absolutely covered with pickel-haubes (*sic.*), sword-bayonets, and other trophies of war. 'Please, sir, I'm sorry I've been away so long, but I've brought you this ring which I got off a dead officer's finger.'

In the evening, after Shadbolt had dealt faithfully with the machine gun, the enemy put down another fierce 'hate'. The little party laden with telephones, reels of wire, rifles, kit, spare food, and Langmead's souvenirs, sallied out as soon as it seemed safe, and made a dive for the trench behind. This was packed with Canadians waiting, with bayonets fixed and set faces, to make another attack. There followed another sprint to a third trench, and then a fourth. Suddenly the air was torn with the crackling rattle of musketry and machine guns. Up got the Canadians in front and in the far distance Shadbolt thought he saw grey forms hurrying eastwards.

Borne down with heat and the weight of the telephone reels there was still trench after trench to be passed, all crowded with anxious, waiting men from whom the words 'Canadians attacking, Germans running', brought a smile of relief and a muttered 'Thank Gawd, sir, for that.' And so wearily home, meeting one of the fresh Highland battalions from England marching up to relieve the Coldstreams. They looked grim and determined enough. Shadbolt had known one of the Company Commanders at home, and shouted him a cheery greeting, but he only stared blankly and made no reply.

Early in June the battery moved to Annequin, where a whole month was spent, without firing a round. Every effort had been made by those at home to supply the much needed ammunition for Neuve-Chappelle and Festubert. At the last named battle some of the 6-inch shells were stencilled April 24th, showing that no time was wasted between the factory and the gun. Actually, since the beginning of the war, about 49,000 rounds had been shipped to France by this date. This compares with 38,000 a month for the first six months of 1916, 290,000 a month during the Battle of the Somme, 840,000 a month throughout 1917, and over 1 million per month in 1918.

The effect of these early battles was to shoot away all the available supply, and for some months after Festubert all siege batteries were reduced to a maximum of twelve rounds a day. At that time the only ammunition supplied to these batteries was some 6-inch gun shell from Gibraltar, which had been condemned as unserviceable in the piping times of peace. To ensure safety these were fired by means of a specially long lanyard, all the gun's crew being ordered out of the gunpit except the hero who pulled the string. A premature occurred in a neighbouring battery, which blew the whole of the front of the barrel off. But owing to the care that was taken when firing these condemned shells no casualties occurred. Whether they caused any casualties amongst the enemy is also an open question.

A few 6-inch shrapnel were also issued, but it was found quite impossible to persuade them to burst at the right spot in the path of their trajectory. This is, of course, just before they reach the ground, so that the shrapnel bullets spray out like the drops from a watering can. Fired from the howitzers they usually burst about a quarter of a mile up in the air, or on the ground, or quite frequently not at all.

Time hung very heavily for officers and men alike. Books and newspapers were in great demand, and the arrival of the mail from home was the outstanding event of the day. The captain sketched, the subalterns loafed and read, and the gunners played 'house' all day. This is a gambling card game, much beloved by the troops, and consists in betting on the face value of the cards dealt out to each player. Part of a second pack is then dealt, the dealer in a sing-song voice calling out the values, most of which have special names. On a hot afternoon, half asleep under a gun tarpaulin, Shadbolt and Alington listened to the droning, unceasing chant: 'Clicketty Click, No. 7, Kelly's Eye, Legs' 11, No. 9, Top o' the House,' while in the distance a regular whine and bang indicated that the enemy gunners were getting rid of their daily allotment. Nearby a battery of French 75s, like irritated terriers, would occasionally reply with a spurt of angry yapping, but elsewhere from the British position all was quiet.

Shadbolt visited the French battery once or twice, and was much impressed by their methods. He never found more than four men in the battery position, one to each gun, though there must have been others hidden away somewhere. On his first visit he was accosted by a friendly-looking tramp in odds and ends of soiled uniform, who appeared to be the only inhabitant. This individual turned out to be a sergeant, and, finding that the visitor understood French and was also a gunner, was only too delighted to show him round and to describe the inner workings. After an exhaustive inspection of the whole battery he inquired whether '*Monsieur le Capitaine*' would like to fire a round at the '*sale Boche*'. Shadbolt said he would. Without further ceremony the Frenchman pushed a round into the bore and told him to shoot. Thereupon he banged into the blue, shook hands with his gallant ally, and departed, still without seeing another soul. Shadbolt could not help contrasting this with the methods employed in his own battery, where the procedure of firing involved a solemn ritual including an officer and six acolytes per gun, and attendant High Priests standing round with range tables and telephones.

The OP for the Annequin position was situated in the wing of a large distillery in the support line. At various times this had been occupied as an OP by every battery in the British army, as well as by the French and Germans in 1914. In the vast cellar lived the signallers and telephone exchanges of no less than five batteries. They had made themselves comfortable with lanterns and stoves, broken armchairs, old French beds, and a piano. The first night that Shadbolt arrived the Germans were putting up their usual evening hate on the village behind. The noise of bursting enemy shells was loud and continuous, but the only retaliation from the British lines was 'Hold your hand out, you naughty boy', played to an accompaniment of much laughter and shouting, on the cellar piano. He decided to sleep upstairs, where the advantages of a large double-bed and plenty of fresh air seemed to outweigh the possible disadvantages of a wandering whizz-bang or a spent rifle bullet. One wall of his bedroom had been blown away, and he looked straight down a long vista of ruined rooms on which the flarelights from the trenches cast flickering, fantastic shadows. The ghosts of all the nations, who had fought and died in this place, crept and peered and prowled. Every so often a brick would fall or a bomb go off, and they would stop and listen – Shadbolt was connected by a speaking tube to the cellar, but it seemed hardly in keeping with his dignity as a British officer to order Gunner Langmead up to keep him company.

Another OP was in a ruined house in Cuinchy, just off the La Bassée road. One sultry Sunday afternoon, when all else was 'quiet on the Western Front', the enemy began methodically to shell the building with 5.9-inchers. Shadbolt and a subaltern from another battery who were both on duty thought it best to retire to a small sand bag dug-out at the back. They stood at the entrance to the dug-out, which was splinter-proof and no more, and watched the performance with professional interest. In the stillness one could hear the German howitzer fire, followed by the long-drawn whine of the approaching shell, and the shattering burst as it landed on a house or a garden wall. They counted the overs and shorts, and the rights and lefts, and were presently joined by Saunders, from Shadbolt's battery, who had come up to repair the telephone wire, which had been cut by the shelling. Suddenly one shell seemed to becoming much closer, and Shadbolt felt a sharp pain in his leg as he dived with the others for the mouth of the dug-out. The blast of the explosion knocked him flat, and when he staggered to his feet he found both the others, covered with mud and blood, moaning on the ground. Binding them up as well as he could, he then discovered that a small splinter had severed a muscle in his thigh, that the telephone wires were again cut, and that the enemy had gone to gun-fire, that is, having found the range slowly and methodically with one gun, he was now firing the whole battery as hard and as fast as he could.

It seemed as if the rocking dug-out would certainly collapse on them with the mere force of the explosions. Saunders was unconscious, but the other subaltern, who was badly hit, kept crying for help in a piteous way. There was nothing to be done but wait. After what seemed to be an eternity, but was in reality not more than ten or fifteen minutes, a figure appeared at the doorway and a quiet voice said: 'Are any of you fellows alive?' It was the Colonel. It appeared that a hysterical signaller had run the whole way down to the battery and reported that three officers had been killed and the OP destroyed. Whereupon the Colonel, who happened to be in the position, had calmly walked up through the shelling to see for himself, whilst an ambulance was sent for by telephone.

There followed for Shadbolt a week of peace in a casualty clearing station some miles behind Béthune, a week spent mostly in an old walled garden reading books and writing letters. After that, being fit to hobble and the brigade short of officers owing to the loss of the two subalterns, he returned to duty.

The effect of shell-fire on the mind is a cumulative one. When Shadbolt and his companions first landed in France, coming under shell-fire did not immediately produce in them a feeling of intense terror or an acute realisation of its dangers. On the contrary, it was regarded as an interesting and exciting experience, with an element of danger to others, but not to any one so divinely favoured as themselves. The relief at finding they were not afraid after all, induced a kind of foolhardy recklessness which was generally the hall-mark of the newcomer to war. As the novelty and excitement wore off, and the horrors of experience impressed themselves on the mind, the fear of death and disablement became ever present realities. It was then that the imaginative man conquered his shaking limbs and with panic in his heart performed deeds which, though insignificant in themselves, were deeds of daily, nay, hourly heroism.

This strain of never ceasing effort to conquer the imagination wore men down more surely than hardship and wounds. The artillery suffered perhaps more continuously than the infantry, for they were always in the line. On the other hand this was more than counter-balanced by the fact that the infantry had a far worse time while they were actually in the trenches.

On his return from hospital, Shadbolt knew that he had lost that first light-hearted feeling of personal invulnerability. This was borne in on him very forcibly a week or so later, when the battery was heavily shelled, two guns were completely knocked out, and he was caught in his bath, a situation in which one feels the extreme of human defencelessness. A company of infantry, who were resting in the village, took refuge in the battery dug-outs and lost twenty-four killed and forty-two wounded. The losses in the battery were miraculously small, as so accurate was the German gunnery that every shell fell in the right section, whilst the two guns of the left were untouched. The Major reported to HQ that he thought he knew the location of the German battery, and was promptly ordered by the Colonel to engage it at once with his remaining two guns. The rest of the front was utterly quiet. Save for the unusual spectacle of a duel *a outrance* between a German and a British battery there might have been no war in Flanders. The German had the advantage of having got the range by aeroplane, and of having already destroyed half his opponent's armament. The Britisher was firing gallantly and probably entirely ineffectually into space.

In the evening, when the casualties had been dug out, and the total damage estimated, Shadbolt and Alington unanimously decided that the glamour and glory of war were definitely things of the past. Henceforth it was to be a matter of doing your duty to the limit of your nervous capacity, of suffering all things, not gladly but grimly, and of waiting patiently for the inevitable end. The light-hearted sense of adventure was over. The romance of war was dead.

EXTRACTS FROM LETTERS WRITTEN AT THE TIME

April 22nd, 1915. I managed to get a letter and a telegram off to you from the docks which I hope you received. We had the most perfect voyage over – smooth as a mill pond, and a clear moonlight night. We were packed like sardines down below. Four of us subalterns shared a cigar box. We had to take turns as officer on watch. When my turn came from 12.00 to 1.00am, I couldn't find my socks in the pitchy blackness. No lights were allowed, not even a match. I stumbled and fumbled about, and woke everybody else up. I laughed till I cried. The others didn't. Then I went on the bridge with the Captain, and watched the stars and the path the moon made on the water and felt wonderfully happy. It is a great thing to have your dearest wish gratified – especially after eight months' weary waiting.

April 26th, 1915. I don't know if you will be able to read this, written on the march. My lorry is swaying like a beast in pain. I have sat on the front seat for two days now, and am sick to death of the straight French roads with their trees on each side, the beautiful smiling countryside; and last, but not least, in my air cushion, which has punctured! We have lost one officer already, Eric Leader, in the A.S.C. He was run over by a lorry the first day and broke his arm.

Later. We got in last night after dark. When I had put my men into barracks (very dirty French ones), got them some food and cleaned up the gun park, I set off down the road in search of dinner and bed. I couldn't find the first, except the inevitable bully, but I did find (oh joy!) a real bed and hot water to wash in. This town (Aire) is only 10 or 12 miles from the trenches, and we can hear the boom of the guns quite clearly.

May 4th. We have been in action the last two days and nights and I am very dirty and very busy still. I am longing for a decent sleep and wash. The first night, moving in, we didn't get any sleep at all, but last night I found an abandoned farm cart in our orchard. I jumped in, took my boots off and instantly dropped into a deep coma, which lasted till I was turned out by the sentry at dawn.

May 18th. Hotel de Lockharts Chocolat Meunier Corner, France. The above is my address until further notice. It is our new observation post, a ruined house, bolstered up with sandbags. The whole place is really one massive sandbag with me in the middle. I am joined to the battery, a mile away, by a piece of telephone wire, and I look out all day on a vast expanse of nothing. At least that is what it looks like at first. It is really a piece of flat countryside, corrugated with miles of trenches and teeming with human beings. Those wriggly, whitey-brown things are the trenches. You can't see the human beings. Yes, those two church spires and that factory chimney in the distance are real.

It is nice to hear you talk of flowers and sunshine. We have had nothing but drizzle here lately, and thick mud, like 6 inches of lukewarm butter, and ever since Saturday one continuous battle.

June 1st. The trenches here are most terribly complicated and confusing to a newcomer. They are much deeper and better built than those where we were before, and have evidently been dug a long time, for grass and even crops are sprouting from them. This is how to get to the OP by trench all the way. Straight up Regent Street, into Glasgow Road, turn to the right across Harley Street, and drop down Hertford Street. Where this trench forks at Marylebone Road, take the right hand turn to Willow Lane, then straight along or rather twist along, till you land in the telephonist's room in this ruined house. There are six of us in here, two officers and four men – all asleep except me and one wretched telephonist. It is frightfully hot and the fug is terrific. I must climb the ladder which leads to the upper chamber and have another look out, and a blow of fresh air.

June 9th. Still at the OP. I think if those at home could see us now, we might forfeit a certain amount of sympathy. The horrors of war seem so remote. Jones and I are sitting in the hall of this fine house, being the coolest and most draughty place. Shirt sleeves and a handkerchief instead of collar and tie are the order of the day. A table is between us on which is spread a very respectable luncheon, including a bottle of wine. Books and magazines are strewn around. We sit back with our feet up. There is not a sound except the birds singing outside, and we are only a few hundred yards from the German front line. Life is very pleasant. It is always changing though. Tomorrow the 'Pip-squeaks,' 'Woolly Bears,' 'Marias,' and 'Johnsons' may be dropping into the poor old house, like tramps into a pub. Today everyone has gone to sleep in the sun.

July 12th. I would love to see *Push and Go* and Harry Tate. I want to get back for a bit now, just as much as I wanted to go out before. I long to go somewhere where I can't hear the shells coming or going. Except for a week in hospital, I've been over two months within easy field-gun range of the Hun, and one's nerves get a bit ragged I suppose. There is an 18-pounder just behind us, which goes through and through my ear drums every time it fires. We were shelled out of our last position and have since then been through all the discomfort of moving and settling in again.

I nearly got shot as a spy yesterday. A subaltern on the staff and myself, finding life at the P.O. overbearingly tedious, went out for a walk round the trenches. It appears that these had just been taken over by some Scottish Territorials. They saw us dodging about behind the houses and crouching in the long grass, so they decided to shoot on spec. Luckily they were stopped by an officer who came along and put us under arrest until we were able to explain. There's a lot of spy mania about.

July 18th. I have got a new job – twenty-four hours on and twenty-four hours off, observing from an enormous slag heap. You never saw such a place. It takes hours to climb to the top and there I sit, or rather huddle, in a little sort of rabbit hutch, with the whole of Bocheland below me, in front, and the whole of France below me, behind. The most wonderful view. When Hans von Spitzbergen makes white and black puffs appear in a certain village below me, I talk down the telephone and similar puffs appear suddenly in Bocheland.

There are some French gunners in an adjoining hutch. Have you ever heard an excited Frenchman talk down the telephone? It is fearful and wonderful business. When I was relieved last night I would have scared a respectable coal-heaver. It had been windy all day, and I was black with coal dust from head to foot.

Later. There is nothing happening and the flies are astonishingly bad. At night they disappear, and the rats come out in hundreds. One of them ran across my face as I was dozing just before dawn. Why any self-respecting rat should trouble to climb to the top of this mountain of slag is a mystery. There can't be much food except what the telephonists throw away. I have been talking to a subaltern in another battery up here, who is just back from leave. We came to the conclusion that after the novelty had worn off, for sheer and unadulterated boredom, war could not be beaten. I also tried to analyse my feelings with regard to the Boche. I cannot feel any strong emotion about him. War from a gunner's point of view is much too impersonal for that. I regard him in the same sort of way as the person who lives at Wigan or at Southend. His ideas are totally alien to mine, and I do not want to live with him in the least. At the same time I do not want all this trouble of killing him. Is it entirely due to him that I live on a coal heap all day and suffer boredom and discomfort and occasional danger? I don't suppose it is. I mean the average Boche has got no more say in it than I have. It is the old gentlemen in brass hats, on both sides, who are responsible.

CHAPTER EIGHT

THE BATTLE OF KUT

By W.J. Blackledge

General Townshend was back in Amarah by the end of August, 1915, from his sick leave to India. Great preparations were being made for a planned advance on Kut, though at this time we were still registering temperatures of 110 to 117 in the shade! Our river transport has been increased, but the important land transport for an advance in such a country was very inadequate. The General recorded this at the time in a letter to Sir John Nixon:

> I am afraid my advance will seem too slow to you, but it cannot be avoided, when I have to battledore and shuttlecock my transport about to fetch up troops and stores in homeopathic doses ...[1]

The troops were being moved up the river in steamers and barges to Ali Gharbi. Apparently the main body of the fighting force was to be concentrated there. Barges were lashed port and starboard of a steamer with the dual purpose of protecting the vessel in the narrow, twisting stream and also to accommodate a greater number of troops. Our company was on a barge starboard of the steamer. We were continually scraping the banks, running so close, in fact, that we could easily have stepped ashore!

Perhaps the most striking feature of that memorable upriver trip was the utterly primitive state of the people who dwelt on the lonesome banks. Those marsh Arabs were conspicuously scanty as to clothing. The children just ran around in their birthday suits, wearing nothing but a smile, while their elders seemed to wrap themselves indifferently in bits of sacking.

We passed tiny farmsteads and ragged habitations. Natives in rags were tilling the land, working ancient water wheels with bullock power, fishing from broken-down jetties – yet they appeared picturesque in a rugged sort of way. At some points we scraped the river bank for miles, and there men, women and children ran alongside our barge to trade with us in eggs, chickens, fish, and any odd ornamental bits they happened to be wearing.

Some of them dropped into the water, awaited our coming, then, one hand on the barge rail, they waded the slushy water, looking about as attractive as scarecrows after a downpour. Trading with these primitive folk resolved itself into a game of chance. The method was to throw your rupees into the sack-cloth of the

1. *My Campaign in Mesopotamia*, by General Townshend, KCB, DSO.

dirty but smiling women – which single garment did duty as blouse, skirt and shop counter – and a small basket of eggs would be handed over the rail to you, if you were lucky!

One charming damsel, with a face like a dockside labourer, waded up to the rail where I was standing. One saw that though she was still young she was as hard and taut and as full of muscle as a prize-fighter. She slipped off her bangle, a bit of beaten bronze and the only ornament she possessed, and offered it for sale. I held up two rupees as a suggestion of the price – then equivalent to half a dollar. The hefty maid laughed her consent, and opened her mouth widely and invitingly. One at a time I threw the rupees into it. Deftly she caught each one. And then – she did precisely nothing! She remained standing, while the steamer continued its way upstream. She seemed to be shaking with mirth.

'Say, Tiger!' laughed Steve, 'I guess you're the funniest thing that dame's seen in years!'

We reached Ali Gharbi, to find the place swarming with troops. All manner of activity was giving the area the appearance of an immense army at work. A vast expanse of the desert was covered with tents of all sizes and shapes – this, we later learned, was merely a stunt to give the enemy's intelligence the impression that the Mesopotamian Force was very much greater that it actually was. We totalled 11,000 combatants and about thirty guns.

It was from this centre that the real hardship began. We were force-marched through the desert for five nights, passing through villages and hamlets without firing a shot. Sheik Saad, Hannah and Sannaiyat we took in our stride. By September 15th (1915) we were massing at Abu Rummanah preparatory to the battle of Kut – which was bigger than anything we had so far encountered. We were then about 8 miles from the Turkish lines.

The Turkish commander, Nur-ud-Din Pacha, had been concentrating his forces throughout the hot months, digging in hard and strengthening his position. He had settled in at Essinn, just below Kut, with three divisions, a mounted brigade and thirty-eight guns, 12,000 regular troops and 3,500 Arabs. At this point the Turks were sitting astride the Tigris with the fixed determination to keep the British out of Kut, since, once we had taken that town, there would be every likelihood of our continuing the advance via Ctesiphon to Baghdad.

Johnny Turk had therefore made an excellent job of his defences at Essinn in order to protect Kut. He was about 8 miles from Kut, had entrenched himself on both sides of the river, and had a bridge of steamers chained together across the stream.

Though the British infantry units were in position for the attack by September 15th, they had to remain idle for ten days while the river transport brought up the artillery and the howitzer battery. It was not until the night of the 25th that the last of these ships arrived. Such was the state of our transport facilities even after months of preparation. We know now that this state of affairs was due entirely to the niggardly attitude of the Indian Government, which was at that time controlling the campaign. General Townshend had begged in vain.

On the eve of this historic battle General Townshend published the following communique to the troops:

> The Secretary of State has telegraphed to General Sir John Nixon (Commander-in-Chief in Mesopotamia), wishing the 6th Division a speedy and complete success, to crown all their previous efforts, and to assure them that their services are not forgotten.
>
> In conveying this message to the troops, Major-General Townshend wishes to say that the Division has fought five engagements in the last eleven months, and has gained in the Empire a reputation second to none, be it on the banks of the Yser in Flanders, or on the banks of the Tigris or Euphrates in Mesopotamia.
>
> There is no need for him to remind the troops of what their King and Country expect of them, and he hopes that a good blow now may well end their Mesopotamian labours.

By a bold and brilliant piece of strategy, General Townshend defeated the Turks at Essinn and advanced on Kut. Briefly, he rolled up the Turkish left flank after leading them to expect the attack on their right. On September 27th the feint was made on the right bank, a bridge was built, the crossing from right to left bank and the deployment of the infantry opposite the enemy's left flank were silently carried out during the night, and the enemy was taken completely by surprise.

Such are the historical facts of that battle. It is always interesting to the soldier who played his little part to learn afterwards just how it was done, for he himself can have no definite idea while the thing is actually taking place. He moves like an automaton. He does as he is told. He is there merely to obey commands. As Tommy would say – 'Orders is orders.'

My recollections of the affair are a little more hectic. I know that our company was part of a massed body that marched mile upon mile through that grim and silent night. The order had gone forth that no man must speak throughout the march, nor fuss with his equipment, nor do anything likely to create the slightest sound. It seemed to me that we were marching many miles into the desert – away from the river we had crossed – and that we were actually retreating!

We plodded on hour after hour, like a great ghost army, crunching the sand with phantom feet. Orders would come along, whispered from mouth to mouth, so that we changed direction like men on a drill square. One had the eerie impression – there being nothing to do but march and think – that the ghostly hand of some all-powerful deity was moving us hither and yon as a man moves pawns on a board.

Anon the platoon commander would turn and whisper halt. The platoon would drop in its tracks, like a row of cards, silently. But there was no 'cigarette space'. Any sort of light was strictly forbidden. In a few moments we were up again – crunch, crunch, crunch. It was the creepiest experience, moving on and on, to heaven knew where or what.

Dull, thudding feet. The monotonous thud-crunch was beaten into our ears. We must have presented a weird spectacle, a giant but ghostly shape looming through the glowering darkness of the night, a grim and sullen thing on a grisly and gloomy mission. No singing, no talking, no smoking – only the monotonous crunch of feet leaping in and out of the sand.

God! How one must fight to stop oneself thinking during the long and ghastly hours!

Though our feet were in step, it seemed to me that bodies swayed drunkenly in the dim column ahead, like stalks of wheat in the wind. And some wag of a fellow would whisper in a hollow sepulchral voice: 'How long, O Lord, how long!'

Afterwards we knew, of course, that that long night march as not a retreat, but a great, wide, sweeping manoeuvre on the enemy's left flank *and rear*. That is to say, we were working round the left of him in order to get behind his trenches before we struck. We were told that there were about 8 miles between Johnny Turk and ourselves when we massed together for the big attack. I'll swear we marched 20 miles that night. A wide enough turning movement, in all conscience!

Dawn came and still we marched. So far as we could see, we were merely marching across the desert, since there was nothing to see but sand and sand, fold upon fold of wretched sand.

'Blimey,' quoth Cockney Joe, 'we're lost!'

At the time we were doing it, it certainly seemed a purposeless thing to do. Nobody ever tells a soldier anything. So we were inclined to ask ourselves why on earth we were being dragged across the desert in this aimless fashion!

Then the rumour went along the ranks that we were taking Johnny Turk by the back door. We were advancing on his rear! The British Army lives on rumours. Nevertheless, as the sun came up we realised that this was one of the rumours that must come true. There was the great golden ball rising on our left flank. We were then marching south. It was an extraordinary experience, to march out of the night into the dawn and realise we were trekking down country instead of up country, as we had been doing for nearly a year!

But with that tell-tale sun rising to greater and greater heat, there was no mistaking the direction. Soon the strange outline of things came over the horizon. We began to pick them out. As we drew nearer they took more definite shape. We saw in the distance the earthworks, the dumps and stations that mark unmistakably a fighting force's rear lines.

No sooner had we got into view than a terrific burst of firing broke out, shattering the morning stillness. But it was not directed against us! Johnny Turk was defending himself against a *frontal* attack. It was then that we fully realised what this night manoeuvre to the rear of the enemy's lines really meant. But surely something had gone wrong? Could it be that the section of our force which had advanced for the frontal attack had so exposed itself that there was no option but to go into action? Looking back on it now, I know that such must have been the case.

At all events, we were suddenly wakened up out of our listless marching. The order went forth to prepare for action. Apparently we were late for the rendezvous. It mattered not that we had marched all night when the order to 'double' came. Double we did, at that steady, military jog-trot that keeps men going indefinitely.

Then we saw the cavalry gallop into action. It was a cheering sight. They seemed to spring out of nowhere, out of the heat haze on both flanks, close in, and race hell for leather towards Johnny's back door. And we ran behind them, deployed into action. At the command of one man the whole desert had come alive. Men laughed and shouted, exhilarated by this sudden springing to life, relieved beyond measure by the action that broke the dead monotony of a night's marching.

When you tap that well of feeling in man which is called 'boyous adventure', you tap more than you know. Streams of excitement and passion and blood-lust are brought bubbling to life. And who shall say at what point these may be dammed?

We went to that job of slaughtering the Turk in the manner of a lot of boys suddenly let loose in the playing fields. To us it was just an exciting adventure after the dread monotony of the hours that had gone before. Damnable as it undoubtedly is, there is a thrill about such a charge. Maybe it is that the beast in man is never far from the surface. It needs no great inducement to make the thing raise his ugly head.

Miraculously the weariness was shed and we were thudding along towards those trenches with fixed bayonets as though refreshed after a night of sound sleep. The thrill of the action had lent us a spurious strength and vitality. We could not get to those trenches quickly enough. We had trapped the other fellow, and that was advantage enough. There is nothing like having the advantage to give a fellow confidence! Johnny Turk was far too busy replying to the frontal attack he had expected and prepared for, to appreciate what was happening behind him – that is, until we were right on top of him.

We swarmed into the communication trenches without meeting any opposition. There was nothing to stop us at that point except the usual motley of cooks, stretcher bearers, officers' servants and such odd men generally to be found behind a fighting line. These we took in our stride. Getting in at the back door like this was no end of a lark!

It was then that we saw how busy the enemy had been during the hot 'idle' months. He had built up a wonderful system of trenches, and had every justification for believing that the Britishers would not be able to oust him. He had reckoned without our back-door manoeuvre. The communication ways led us through wing trenches, third and second line trenches up to the main fire trenches.

To appreciate fully what that fighting below ground was really like, one should have some idea of a trench. Not everyone has seen a trench. Briefly, it is an elongated grave (how true!), deep and narrow, so that two men could hardly pass each other in the confined space. The communications were at right angles with the front line trenches, and from one to the other were turnings and angles leading to rests and dug-outs. All along the subterranean passes we were jumping upon surprised men, the bayonet would strike once, and we would pass on. The trapped men, busy defending themselves against the frontal attack, had hardly a chance to turn to those who were paying a morning call by way of the rear entrance.

The result was those trenches became a veritable slaughterhouse. Our sudden appearance brought the greatest confusion to the hapless men unable to face both ways. The dug-outs behind the main fire trenches were raked with the bayonet. Men dropped their arms and threw up their hands, thinking naturally that we had come over the top from the frontal attack, and that being so, the show was all over.

Here was the element of surprise with a vengeance! I cannot forget how extraordinarily thrilling it was suddenly to turn a bend in the trench and come face to face with an astonished Turk! I never saw so much surprise revealed in the faces of men as during the hectic hours of that memorable morning. One after another we came upon them, all registering that rather silly look of amazement. It is so easy to down a man when he is taken by surprise.

Nor was the manoeuvre without its element of humour. I came upon Cockney Joe, that under-sized little devil all wire and thong, at the door of a dug-out, busily cutting the buttons off a Turk's trousers! Already he had four prisoners standing in a line, each one holding his waistband to prevent his trousers falling down! And he was at work on a fifth. There were more Turks inside that dug-out, but the little Cockney – himself hardly more than half the size of the men he was taking prisoners! – would only allow one man to come forth at a time, for he held a hand grenade and was quite prepared to throw it in the dug-out should the Turks fail to understand him. He knew that so long as his prisoners' hands were occupied holding up their trousers they were helpless. He told us later that by such means he managed to capture a score of men single-handed. It is probable that he exaggerated. He had a tendency that way.

We reached the front-line trenches to find that the fire of our own force was still coming over. In such an expediency there was only one thing to do. We had to silence these Turks who were busily replying to the fire of our brothers-in-arms out there, lest we receive some of the fire ourselves! To be shot by our own men was hardly the thing we had bargained for. I fear that in the desperate circumstances we went to it with unusual ferocity. The majority of the Turks were standing on the fire-step, their backs to us, heads down on the rifle-butts, pressing the clips and firing as fast as they could go.

They were stuck in the back and pitch-forked unmercifully to the floor of the trench, for all the world as if one were stabbing sausages and dropping them into a can! Thus we passed along the front-line trench, sticking and dropping these unwary men, trampling them under foot in a frightful scramble of blood-lust and sickening death. In that shambles the yelps and grunts and squeals, the cries of pain and the curses of Allah, made an appalling chorus for the crackling fire. True, as we progressed, those on the fire-step ahead were made aware of our presence. Many swung their rifles round and fired into their own trenches.

The raid went on for hours, scrambling up one trench and down another, and it was difficult at times to avoid clashes with our own men. Presently we realised that the fire was dying down. We rounded up the prisoners, collected our dead and wounded – a surprising number! Then a concerted thudding of feet, and we knew what it felt like to have a body of men charge and bombard one's trenches. They, however, had been warned of our presence. We joined forces and set to work to clear the entrenchments.

The Turks, we learned, had been working on this entrenching system since June. They had made elaborate use of plates, sleepers, timbers and other railway material that had been specially brought down from Baghdad to strengthen the field fortifications. And after all their work, a simple trick of military strategy had beaten them.

We had no means of knowing at that time what had happened on the front as a whole, since our responsibility was the left flank situated 6 miles from the Tigris. We knew vaguely that the river had been blocked by the Turks and that the enemy had a strong force on the right flank – where they had expected to fight the big battle. Nor did we care. By noon of that memorable day most of us were exhausted. We had marched all night, made a charge and stormed the trenches during the morning, so that it was not surprising to find men dropping down with sheer weariness. Added to which was the problem of water. The heat was blazing down and we were too far from the river. There was a marsh some distance from the entrenchments, but the water was poisonously bad. Just the same, many of the men were in such a state that they would drink anything, however filthy. Finally the order went round that we might rest for a while. We sank down in those trenches that stank of blood and the unhygienic habits of Johnny Turk and slept the sleep of the exhausted.

It seemed that I had hardly closed my eyes when I was being booted to my feet again. We were going straight into action! The Turks had brought up their reserves from the right bank of the river and across their bridge of boats near Kut with the intention of restoring the battle on the left wing. We climbed out of these fortifications and went to meet them. That was at sunset and some twenty-four hours since we had started out on this ghastly job.

We met Johnny in the open and gave him all the lead he asked for. He was not keen on a fire-fight in the open, and less keen about our advance with fixed bayonets. He retreated. He drew us towards his artillery fire – and we didn't like that. We dug in, each man working feverishly with his entrenching tools to make a hole big enough to shield himself. It is somewhat surprising to find how quickly one can make a trench, piling the dug earth in front of oneself the while, in such circumstances! Men do astonishing things under the stress of fire!

Darkness descended. The scream of shells was dying down. We burrowed and burrowed like great moles, sank deeper into our holes. Johnny Turk turned off the fireworks, at least so far as our bit of front was concerned. We could hear an intermittent phut-phut in the distance, but evidently not meant for us. So we sank down and dozed while nursing the rifle-butt.

Steve, who had used a gun in all sorts of odd spots while I was still at school, was of the opinion that the battle of Kut was over. He argued that Johnny Turk would have driven us back and back in order to regain his trenches, if he had been strong enough to do so. He was right. When daylight came we were given the cheering news that Johnny had abandoned his defences and had passed on under cover of darkness.

As to the obstruction across the Tigris – thereby hangs a tale of wonderful determination and courage on the part of Lieut. Commander Cookson, who was in charge of our naval unit. It should be noted that the river at this point had a navigable channel only half the width of the stream at Basrah, and that the trenches on both sides reached the river banks. The Commander went forward with his three gunboats at dusk under tremendous fire. The obstruction was found to be a flying bridge made by an iron lighter running on chains.

The Commander left his ship in a small boat, axe in hand, paying no heed to the terrific fire blazing all around him, an enfilade that riddled his ships and the little boat in which he worked. He was shot dead while in the act of severing the cable.

We captured 1,158 prisoners and fourteen guns in the battle of Kut. Altogether the Turks lost 1,700 killed and wounded, and our casualties amounted to 1,229 killed and wounded.

General Townshend became the hero of the hour, and deservedly so. The men swore by him. Their confidence in him was nothing short of amazing. Even the Turks began to think him irresistible. The attitude of our prisoners was one of reverence. This great General had achieved the impossible. He had routed the enemy from fortifications they had been building for months! Thus far, his troops had never been beaten. They had taken everything before them – thanks to his splendid generalship. But no thanks were due to the Indian Government for its niggardly attitude in the matter of adequate divisions, munitions, transport and general supplies ... This attitude was yet to prove the downfall of Townshend and his gallant troops.

In his story of the campaign, General Townshend wrote:

> The battle of Kut-el-Amarah can be said to have been one of the most important in the history of the British Army in India. There had been nothing of its magnitude either in the Afghan war or the Indian Mutiny, for it was fought against troops well-armed and of equal numbers to ourselves. In addition we ejected them from a very strong and up-to-date position commanding ground as flat and as open as a billiard table with nothing to check their fire-sweep.

CHAPTER NINE

A PERSONAL RECORD

By R.H. Mottram

They say we change every seven years, and are renewed bodily. If this is true, then twice over have I ceased to be that incredible person, strapped about with a set of contraptions that are already beginning to look queer, to date unmistakably, as I lay them out on the table, who, shivering, cold and wet, desperately perplexed and very much in earnest, on an autumn night of 1915 found himself commanding a company of infantry, that held the fire-bays of a front line trench in Belgium. And yet, although I have twice outgrown that body, and many more times the mind of that chap, I am linked to him indissolubly by an identity to which the proper persons at his baptism gave the name which I now sign. Here is that name engraved on the butt of the clumsy Smith-Wesson revolver, and here, marked with indelible pencil on some frayed straps of 'Webb' equipment, are the names and regiment which were mine, and his. Against every feeling of probability I sit down to write out what happened to him during those years as nearly as I can remember them. The difficulty I feel in getting back to his almost alien personality is evidently not peculiar to me. Here are two others trying to do the same, and many more have tried. The avowed reason is the fact that, unless done soon, it may be too late. We have all got to die – amazing as it will seem to us who have survived, sometimes almost alone, out of a battalion – and long before that, the process of time may make it impossible to get back, as I am now trying to do, to the man I was on that night, and the days and nights that followed it. For although they were dreadful, I could not have forgone them. I must differ from some of my colleagues who have written on the subject, in their insistence on heroics and horrors. My impression was that most men were heroic. It was quite ordinary. The behaviour, I will maintain in the face of the whole world, of volunteer amateur infantry in the face of unparalleled dangers was heroic, if you like, but so regular as to become unremarkable. Again, cosmic murder is always horrible, but if every middle-class civilian like myself had received a fresh shock from each village street he saw full of dead bodies flung down like so many sacks of bad potatoes, he would have gone mad. He didn't. He got used to it. And, above all, I at least am recording fact, not constructing drama. I wish I were.

Here follows, then, no work of art. The true experiences of one individual can never be so interesting as the selected, arranged and properly presented contrasts of created character. The purpose, here, is not quite history either. It lacks the scope and documentation. It is not autobiography, for the War of 1914–1918 was not something that happened to a man or men, but something in which the major part of a generation was involved. It is, what the title says it is, a personal record. Even so, I should not have thought it worth writing, had I not discovered in the course of hundreds of conversations, that mine must have been amongst the longest and most continuous memories of the Western Front, for while I never did anything remarkable, or had any ambition for rank, I seem to have remembered more than most men. I was mainly just above the trench level, where men could seldom see or hear many yards, and often did not know the names of the places where they fell down and slept without taking off their equipment during those quaint interludes called 'rest' – and just below the official administrative world which is bound to take a view dictated by policy, and constrained to take one dimmed by distance. I was never, from the autumn of 1916 onward, quite buried in the mud, nor ever, for more than a day or so, out of range of shell-fire, as all administrative staffs and all troops 'in rest' were. But strongest of all is the reason that, for lack of opportunity or other cause, not twenty men have written anything intimate, either shaped into fiction or left as raw fact, about the geographically and numerically biggest military effort ever made by Great Britain, and one more can hardly be one too many.

Do I and others, then, presume to be Rifleman Harris of the Peninsula, or Kinglake of the Crimea? Indeed no. We only suppose, in all humility, that those who are deeply interested in our country would be glad enough were there a dozen minor Harris-Kinglakes to give some ampler day-to-day account of those periods of national struggle. For our subject is our justification. However earnestly we may desire the end of all war, however faithfully we may believe that the ineffaceable shock that humanity received at that time has had lasting cautionary effects, we cannot avoid the conclusion that men and women, and especially children, are still deeply interested in war. Only religion and love share its fascination. The very nature and immediate results of this which we call the Great War make it desirable that the impressions of eyewitnesses should be available. So far as I am concerned, they cannot be more than that. I observed literally the injunction against the keeping of a diary, and also that as to not divulging my whereabouts on the Western Front. My letters home, carefully preserved by loving hands, contain chiefly requests for socks, good thick hand-knitted ones, a lot of interest as to what was happening in my native city, and little else. One word more. I have tried to be elementary, for the sake of those who never saw, and one hopes will never see, what war was like.

It is, then, almost entirely a spiritual journey on which I set out tonight, sitting in comfort that is all the greater because of the weather outside – a journey back to try and recover and re-enter the body and mind of that fellow on the fire-step. The only tangible guides I have at all, besides my revolver and bits of equipment, are a map (which I subsequently 'won' from Corps Headquarters), which gives me the actual spot on which I stood, and, by some miracle, a pink field-message form, addressed 'O/C D Coy.', asking how much SAA and what grenades he possessed. This piece of paper, torn from a pad of some signaller, long since, I fear, dead, and brought to me by a runner wading in the darkness, who might have been a German, for all I could tell, except that he asked of the star-shell-chequered night if Lieutenant Mottram was there, does help me to get back to that hour. It enables me to set down the actual condition of a portion of the Western Front, as I found it, just as trench warfare set in for the winter, after the disaster at Loos, which effectively paralysed – and no wonder – such initiative as the Allies had maintained during the summer of 1915. The exact spot was to the north-east of Ypres, and was a section of the roughly semi-circular line of defence around that mediaeval city which, beginning at Boesinghe, on the Fumes Canal, due north of the town, and passing eastward through Hooge, at a pretty even radius of a little more than 3 miles, ceased to be called 'The Salient' somewhere near St Eloi. The importance of the place, at which two of the outstanding 'battles' of the War had already been fought, will hardly be missed by posterity. One of the main objectives of the German Armies may have been Paris. The other, competing and sometimes overriding one, was the Channel Ports. The direct corridor to these (with the exception of a tiny strip of coastland well within range of fire from the sea) lay between the Belgian inundations that came nearly down to Boesinghe, and the queer geological accident, the gravelly Flemish hills, that began to mount a very short distance to the south of Ypres, and which indeed proved a sufficient obstacle in the critical days of 1918. Beyond that, southward, were far more indirect and heavily fortified routes, through the French Black Country and those very Picard downs that were our own sticking-place in the Somme battle. Thus the 6-mile semi-circle, of which Ypres was the axis, was of prime importance. These facts were of course even plainer to the well-informed German staff, and account for the enormous squandering of men in the cramped area of the Salient, by both sides, in conflicts more frequent, continuous and ineffective than were ever the more spectacular battles around Arras, at Verdun, or on the Somme. From this has arisen the now fashionable detraction from the importance of the Salient, with which I hasten to agree. Neither side ever got any credit from that miserable slaughter-yard. The one thing that rendered it permanently fascinating to strategians of both sides was the impossibility of fortifying it. Over most of its extent, 18 inches beneath the surface brought one to the water below, while the grey skies above never seemed to cease their weeping. Many of the trenches, in those best days of the trench system, were mere breastworks. Men who came into the War later, went to the Somme or below it and never knew anything but deep burrows in the chalk there, can form little idea of what it was to have no dug-outs measuring more than 2 feet in each direction, with 6 inches of water already over the 'floor', which had in any case to be reserved for the two boxes of small-arm ammunition, and one containing twelve hand-grenades of the 'ball' pattern, long obsolete, which were all that I could discover, in response to the message I received on that, my first tour of duty.

   I notified this fact to battalion headquarters, and should have been much more worried had I known more of the general situation. I was by no means so clear as I am now as to the importance of that mile or two of trench line. I knew roughly that we stood in trenches that had been built after the British line had been pushed back some 2 miles by the first use of gas in the preceding April. The remains of the Canadians' artillery, which they were unable to withdraw, and which were subsequently destroyed by our heavies, the Germans finding it impossible to move, lay in the waste of no-man's-land, here very wide and disputed, being too marshy for either side to consolidate. The sickly disheartening smell of gas still clung to the rank grass beyond our sketchy dilapidated wire. The most important thing, according to the training we had received, was to establish contact with the units on either flank. To the south, after some wading, I was able to find C Company holding isolated fire-bays very similar in general appearance to those held by my own company. Northward, however, the firing-line appeared to have dissolved. It came to an abrupt end at what had been described to me as a bombing post, and limit of the company sector, by a sleepy and hurried subaltern from whom I took over, and who was chiefly concerned with the fact that we were, in his view, late, as always (it was impossible not to be late in the eyes of those who had been standing in water for a week). I sent my bombing sergeant to man this position with two of his crew, and with orders, when he had made himself at home, to find out where A Company continued the line, but not to go forward on patrol until I had seen him again.

All this sounds no more complicated than carrying out some specimen dispositions on a parade ground in England. But these simple operations were conducted in just those different circumstances that make up the stupefying contrast between War and Peace, and even more between Modern War and Traditional War, most of all between War in practice and War in rehearsal. Not only was the place utterly strange to all concerned, but everything had to be done below the level of the ground, and not so much in utter darkness – that might have had certain advantages – but in an intermittent, dazzling, enemy-dictated alternation of darkness and light created by German firework star-shells that rose every moment or so, hung some seconds, illuminating that waste of undulating uncertainty, and sank, leaving one momentarily blinded. We had, of course, an insufficient supply of our own 'Verey' lights that, shot from a sort of blunderbuss, whizzed away like a rocket, and illuminated nothing. But the main fact of that place and time, which cannot be too heavily emphasised, was that the Germans had complete superiority of fire. It was not merely that we, a relieving division, desired to get to our positions and to allow those we relieved to go out to rest with a minimum of casualties, and, consequently, refrained from gun-fire and 'Verey' light firing as far as possible. It was a far more grave and permanent factor in my first experience of a command in the trenches. Partly from the way in which they held their lines, with great economy of men but with relative nervousness, partly because of our 'containing effort' at Hooge a week or so before to prevent them withdrawing all reserves to meet us at Loos, partly because, as I heard a brother officer say, they had nearly a machine gun apiece – most of all because it was the Salient, the Germans fired continuously and with very great map-accuracy. This was later the one safeguard. One did learn, after a time, on what points their machine guns were trained or traversed, and could avoid them. Heavy shell-fire for demolition purposes was not common at night. Field-gun shrapnelling, on sights taken with great pains and care during daylight, was, in ordinary trench warfare, frequent enough, if rather sporadic. Its effect depended, in darkness, on pure chance. Of individual sniping I shall have something to say later. But the superiority of machine gun fire alone was a very serious problem, and I had not, in those first hours, learned to dodge it. New Army officers like myself, who had arrived in such a situation as that above outlined, only with the intention of fighting, thought it was of paramount importance to overcome this superiority. While it existed (and it lasted all the winter) it meant that casualties had to be incurred in such daily necessary tasks as rationing and supplying the firing-line, through fatigue parties getting out of the trenches and going 'overland' as it was graphically called, or else the delay, and only doubtful avoidance of casualties by using the unpassably-bogged communication trenches, which were 'registered' for shrapnel. Now, casualties incurred in trench-warfare meant a lessening or delaying of our power to attack and drive the Germans back, the only conscious motive that had brought the new armies into being. Because of this, and because in many cases the officers had been the recruiters of the county battalions, every casualty constituted not merely a drag on the whole machine, a gap in section and platoon that could not be filled for days, but in the ultimate, something like a breach of faith with the men, the nation, and the whole principle of entry into the War. It may be imagined, therefore, how urgent I felt it to reverse this state of things immediately. I think it was from this moment that I began to feel that utter helplessness which grew on me until at the Armistice it was my prevailing impression.

    Among the general instructions given me was one that only absolutely necessary rifle fire was to be allowed until the relief was complete. Indeed, looking over the parapet, into the impenetrable blackness, or at other moments glaring light from which so much lead was being emptied upon us, it did not seem likely that individual rifle fire would produce much effect. The difficulty of sighting the spot from which a star-shell had just risen, or attempting to gauge by the sound the direction and range from which a machine gun or fixed rifle was being fired at us, was obvious. Yet there they were, the former continually traversing our parapet, and sounding like long spikes of steel being rolled from right to left, or left to right, while the latter hit every vulnerable point – gaps in the sand-bags, the communication trench entry, the latrines – with a steady punch which I timed approximately at one a minute, followed by the whip-lash crack that is only produced when the listener is in direct line of fire. There remained two alternatives – reliance on the everlasting artillery battle – or a raid with grenades, which required more organisation, such as the warning of battalion headquarters, and our supporting artillery, than I felt inclined to undertake until I knew the relief was complete, or the efforts of our own machine gun fire which might cause the industrious enemy to keep their heads down. (I pictured the Germans as standing precariously in open ditches like our own, and did not for weeks after know of the experiments they were already making in concrete emplacements, the embryo of the pill-box.) The difficulty in this case was that, of our machine guns – we were supposed to have Maxims and Lewis guns – the former had been removed from the jurisdiction of company officers and placed under brigade orders. Leaving my platoon sergeants busy making a sort of miniature order of battle, so that I might see at a glance how our sections were distributed in the tenable fire-bays, I sought out the dug-out of the battalion machine gun officer, but found only a sentry, my friend C – having taken his guns along to C Company first. Of our own 'Lewis' weapons, one was either on a course of instruction, behind the lines, or had been lost at Loos and never replaced, I forget which. The surviving one was already jammed by the omnipresent mud in which its bearer had fallen while taking over the sector. Moreover I was soon aware that an eight-hours' fast and a march (if entering the trenches of that date could be so described) of 10 miles had seriously fatigued the men, and I was making up my mind to be content to keep them under cover until rations came up when I became aware of a commotion to the left. It was my bombing sergeant, wading staggeringly, and muttering, when accosted, that he had been hit. In fact, a bullet had ploughed his scalp from front to back and done away with his cap, but I considered him more startled than hurt. A more serious thing was his report, which I think was: 'They've got that place absolutely taped, sir; there's nothing to be done with it!' I left him in the hands of the stretcher-bearers, to be iodined and tied up, and resume his guard without running undue risks, until I could find on what, if anything, our left flank rested. There was another matter I wanted to clear up. Not far from the communication trench, a big elm had fallen right across a fire-bay, and under cover of it a listening-post had been dug, running out perhaps 20 yards into no-man's-land. As it was already full of water and was therefore useless, I had only been concerned to see that the NCO next it kept a sharp look-out for enemy bombing-parties that might use it for cover. Now, however, I had a chance to see more of it, and as my own servant had been chosen on account of his being a valet in private life, and not for sprightliness, I took the corporal from that bay, a youngish, athletic fellow, and scrambled out. It is not so easy as it sounds to crawl and climb over ground covered with liquid mud, in winter clothes, with equipment, weapons, and various utensils strapped upon one. (There were no regular bye-laws for raiding, then.) There had been, during the summer, a proper entry from below the parapet to the now flooded mole hole, but as I had found water flowing thence into our sufficiently inundated defence works, I had it blocked up and took the higher way. I became suspicious directly we got through our ragged but sufficient wire, on account of the lack of enemy fire against that portion of our defences. Even when we got beyond the tree, and were trying, by the aid of the illumination provided by the enemy every other moment, to see the nature and extent of the listening-post, we seemed to be in a wedge of quiet. Reports, thumps of bullets on the parapet, the shriek of ricochets, went on on either side of us, but nothing near us for some yards. This facilitated our feeling our way round what seemed nothing but a big shell crater, full of noisome water, which constituted, apparently, the listening-post, and had been left unwired, I suppose, for inconspicuousness and egress on raids. We were doing this in the most treacherous light, as no star-shells were being fired opposite us, but only at a considerable distance to each side, thus throwing very long, faint and indistinct shadows, when there was a commotion and a splash on the other side of the listening-pond. My corporal and I both fired, more by faith than sight, and falling star-shells left us in total blackness and further commotion. I suppose we both thought of making a prisoner and jumped forward, with the result that we both lost our footing and fell into the water. I don't know how long we took to scramble out, not many seconds certainly, if only from utter disgust at the horrible-smelling mixture, but it was time enough for the enemy to depress his fire so that the air above us and the ground all round seemed to be tightly laced with whizzing bullets, striking sparks from any hard object, or going so close to our heads that we had the sensation of tiny draughts blowing. This may have been mere nerves, but the impact all about was actual enough and made us bury literally our noses in the slimy weed-grown earth. I have a recollection of my fingers finding some hard material just in front of us, which may have been the edge of a small farm track known as Admirals Road that ran near that spot. The camber of this long-since-destroyed byway was perhaps 4 inches, and I can only think that this saved us. I do not know how long we lay there, while scores of star-shells now blazed continuously along the enemy's lines, and I kept my face down. My corporal gave a sort of grunt, and in answer to my enquiry, said he thought someone had got hold of his heel. Eventually the racket subsided, the lights lessened, and we were able to crawl back, an inch at a time, to the tree, and thus, calling as loudly as we dared to our sentry over the parapet, into the fire-bay. The men of the half-section that held it had not, luckily, fired, for fear of hitting us, and were glad enough to see us back. This experience was a lesson. It was also a great benefit, and was the only time I was thoroughly warm that week. The corporal found his foothold lopsided and said: 'Look here, sir, what them B*******s ha' done to me!' I bent down and my torch revealed that the heel was shot off his left boot, so that I suppose we lay out there with heels higher than our heads.

On going to see the rations, that had now come up, distributed, I found that we had two men killed, both shot through the head, I am afraid from looking over the parapet into the machine gun traversing. When assured that the bodies had been placed out of the gangway, which ran along behind the fire-bays at a distance of some 5 yards, and that an NCO was making up those pathetic little bundles of 'deceased's effects' for transmission home, and that the remainder of the two platoons were eating such a meal as was possible, I got into the dug-out that was more or less sheltering the reserve ammunition, to which two further boxes had now been added, and took my first bite since noon. It was nearly midnight, and although lighting a fire was out of the question, I can only say that I even now vividly recollect the zest of that meal. Eaten by the reflection of the enemy's flares in the stagnant water outside, it consisted of bully beef dug out of the tin with my knife, bread that had, of course, been carried in a sand-bag whose bearer had fallen into various shell-holes from darkness and fatigue, if he had not been hit, and which therefore tasted of the contents of shell-holes, that is, human remains, various chemicals, excreta, well-manured Belgian farm soil, and rainwater – and, to finish with, cheese that survived it all. Against such disadvantages must be set youth and health, and an emotion I simply do not know how to describe without distorting it – a pride intenser than I had ever felt or shall ever feel again, in the responsibility of even so subordinate a command in a fight against what one felt to be not so much national or racial antagonists as Tyranny. I do not recollect that I took long, however. The situation was too urgent, and I suspect too wet and cold. I went along the sector, and saw, for the first time, that typical scene. There was nothing whatever to be done. Even had shovels and bags, wires and pickets been brought up – and the tour was yet too unorganised to permit of it – I cannot believe that work could have availed much, for it only meant adding fresh gobbets of liquid mud to our dissolving defences. There was at that time no wood available for building purposes, save a few 'duckboards', but the lack of another sort of wood – kindling – was already hastening their destruction, where shell-fire spared, or the swamp failed to engulf them. I little thought how the problem of firewood was to influence my view of the War. The lesson was learned that first night, and never again did D Company fail to relieve in the line without pieces of dry wood inside their shirts – the one safe place.

As it was, on that night the nervousness, or whatever it was that kept the Germans so energetic, forbade lighting fires in the open, and there was no overhead cover in the battalion sector. Thus there was absolutely nothing for the men to do but crouch against the parapet and smoke, with one sentry per fire-bay. The NCOs had lists to complete, sixteen pairs of already holey rubber wading boots had been discovered, and were distributed to stretcher bearers and other specialists, and we sat down to wait for the dawn.

It came, heralded by a sudden increase in machine gun fire, and sporadic shelling. I went along myself to see that everyone was standing-to and that fires were being lighted, now that their glow was less noticeable and before their smoke was visible. At the foot of the communication trench I was to meet F., the company commander, just back from some stunt – I cannot remember if it was a course of training or the distribution of the MC he had gained at Loos. S., the commander (*pro tem.*) of C Company, met me there, as he was also expecting to be relieved. I remember the faint flush in the sky, the racket all round, the murmur of our men stirring about, and S., standing knee-deep, solemnly lifting up first one leg and then the other, to empty the water out of his waders. This was purely a ceremony, as they filled again immediately. F. arrived punctual and cheery, with the commander of C Company, and I pointed out the principal elements in the situation, the whereabouts of supplies, the need of further indents, and the disposition of sections and the NCOs. S. did the same on his side, and he and I were then free to scramble up the CT to the support line where hot drink awaited us; we were still very military, and there was no provision for food for officers in the fire-bays, nor could they sleep during daytime, as some proportion of the men were supposed to do. Imagine, then, the sensation of arriving in the support line after much dodging and ducking, for the CT was enfiladed by machine gun fire, as well as shelled, and was, moreover, nearly impassable, so that S. made all the time-honoured jokes about swimming the Channel and seeing the lights of Calais ahead. I crawled into one of the dug-outs of the period, which contained my head and shoulders, and took off my sodden boots, puttees and breeches, and wrapped myself in a blanket. F.'s servant brought me some gritty bacon, toasted over a candle, biscuit, marmalade, 'butter' and a tin of hot tea. He also pointed out that, on the ledge above my head, was a mug of rum. I drank it off and lay down and slept deliciously. It was not until midday that I was roused, and it was made plain to me that I had consumed the rum ration issued for six officers supposed to be with the company. I cannot say I felt any ill-effects. On the contrary.

Such was my first night in the line. It seems necessary now to describe the organisation in which I played, and was to play for years, a subordinate part. The Ypres Salient, a curve of which the base, from Boesinghe to St Eloi, was about 11,000 yards, was held by two out of the fifteen Army Corps of the entire eventual British Army. Corps were at that time almost stationary, some of them held the same Corps sector for years. Of these two, one ruled from Boesinghe to the Menin road that runs roughly east from Ypres to Hooge, and divided the Salient in two, the other from thence to St Eloi. Each Corps was nominally, and then in fact, composed of three divisions, one of which was at least 10 miles back, at Corps Rest. The divisions holding the trenches were very much more self-complete then than they subsequently became. They still bore traces of their recruiting districts, Highland, Lowland, Yorkshire, Midland or London, Welsh, Irish. Each contained three brigades or twelve battalions of infantry, approximately 10,000 bayonets, or nine batteries of field artillery, thirty-six guns, two field companies of engineers and one of signals, three field ambulances, four companies of ASC. There were also, then, at the divisional commander's disposal a squadron of cavalry, some cyclists, heavy guns and transport details, all of which were later detached one by one and placed under Corps or Army command.

Of the three infantry brigades that shared each divisional section of the Corps sector, one would be back in divisional rest near rail-head, two occupied the Divisional Sector, placing two of their battalions in the line. Each battalion usually put three companies into the trenches and kept one not further back than the Canal bank – that is, out of bullet range, but within that of enemy field artillery. Each company put two platoons into the fire-bays of the advanced or firing-line, one in support, and one in reserve. In theory, battalions should have relieved each other every four days, and brigades at intervals of a few weeks. Whole divisions should have changed from the line to the Corps rest area, miles away, every three months; but this was rarely possible until later in the War.

Such at least was the scheme, on paper. Even so it was open to the grave criticism that men, and volunteers at that, were being used for a very wasteful, stationary, and purely defensive war, which Germany carried on chiefly with machine guns, and France with its celebrated 75 mm. field-guns. In practice it worked, in patches. Divisional Reliefs were carried out, always late, but with fair regularity until the major offensives abbreviated them so that they were unrecognisable. As a rest, they were, however, effective as far as they went. Brigade relief meant sleeping during the day in towns like Poperinghe or Bailleul or Bethune with a certain amount of shelling and bombing, and going up at night to dig. (Bombing we then thought a treat by comparison, and the bombs, truly, were not the monstrosities they afterwards became.) Still, games were possible, and certain entertainments flourished, Pierrot troupes, boxing tournaments, cinemas, and it was possible to supplement rations by purchases or by frequenting restaurants. Battalion rest seldom got back farther than one of the camps that were liable to shell-fire. It was possible to walk about upright in daytime, with care, even to march to the nearest bath-house to change clothes and de-louse. But the digging was nearer and more incessant, and as the distance was short, it meant marching instead of using the train that assisted the efforts of Divisional reserves. The actual reliefs between companies and platoons in the line were simply moving from one wet patch to another. When it was discovered – and it did not take many days – that men who have been standing in water for even forty-eight hours are no longer in a fit state to march as a soldier is supposed to be able to do, not to speak of undertaking offensive operations, these reliefs were made to recur more frequently. Even so, the sickness at the end of our first turn in the line, which was eight days, was very heavy.

Here I must diverge to describe what sort of people we were who officered the New Army, as it was still called by real soldiers. F., the company commander, was typical of what I may call the semi-soldier type. The military type proper were either officers in reserve, or Sandhurst cadets who would have been soldiers by profession in any case. F.'s was the type of public-school men who were probably destined for some other profession. He may have been of age, but I doubt it, and many of the graces of his University hung about him, sportsmanship, conscious and boundless ability, a contempt for any tobacco save very good cigars. He was one of the few who seemed to enjoy the War with an almost righteous satisfaction. Of the same sort was A., a platoon commander, merry, but not of such Spartan stuff as F. He lamented over our baths in a brewery vat, our 'comic' food supply. I remember his saying to a harassed mess-orderly, 'I want a knife – the thing you cut with, y'know!' Another platoon commander was B., a civil servant, I believe, taciturn, competent, but with a curious undercurrent of feeling, due, possibly, to the fact that his elder much-loved brother had just been killed. These were the only four officers with the company. I do not think we were ever up to the establishment strength of six officers, except, perhaps, just before the Somme. Thus, holding our company portion of the battalion sector, with two platoons in the fire-bays, one in support and one in reserve, as officers had to be on duty the whole time, it was necessary to change them frequently, and F., A. and I had to 'live' in support, and take eight-hour shifts in command in front. This left each of us eight hours' sleep and eight hours to superintend the digging and other work of the platoon in support. B. had his platoon in reserve, 1,000 yards back, and could sleep during part of the day, and be ready to superintend ration and other arties which he had to find from his command, because the battalion dump, to which horse-transport brought rations and supplies, lay in his 'line'. So far the officers. The men had less responsibility, and as it turned out, less danger. In my regiment the eventual total of officer casualties was five times as large as that among other ranks, in proportion to numbers. But they had, through their comparative immunity from moving about in exposed places, the disadvantage that they could seldom move enough, in winter time, to keep warm. Thus, although less fatal, the actual disability, while they remained unhit, was greater. Next to the military type proper, and the semi-military that contained F., A. and B., came the bulk of New Army officers, men like myself, over 30 years of age, and mainly with some years of professional or business career behind them. How had we come into the War? We had nearly all enlisted in the ranks, and although there must have been great variations, amid so many hundreds of thousands, in the motive, I believe in the main that none of my sort had any military instinct and very little class consciousness. Had Germany attacked Russia, and remained on the defensive on the Rhine, I doubt if we should ever have enlisted. The invasion of France and Belgium and the bombardment of our own coasts decided us and we went to put things straight again. I never heard the invasion of Germany mentioned except in joke, and I am quite sure that if we had had any inkling of what the last year of War and first of Peace were to be like, most of us would never have gone, and we should have been an awkward lot to conscript. How were we enlisted? In 1914, so utterly unprepared were we that the dominant note of those days was one of uncomprehending enthusiasm veiled by comedy. The NCO who received us in the Drill Hall, that August, began: 'Now, then, answer your names, those of you who can remember the names you enlisted under!' He took us for 'Tommies', as Wellington said, 'enlisted for drink!'

Again, the Territorial Officer in charge of recruitment, who was also a magistrate, fixed one of us with his eye: 'Where have I seen you before?'

'You was on the Bench, sir.'

'Poaching, was it?'

'Yes, sir.'

'Will you go straight if I let you enlist?'

'Yes, sir.' He did, to Gallipoli.

And between the poacher and myself, the bank clerk, stood one for whom a large car called to take him home from drill, and who gave sumptuous dinners after which officers were invited to take wine with him. Other recruits were forcibly reclaimed by female relatives and employers.

The Regimental Police Sergeant also had his joke.

'Mottram, have you been to the recruiting room this morning?'

'No, Sergeant.'

'Well, I have. They were a dirty lot to-day. The MO was ordering them baths. Just as I came away I heard him ask one of them, "Which bank do you say you come from?"'

I, at least, was more serious, and, as soon as I could, took aside one of the few veterans, on the breast of whose tweed jacket were sewn the South African ribbons.

'Look here,' I demanded, 'this drill is all very well, but you don't tell me that when you find yourself under fire, you give the order "At the halt, on the left, form platoon!" What did you do when you found yourself in the scrap at Paardeberg?'

'I got under a waggon,' was the reply, which I am now persuaded was both sensible and true. At the time I didn't believe it and could see no possibility of driving the Germans out of Belgium on such lines.

Training was healthy and enjoyable, and the feeling of defending one's own coast a proud one. With what dismay, then, did I, a platoon sergeant, hear the gruff voice issuing from the beribboned chest of the Regimental Sergeant-Major – not the waxed-moustache, bulgy-eyed type of caricature, but an older, graver, almost sacerdotal soldier.

'Young fellow, you ought to take a commission!'
'I'd rather stay with this crowd, sir!'
'Can't help it. You ought to go!'

I filled up some forms, received the colonel's benediction, and was astounded to find myself gazetted and posted. I had become an officer, I perceived with resolute consternation.

Followed more training, learning the things I had taught as a sergeant. First there was the OTC at Harrogate. Here I learned to be knocked over by gigantic Toronto Highlanders in bayonet charges that never occurred in any field of battle. Here also we got news of the landing in Gallipoli, and, simultaneously, it now seems, of the first gas attack at Ypres. The Canadians left us that night. I can see one of them, white as a sheet, reading some communication that had reached him from the First Canadian Division.

Then there was the Reserve battalion at Colchester, the immense parades and marches, range practice and camp life. Most of us enjoyed it, I believe. We were immensely fit, if occasionally impatient. It created one notable illusion – that the War would be fought with the rifle. This was no one's fault. It was a most plausible view.

On the morning that the Battle of Loos began, being assistant adjutant, I opened the mail in the Orderly Room at the barracks and found myself ordered to France with others. So it had come at last, and most inopportunely, as my father lay very ill, dying, in fact. This sounds bathos, but I do not know how else to convey the first realisation of what War was, the utter dislocation of the decent, steady life that I and mine had led for generations. I got a few hours' leave, and then dashed off for Folkestone.

It was there and at Boulogne that I first found out for what I had enlisted. The arrangements were puerile in their inefficiency, and it was with great difficulty that I and others found our way to the Base Camp at Etaples, which was full of officers and men and bankrupt in accommodation. It was filled with a great mass of volunteers, eager to fight, and deep down beneath them could occasionally be discerned the thin ossified structure of pre-War military organisation, whose executives bickered among themselves while we stood about in the rain. There were awful scenes when the Director of Reinforcements tried to post Highland officers to county regiments they had never heard of.

There were neither baths nor canteens available, and although gas had been in use for months, there were still being issued, as protection, lengths of black veiling, with a little pad of cotton wool, which we were instructed to moisten in a primitive manner. At last we got 'orders' (indecipherable), found our way to a train and set off. Arrangements were so bad that we had to live on iron rations until we got to Poperinghe.

For we did eventually arrive at that village of unprecedented importance. In the evening sky a plane hovered, surrounded by puffs of smoke, the station was deserted, and above a distant rumble and popping that had been audible for some time there arose a regular, near and drawn-out crash. Around the Flemish-School picture made by the towers and gables of the town, a great cloud of brick-dust bellied out, while in measure with it rose a clamour of shrieks, falling masonry, footsteps and scatteration. It was our 'baptism of fire', totally unlike any such ceremony in history, typical of the War. The Germans were firing from a distance of nearly 20 miles with the regularity and precision of a machine in a factory. I enjoyed it, and felt perfectly confident of dodging such a demonstration and of presently going forward and putting the gunner out. At the moment, the thing was to find the battalion which I had no doubt was in action, and after some search in silent and deserted streets we did find a limber from the transport lines, hiding.

It grew dark as we rattled over the pave, and after an hour's jogging were decanted into a wet field at the end of which glimmered the lantern of the guard-tent. We went into the farmhouse and reported, and I could not at first understand the warmth of our welcome. It was only after I had eaten and drunk that I discovered that the dozen officers round the table were the survivors, just dragged out, of Loos, and that we four newcomers did not make the battalion establishment up to half its strength. Some of the men were in a dreadful state, without rifles or equipment, and it had not been possible to ascertain the number of casualties. The following day, after standing about for an hour, I asked F., to whose company I had been posted, whether there was anything for me to do.

He replied, 'Nothing', and his silence and gravity gave me a first glimpse of what he had been through.

Next day, however, I managed to get taken into the trenches with the guides for the next relief. We got a lift to Brielen (further than ever again, as the leaves were still on the trees, and screened us), found a pontoon bridge over the canal. The peculiarity of the modern battlefield struck me at once – the enormous noise, continuous explosion, deserted landscape, complete immobility of everything. We then engaged in a narrow ditch called a communication trench, and soon, overhead, came that fateful whispering of bullets with an occasional thump, or the 'whee' of a ricochet. Under a barricade we came out into the trenches of a regular battalion. Gullies branched on all sides, mostly very wet. Men were eating, smoking, doing odd jobs. No one was fighting. A few were peering into periscopes or through loopholes. I tried both and could see nothing whatever but upturned empty fields. Then, suddenly, there was a terrific crash that flung me yards. I picked myself up and did my best to laugh. Nearby, a man lay with a tiny hole in his forehead, and close to him another limped and crawled with blood pumping out of his leg. They were carried away, the latter bandaged, the former now beyond it. These were the first casualties I saw and were typical. I shall not describe the subsequent ones at length. I was quite clear that a casualty was not a matter for wonder or horror but for replacement. I regarded the incessant bombardment as temporary and expected every moment to see men going over the top to put the guns out of action. Nothing happened, however, and I went on with the guide, between narrow, sand-bag walls, blood-and-dirt-stained, frequently collapsed or knocked about, ill-smelling, inconvenient and full of racket and humanity, everywhere bombarded. I took some notes and made my way back to my battalion. That was how I first saw the War.

* * *

Wet day succeeded wet day of that cold and premature autumn. After forty-eight hours I found many of the men to be in such a bad state that I spoke very urgently to F. about it. And then, at that early date, the disadvantage of the structure of the New Armies, and the type of warfare in which they were engaged, came to light. I was well enough aware of the shortness of my training and total inexperience of war. I had expected to be guided by orders from old regular soldiers like the Colonel and Adjutant. In practice, however, we were almost as much cut off from Battalion headquarters as from brigade, which seemed as distant as England. You could wire to either place, but to get there and obtain any detailed information meant neglecting either frequent and urgent turns for duty, or the short time available for sleep and food. Above such considerations was the stronger one that a platoon commander who took the matter as seriously as I did then, could not go hanging around battalion headquarters. His company commander was his direct chief, and could not be missed out. I therefore had a very serious conversation with F. on the third morning when he relieved me at dawn, as to the condition of the men, and their total unfitness to undertake any offensive operation. He pooh-poohed, not so much the facts, as my attitude of mind. The men would do as they were ordered. There was nothing for it but to shut up. But after sleep and food and reflection – if one can be said to reflect crouching in a wet rabbit-hole, with considerable if irregular gun-fire going on, and nothing dry about one, as the water was now standing in the support line almost as much as in the fire-bays – I wrote out a report in my field message book, in the approved style we had been taught in the OTC, setting out the state of affairs, and suggesting a system of moving patrols to hold the fire-bays. This was not pure invention, but was partly prompted by the fact that I suffered less from exposure than the men, owing to the fact that my responsibilities as an officer kept me on the move, and partly from study of the enemy movements and habits. Such crawling about No Man's Land as we had managed to perform since my first essay in the listening-post, had revealed nothing but the dense hedge of German wire, and the fact that the continuous machine gunning and star-shell illumination came from a long way back – nearly 1,000 yards, so far as I could judge by the fall, at a very sharp angle, of bullets behind our parapet. That enemy patrols came right up to our wire at times I did not doubt after the first night. It followed that the trench, whatever it was called, that the enemy had most advanced, and just behind his wire, was not regularly held at all. At least we could see and hear nothing, and grenade-throwing produced no response. I was merely combining this fact with the obvious advantage of keeping our men fit and – shall I say, interested – for the utter disgust and disappointment of those volunteers was audible enough to any officer who kept his ears open during his peregrinations. They had come out to fight, not to sit still and be shot to bits. The trouble was that there was no decent opportunity to discuss such a matter. I only saw F. when he was preoccupied or nearly dead with fatigue, and could hardly ask him to consider a report in either state of mind. Nor was there any place for debating ways and means. So that I simply handed in my report and asked him to read it at leisure. I did persuade him to carry out an inter-platoon relief, those from support and reserve going down into the fire-bays, and the first occupants coming back to places in which at least their puttees could be changed. It made no difference to the officers, of course. F. went back to reserve, F., B. and I taking turns to command in front, in support, or to rest a bit.

It was only on these occasions – in my own case, between getting up and eating anything that could be found under such conditions, for our company mess, and general stand-to at dusk, when I took over the front line until dawn – that I could get any idea of what the place looked like. In the northern half of the Salient there was a gentle undulation of the ground, not sufficient to be called a hill, that hid the town of Ypres from the German lines, except on the extreme northern flank. As our trenches were on the eastern, or outer slope, of this, we could see nothing but the solid bank of enemy wire, and the endless complexities of his parapet, mound after mound rising away to the sky-line and always seeming higher than ours. Beyond that, the mist or rain, always one or the other, hid the horizon, and nearer were shattered trees, splintered into incredible fan-shaped stumps, here and there some faint remains of brickwork or paved or metalled roads. Flanders is not a country of hedges, and in any case the involved windings of the trenches half simulated, half hid, any that existed. So much, in fact, had the ground been disturbed by digging and shell-fire, that any clear-cut picture is impossible. It was incredibly easy – in fact, it was usual – to lose oneself in what appeared to be a maze of collapsed sewers by day. By night, over and over again, parties got out of the communication trenches, and struck across the open, sacrificing some small protection for the sake of freedom of movement, and, as time went on, the greater protection of being away from any object the Germans could photograph and so shoot at. Their firing by map was wonderful. They must have had the completest scheme of our defences and registered every vulnerable point. After losing many men in latrines, those in front line threw their sewage over the parapet into the wire, those in support used the spoil-pit behind the trench. Thus even our little company cemetery was a dangerous place, some cautious German gunner having found traces of digging there and registering upon it with great care. This he did with such perfect discipline that it became a safeguard. Early in the day, obviously just after a good breakfast, one could almost hear him carefully measuring off the range of the appointed spot. Pop went his gun, but before that there had already reached us, whizz, bang, his shell. It fell 20 yards beyond some forlorn attempt to get two sand-bags to stand above water. Two minutes would elapse. One could almost hear the conversation over the telephone, the meticulous altering of the elevation. Whizz, bang! This time 10 yards short! (Here we saw what he was after, and moved our men). Another short interval of almost prayerful preparation. Whizz, bang! Plumb on the spot. That was German gunnery. Now, even at that period we could reply with artillery, and did most effectually. But the point which can never be sufficiently understood is that infantry are helpless before all artillery and most machine gun fire. Our artillery could reply to the German artillery, we could reply to their machine gun and rifle fire, but neither of these efforts could be any real protection. The men who carried out any duty in the least exposed were hit just the same. Again and again I tried to evolve some scheme for obtaining superiority of fire, spending hours lying out in various selected spots. My eyesight is extremely good. Even today I wear no spectacles. I had a very good pair of binoculars and had qualified pretty well in musketry. But it was the rarest thing to catch a glimpse of something moving amid the confusing dim heaps of soil and debris, wire and tattered trees. Sometimes I tried a shot. There was no such close liaison between infantry and artillery on our side as on the Germans', partly because of the nature of the ground, partly on account of our guns' heavier calibre and longer range, partly because the Salient having a bad name, few artillery commanders would trust their guns eastward of the Canal. I had therefore to judge the range (the sort of places in which I lay up were not suited to a Barr and Stroud rangefinder), and the only satisfaction I can record was that whenever I fired I saw no subsequent movement. Caution, perhaps. Even so, this sort of thing could not be practised on any large scale, points of vantage being too few, enemy machine gun fire too insistent.

Much has been said about the deadly German sniper. I saw little evidence of him. I know that subsequently very finely-equipped rifles were found in their trenches, which gave colour to the idea. I cannot imagine the German being so unbusinesslike as to fire by sight when he had abundant machinery to put up regular barrages that were far more certain of hitting somebody than the finest single shot ever was of hitting anybody under trench conditions, I frequently found I had exposed myself while busy over some problem of drainage or storage. No sniper ever shot at me. On the other hand, I got a bullet through the peak of my cap in the middle of the night, moving carelessly into what I knew to be an enfiladed spot, to see to the housing of a relief of machine gunners. This problem was confined, of course, to sectors where the trenches were relatively far apart. Where No Man's Land was only a score of yards, the rifle went clean out of use, and grenades of all sorts were the weapon. There was plenty to be done. Pumps appeared on the scene, carried up by laborious parties, but it was weeks before the work was organised on a sufficiently comprehensive scale to be other than the emptying of water out of one trench into another. We tried what is called in Norfolk 'Dydling,' scooping out the liquid mud with shovels, when, eventually, these implements reached us. But wherever a shovel appeared, or a pump nozzle, there was the same painstaking registering by the enemy, the same hurried removal of our men, the interruption of the work until nightfall. There was no effective means of improving our conditions without far better organisation and many more supplies than we then possessed.

Have I conveyed the preliminary impression necessary to understanding the war we then waged? I do not know how else to render its utterly novel and perplexing character. The remoteness of the unseen enemy, the impossibility of personal hatred, the invasion of all the usual tactics, so that the 'brave soldier' of history, marching forward with his bayonet fixed and his rifle at the 'engage,' was no longer a hero, but a fool and probably a criminal – such were the factors of the situation in which we found ourselves.

I hope I do not sound as if I complained of any one. To make this clear, I must next go on to describe a journey (it was about 500 yards in a straight line) I made at F.'s suggestion to battalion headquarters. It took over an hour, with elaborate precautions. Even so, I and the 'runner' I took with me, feeling that one could not have too many people with some knowledge of the way about, in view of our daily casualty list, blundered into two other battalions before we crawled and slipped (there was no question of going overland in daylight) into a largish dug-out on the summit of the undulation. Here I found the Colonel, the only surviving Major, and the Adjutant. As I look back on it now, there is something touching about the picture they presented in the candle-lit subfusc noon. All regular soldiers, their faces were masks of the approved pattern. All of them had been under fire in South Africa, Egypt, or on the Indian Frontier. Their servants had brought up their camp beds and paraphernalia, and there they sat, commanding the battalion. That is to say, the helplessness of the rest of us was relieved by the necessity to eat, drink and sleep, even to make some sort of toilet, all difficult and dangerous adventures. These senior officers had nearly everything done for them. They had, therefore, absolutely nothing to do save to pass on to Brigade the indents for stores and reports of casualties. There was a rumour that the commander of the preceding battalion had had his horse brought up to the dug-out in daylight. I myself thought that the tremendous smoke made by the battalion headquarters mess kitchen, adjoining the dug-out, was sufficient to make them a mark to German gunners. Anyhow, they were being shelled. It was 8- or 9-inch stuff, steady, persistent. And they could not shift, as we, in the lines, shifted our men. They bore it, even if they did not grin, with admirable stoicism. I shall never forget the Major sitting there with all his English-field-officer plus all his English-country-gentleman's contempt for the expression of any feelings whatever. A lump of shell-case, result of an explosion that scattered all the objects on the table, came through the wall above his head, and embedded itself with a 'whump' in the opposite wall. Where it cut through the sandbags it let a thin trickle of dark Flanders earth fall on his crop head and strong red neck. He stuck it for a moment or two and then moved, with an exclamation of annoyance, wiping himself. Clearly his annoyance was not with the shell, but with the fact that he was obliged to notice it. I am not, for one moment, laughing at him. His *sang-froid* was precisely the quality that has maintained, in odd corners of the earth, tiny British armies in the face of enormous odds. His sort had died fighting, to a man, at Maiwand and Isandhlwana. Had it been possible he would have led us, I feel sure, to gallant extinction in front of the German wire. But the nature of this new war forbade him. Or, had the Germans only attacked as they were supposed to attack, in dense mass formations, with what coolness would he not, I feel sure, have ordered me somewhat to this effect: 'Hold your fire, Mottram, until they come to 200 yards. You have your range-finder!' as I was always hoping he would.

Alas! That also was impossible. All that he and the Colonel could do was to ask about the condition of the men and the state of the line. I replied fully and correctly as I could. I was only too pleased to do so. It seemed like getting something done. I did not reflect that F. had already passed them my report and that they considered it grossly unmilitary. Nor did I grasp that they found me – I was wearing a woolly sleeping-cap, my uniform one being soaked and cut nearly in half, a blood-and-muck-smeared raincoat, with a private's Webb equipment over it, sand-bags bound round my shins while my puttees were drying, boots that squelched as I walked, and was leaning on the branch of a tree I used for testing the depth of the water we had to wade – more like a scarecrow than an officer in a celebrated line regiment. In fact, it was easier for me to adjust myself to the actual conditions, by inexperience, than it was for them to do so by their twenty or thirty years' knowledge of real 'soldiering'. They heard what I had to say, and silence, punctuated by terrific shell-bursts, succeeded. They offered me a drink, which I accepted, and then asked if I might go back to my company, as I was nearly due to relieve B. in the fire-bays. I was dismissed with nodded approval. In spite of the unhealthiness of the spot, I had a good look round. Our own artillery was now tuning up, in retaliation, and I noted with comfort big bursts beyond Hooge on the right and over Pilkem on the left, then dived for the CT to resume my duties.

I think it was on this occasion that I met B. at the foot of the CT in the front line. He wrung my hand and said 'Good-bye, old chap, if I never see you again!'

I treated it as a joke, but found when I got about that there had been a good deal of shelling, and that the horrid job of lugging bodies (always of one's best, that is, most active men, necessarily) on to a collapsed dug-out which we used as a mortuary until burial was possible, so that they did not impede the work and lower the morale of the rest, had got on his nerves, upset by his brother's death. Nothing happened to me, however, except that I committed a gross breach of etiquette by accepting a drink of 'pozzy'[1] (?posset:[2] hot tea, rum and sugar) from the sergeant of the nearest platoon. But B. was queer in the head next day, and F. and I divided his noon-to-dusk turn; and it was then, to my astonishment and pride, I suddenly found myself face to face with the Brigadier. There he was, red tabs, cap and all, an orderly from BHQ as guide, not an attendant officer. He sploshed about in our filthy sty, asked questions, peeped in periscopes, spoke to everyone. I can only recall his saying 'Remember, Mottram, this line must be held at all costs!'

How much my precious report had to do with it I have never known, but certain it is that the same night, long after rations and battalion carrying and working parties were up, there suddenly appeared what seemed a whole field company of Sappers, with timber, wire, tools, and all sorts of things we had never

---

1. 'Jam. Issued as part of the British army field ration, tinned plum and apple pozzy was much in abundance in the early years of the war, being supplemented later on by such exotic mixtures as gooseberry and rhubarb.'

2. A drink made of hot milk curdled with ale, wine, or other alcohol and typically flavoured with spices.

had; solid platforms of wood were built in the half-dozen habitable bays, extra wire put out, the CT cleaned and strengthened. The enemy was unusually quiet while the whole place bummed like a builder's yard. And the very next day, the first in which we had been decently comfortable and capable of some effective resistance, we were relieved by the next battalion.

It took hours. Instead of relieving section by section, the newcomers (green, I suppose, as we had been) flocked into the narrow gangway, cursing when their packs stuck against the traverses, falling into pools of 'water', demanding dug-outs, stoves, heaven knows what. It became extremely difficult to get my men out. Some were in a sort of coma and could hardly move their legs. When they grasped that they were being relieved, they slouched away, without passing on the word to the next bay. I had to scramble along the parados and pick them out by the lights of Boche flares from among the moving forms in those dark gulleys, tripping over signal wire, barbed wire, and the unnameable encumbrances of the spoil-pit. NCOs were undiscoverable or helpless. I do not know at what hour we finally passed battalion headquarters. I was with the rear platoon of the rear company, and no sooner did we get on to a hard road, full of shell-holes, by the reserve lines than the condition of the men revealed itself. Their feet could not bear the contact with paving, their senses failed to warn them of unevenness and obstacles, they could not support their packs. By the time we reached the Canal bank and were out of bullet range, but under heavier shelling, I was driving along as best I could a crowd of limping, staggering figures who, unless watched, were likely to drop rifles, packs or themselves in sheer abandonment. We were not making a mile an hour, and I knew that our destination was 4 miles away at least. Some ancient military superstition made it necessary to form a proper battalion column on the Brielen road just behind the Canal. Here, about midnight, we mustered, and I sought the Major at once (F. having gone on to prepare billets and left me the company), pointing out that I had at least two-score men who needed ambulances to move them. His reply was: 'I don't keep ambulances in my pocket!'

There was nothing for it, therefore, but to make the unfortunates march. How we covered that distance, on the pave road, to Steinje Molen (Stone Mill) I cannot make out. Somewhere along the road I found a dressing station and dumped some of them there. Of the others, when at last we came in sight of the lantern that marked our camp (it seems incredible that such lights were allowed), some were still going with me on hands and knees rather than put the soles of their feet to the ground, so swollen were they with wet and cold and continual standing. It was impossible to check casualties, and I rolled into the hut, where some wire stretched on poles represented bed for company officers. I drank something and went to sleep. This ended my first turn in the trenches.

* * *

I remember that I seemed to have slept less than two minutes before being roused by my servant with a mug of tea and the information that breakfast was ready. It sounded queer enough to waken me, and I staggered out of the hut in which we had slept, from which other officers were turning out. I could hardly see or walk,

I was so sleepy, the live hours, I had had having been as nothing against the arrears I wanted. But the sheer delight of being able to walk upright, without dodging along a sketchy trench and offering myself as a registering mark to the enemy, was so pleasantly novel as to keep me going in the direction of a smell coming from a larger hut under the trees. On the step I was met by the Major, who eyed me severely and remarked: 'You haven't shaved.' It was true, and comprehensive, indicating my general appearance, which was simply that of a company officer just out of the trenches. I suddenly realised that we were soldiers again, ran back, gave a hasty scrape to my face, took off my sand-bags, raincoat, equipment, and woolly cap, and reappeared. This time I was correct, apparently, and sat at a wooden trestle-table on a bench, and ate everything passed me. Not only was the food properly cooked and eaten in comfort, and, better still, in the exhilarating company of companions I had not seen for a week, but the day was drier and less cold, my clothes had dried in the night, and the spirits of all rose rapidly to the boisterous with sheer reaction. The Major was good-humoured enough once a certain minimum tenue was adopted, and the only shadow on that unforgettable meal – besides the shadows cast by thin autumn sunshine coming through paling poplar leaves – was the Doctor's grumbled commentary on the sick parade. It seemed that it was bad for men to be wet above the waist for days together.

However, some two-thirds of the battalion were able to stand up, half an hour later, for arms inspection. After that, weapons and equipment were placed in racks, and we moved off, by platoons, to Poperinghe, to have baths in the brewery in the Grand Place. A keen wind cleared the sky, and the vigorous motion was intoxicating. In the open fields between Poperinghe-Ypres road, still tree-lined, and the Elverdinghe road that bounded the camp on the north, all the brigade reserves like ourselves of two divisions, and divisional and corps troops, were going through various routine jobs. To add to our good spirits, there was the heartening effect of numbers and efficient appearance. We no longer felt like a handful of sodden despondents, hoping to hold the line by the use of our rifles. Here were, besides seemingly thousands of other infantry, divisional artillery, even corps heavy guns, engineers with pontoons, a sort of Smithfield-cum-Covent-Garden by the new railhead, crowded with ASC, medical units and divisional cavalry. So one was part of an army, after all, not an abandoned waif! On one side was the cheerful rat-tat of a machine gun range, and on the other a divisional band practising. We covered the 4 miles in record time, singing as we had not done since England, and carrying nothing more lethal than towels, soap and clean pants.

Poperinghe, a solidly-built, rather-more-than-village of horse-dealing proclivities, stood ample and welcoming beneath its three gigantic church towers. In the big brewery the men went into the vat, and the officers had individual mash tubs nearby. Here I learned A.'s distaste for this sort of bath: he stood stark naked, pretty as a girl, bitterly complaining that I had made a mistake and led him back to the trenches: 'Same water,' he cried, pointing to the dark brown liquid steaming in the mash tub.

'Only hotter,' I ventured.

'Shows we're nearer Hell,' was his comment.

I don't know what we did after getting the men together – they wanted to go shopping or sight-seeing, of course – and marching back to camp. I strongly suspect that we ate all we could, and went to sleep. If my memory serves, we did the same at and after dinner. I fancy I was still serious enough, or still sufficiently aware of sounds coming to us from beyond Ypres, 4 miles away, sometimes making the roof of the hut rattle, to talk straight to E., the bombing officer, and C., who had the battalion machine guns. Both assured me that things would be better next time. E. had actually got some 'Mills' grenades at last, had secured a practice pitch, and had been exercising his bombers until sternly ordered by the Major to take them further off. I'm afraid he argued, and he admitted that the next thing the Major said was: 'Do you understand the nature of an order?' C. was even more helpful, explaining that he wasn't going to play squirts with his guns in my nasty drain, as he characterised the section of line I had held. But proper machine gun protection was to be organised, he said.

The following day parades were ordered, and shortly after lunch came orders for carrying and working parties. I had to take a platoon to the petrol tanks at Ypres. I asked the Adjutant where they were. He took out a map and put his finger on a spot marked clearly enough, Ypres. As I knew what it would be like, that night, I asked for the map. It was his only one so I couldn't have it. After tea, therefore, I set out to that town to which I had never been, to find a place I had never seen, in the dark. The men trailed behind cheerfully enough. It began to rain and the paths we followed to the Brielen road were simply a quagmire. But the greater difficulty was that practically the whole of Corps and sub-Corps artillery was packed along our route. Between the roar of big guns firing singly or in sections and of 18-pounders in salvoes from all the fields around, and the bursting of German shrapnel retaliation overhead, it was impossible to hear anything said, or to tell by sound if the men were keeping together. I had Sergeant H. at the rear, but he was as helpless as anyone else. This meant that at every shell-hole – and there were countless ones and more being made eve minute – it was necessary to stop to let the rear come up. We were no longer soldiers as on the morning before, but a party of explorers, slouching under mackintosh sheets and with oozing extremities. Under these circumstances I suppose we were about four hours covering the 4 or 5 miles, and arrived at Ypres in the midst of a wonderful pyrotechnic effect. I now began to inquire of individuals and parties we met, the direction of the petrol tanks we were destined for. Some said one thing, some another, some were truthful and professed ignorance. It was often as much as I could do to keep my party disentangled from others, from convoys of lorries and horse transport.

We must have walked over every inch of Ypres, which, seen subsequently in daylight, is a small compact town. Finally, having visited the ramparts and applied to all the REs that could be found, including some who were playing the piano in the fastnesses of dug-outs such as I had never seen up to that time, we emerged by the Menin Gate, and came back upon the Canal by the Thourout road. Here, about midnight, I found the RE to whom we were supposed to report, but who, owing to some hitch, was not requiring our services. We were able, therefore, to

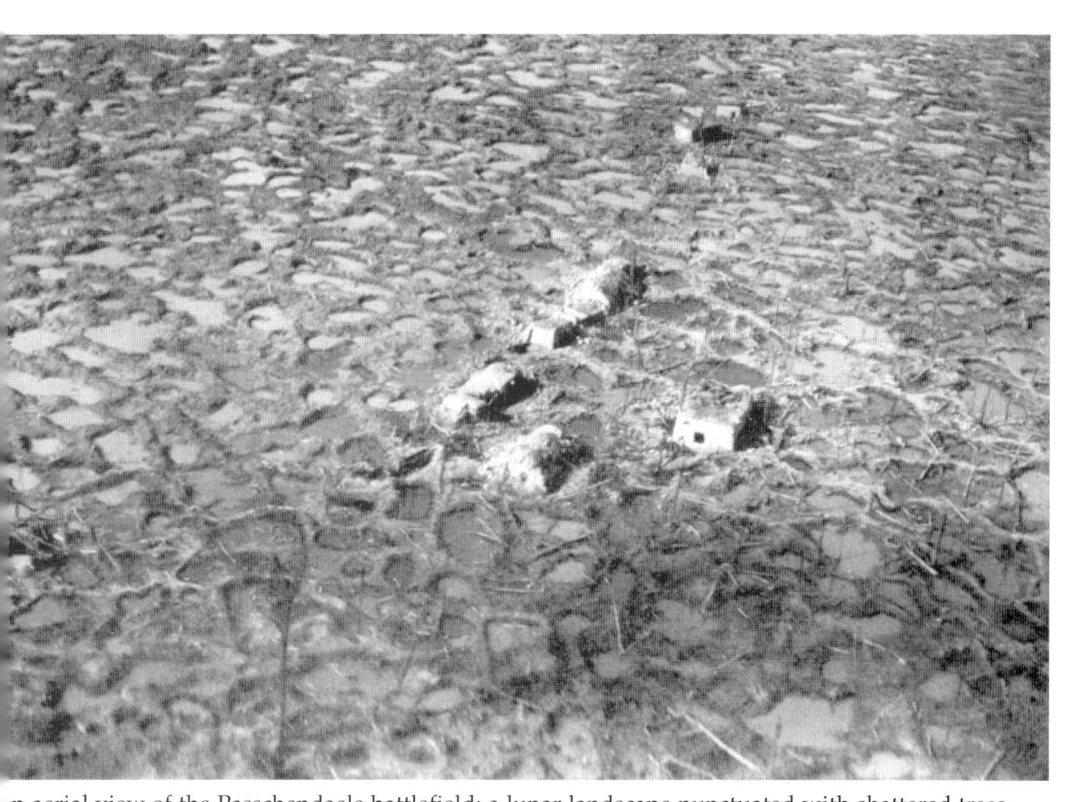

An aerial view of the Passchendaele battlefield: a lunar landscape punctuated with shattered trees and the remains of German fortified constructions. In conditions like this falling into a shell hole could mean drowning in mud unless there was someone there to help.

An earlier view of the same Passchendaele battlefield before craters filled the land.

German artillerists manoeuvring a large artillery piece during the Spring Offensive of 1918. It is camouflaged to blend it in with the foliage.

German stormtroops during the Kaiserschlacht of Spring 1918. In the front is a soldier equipped with a portable flamethrower, used to break down points of resistance.

After the battle had moved on during the 1918 German offensive. Troops resting in the remains of a shattered village.

There were so many prisoners in March 1918 that the Germans often left them to make their own way back.

British troops with tanks moving up to the front in late Spring. These were the sort of tanks that fought the German A7V tank.

British artillery in 1914 during the mobile phase. They are not dug in and are camouflaged by the autumn trees and a thin fence.

om August 1918 large numbers of German troops were captured. As their offensive failed many illingly gave themselves up, often whole units at a time.

ırkish troops attacking British positions on Gallipoli.

In Flanders it was difficult to dig trenches because of the high water table. Here, British troops are sheltering behind an above ground trench made of sandbags filled with soil.

By late November both sides had become entrenched. Here German troops are in a temporary position that allows them to see above the parapet. Increased sniper activity meant that the men had to remain below the surface until dark.

French African troops waiting to go 'over the bags' in 1915 during the Gallipoli campaign.

French troops in Gallipoli.

A French officer giving orders to French African troops before moving up to attack positions.

General Townsend, the officer in charge at Kut, with his staff. He was well treated by the Turks, unlike many of his men after their surrender.

A British soldier resting at a dugout somewhere on the Somme in 1916.

A tank moving to the front to support the attack. Initially tanks were feared by German troops, but quickly methods of dealing with them were devised.

This photograph clearly shows the devastation caused by artillery on the Somme.

British troops resting after an attack somewhere on the Western Front.

Guerre 1914-1916
264 — ALBERT (Somme)
La Basilique d'Albert (côté ouest)
après 15 mois de bombardement.
The Basilica of Albert after
15 months of bombardment.

GUERRE 1914-1916
266 — ALBERT (Somme)
Clocher de la Basilique
de N.-D. de Brebières
The Steeple of Basilica
after several bombardment.

The 'Leaning Virgin' at Albert. The British legend said that whoever made the virgin fall would lose the war, the Germans thought the opposite. When the British withdrew in March 1918 it was still in place, but in April the area was shelled by the British and the statue fell.

German troops being sent back to PoW cages during a British offensive.

A German spotter plane above a British tank, partially obscured by smoke from shelling in the area.

The Germans were not impressed by their own cumbersome and slow tank, preferring British ones instead. Damaged captured British tanks were cannibalised to provide working machines for German tankers to use.

The unpopular German A7V. It weighed 32 tons, had a crew of 18 men and had a top speed on roads of 9mph (4mph across country).

With the Armistice, the Germans were given only two weeks to return to Germany. Here, troops fill a train in an attempt to return home.

British cavalry in Salonika.

urkish troops entering the trench system in Gallipoli.

adly wounded British soldiers guarded by German troops during the Festubert battle.

While most of the Kut garrison marched to captivity, General Townshend was taken by car with a personal escort.

The Cloth Hall and the Cathedral, Ypres.

turn our faces campwards and tramp back, through a lessening activity of the guns. There was not really much in this experience, save that it gave me my first idea of the utter inconsequence of infantry in modern warfare. In the front line one felt oneself to be of some use, but back, out of bullet range and amid the gun-pits (and the total weight of artillery was then a fraction of what it subsequently became) one saw clearly for the first time – and did not grasp what had happened – how this enormous steel plant could go on working against the other steel plant, over on Pilckem ridge right along to Messines, without our interference, and only regarding us as a target. Herein lay the possibility, so fully exploited later, of always taking trenches at will, whenever sufficient artillery was focused upon them. The prowess of individuals, of platoons, and battalions even, and subsequently anything up to a division, with its bombs and rifles and bayonets fixed, was grotesquely irrelevant. The infantry didn't matter. Such, however, was not then the opinion. I think we were only four nights in camp, and then paraded at dusk and marched to the railway near Vlamertinghe, and were taken up to Ypres by train. This was a novel and cheering experience. We thought the glassless compartments a great luxury, and the bulk of the train a perfect protection. When shrapnel came through the roof and hurt no one, it was considered a great joke, to the horror of the RTO, who implored us not to make so much noise, lest the Boche hear us. This only made men who had been living within earshot of the enemy laugh the more.

The company was this time in battalion reserve, and therefore held a 'keep', or fortified position, behind the reserve line and facing not only forward and to either flank, but, at a pinch, rearward. It occupied the village of St Jean, about 2km north-east of Ypres on the Thourout road, and straggled from the summit of the slight eminence that filled the north half of the Salient some hundreds of yards down the west or sheltered side of this. It was just within bullet range of the enemy, but as most of the buildings, except the church, were still standing, it afforded a good deal of cover from view and from weather. What seemed to us sand-bag shelters of immense strength had been constructed in the cellars of all the larger houses, while the then continuous double line of cottages made the street, at its western or lower end, a fairly safe dump to which horse transport came every night, while company headquarters, under the lee of a rockery in some old gentleman's garden, appeared to us nearly as commodious as the camp. On the northern side of the street was a good aid post. At the eastern or exposed end was a barrier of paving stones across the road that would certainly stop a whizz-bang or field artillery shell. Through the gardens behind the houses on either side ran the flank trenches that also served to give access to CTs that were supposed to connect with the front line. The whole place was thoroughly registered by machine guns, but the protection seemed ample, and we had learned the trick of listening and dodging those systematic visitations. What we did not realise was the rhythm of the war: how one side was perpetually inventing some defence that stalemated the opposing gun-fire, and how the other side immediately took steps to find a way of penetrating that defence. We did not grasp, not being professional students of tactics, that in losing the surprise of the first few weeks both sides lost the War. There remained a very different thing, the War of Attrition. It took a long while to learn that attrition was not merely a matter of decreasing manpower and materials, but something that affected the spirit.

That evening being dry and fine, with a magnificent moon, we all felt in good spirits. It is true that, after we crossed the Canal and divided into companies and were half-way up the fields to St Jean, we were stopped by A company coming clean across our route. Captain R., who commanded, asked me if I knew where we were, as his guides (runners sent by the battalion being relieved) had not turned up. I told him what little I knew and went on with D Company, F. being busy elsewhere. I had seen St Jean twice for a few minutes, and was not at much of a loss in identifying it. There followed the distribution of the sections, and the telling-off of parties to carry rations forward as soon as these arrived at the dump. Then we listened to the tramp of the – shires whom we relieved, 'going out', platoon by platoon, with that timbre of footfall so ominously different from that of troops 'going in'.

Next came the rumble of limbers, the muffled hurried voices of transport men anxious to be quit of their burdens, turn, and set their willing beasts galloping back to their lines. This was always a moment at which it was quite possible to lose a lot of men. The enemy could not fail to know what was going on. To begin with, he was doing the same thing himself, probably more efficiently. The noise of traffic on the broken pave was audible for miles, the spot known by air photos as well as if it had been measured with a foot-rule. I took care to keep most of the parties back until the first one or two were clean away. There remained Battalion HQ mess, machine gunners, and such special details. When they were all gone I found the valuable Barr and Stroud rangefinder still lying in the mud where it had been thrown. I folded it up in my raincoat and carried it back to Company H.Q. dug-out, where it was carefully put away. I still cherished the idea that someday I should be allowed to use it.

The night passed off quietly, and by daylight, from our situation, we had the novelty of enjoying a view. From Company HQ looking west, or rearward, we had in the foreground the white bones of Ypres. It appeared to be all built of stone, but this may have been because the brick buildings would naturally go first, much of it still dignified and marked with that intriguing decay which, allowing for utterly different sentiment at the root of two opposed styles of architecture, makes the present Parthenon so much more appealing to the imagination than the completest theoretic reconstruction of it. At our feet the Canal ran northward, and beyond it were the fertile plain of the Yser, bounded by Elverdinghe woods in the north, the slight rise of the ground by Poperinghe in the west, while southward rose the gravelly ridges of Mont des Cats with its convent, Mont de Boeschepe with its windmills, and Mont Noir with its pine trees. Most of the farms were then still standing, Vlamertinghe, Brielen and Dickebusch were intact barring a few roofs, and in the pale sunshine the whole made up into one of the landscapes of the Flemish School one had been brought up on. The one disturbing element, the railway, was deserted, thus helping the illusion. But nearer to us, of course, were incongruous traces of the strife we were engaged in, with its wholesale destruction and its extraordinary erections, or rather burrowings.

I think it was on the second night that, having seen all duties dismissed, rations distributed and the dump cleared, I was astonished to find more commotion than ever, Ypres-ward.

The keep was closed on this side by C.'s reserve machine gun post and 'knife rests' (roughly, hurdles laced with barbed wire). These had been pulled aside, and I found artillery transport coming through. An officer commanded the party, and I told him I didn't want him up in our lines, bringing down a lot of unnecessary shelling. He replied: 'That's what you're here for!' and I think a truer word was never spoken. That, precisely, I was beginning to see, was the place of infantry. The gunners were supposed to have a gun hidden somewhere in St Jean for the purpose of registering. I never discovered it, although I crawled over every inch of that rapidly collapsing village at one time or another. But the enemy had the same idea. The next night they started in to find that gun, and never was German character more clearly revealed to me. They employed a battery of 15cm guns (5.9 inches) of which one section seemed to be behind Pilckem and the other near Gheluvelt. They fired in turn rather more than once a minute, searching the entire place methodically yard-by-yard. At the same time their field artillery was directed upon the trenches forward. Soon a trickle of walking wounded, followed by the more laborious stretcher parties, began to wind down the street. The bombardment was so regular that I cleared most of the men from the dug-outs on the top of the slope (east end of the village) and made them lie down in the fields adjoining; even so, the platoon near the barrier lost fifteen men immediately by the destruction of a big house. We got together a party, under the company-sergeant-major, to dig for them, but some of the bodies were, I believe, never found, and were probably victims of a direct hit. After this, I stood by the barrier turning the stretcher-bearers off the road. About 50 yards away on either flank they were in comparative safety, and could reach our aid post, and when, very soon, that was overcrowded, the larger dressing station near the Canal head. I had several near shaves and was frightened out of my wits, but managed to stick it. There were, at moments, interesting things to see. A fair-sized, brick-built shop and dwelling-house was struck by a shell which appeared to land just inside the doorway. The building seemed to rise an inch or so, like a sponge filling with water, and then collapsed in a mere heap of ruin. One house began to burn, but water was not lacking, and we baled a CT on to it with waterproof sheets and buckets, and prevented it from being much of a mark. After about three hours the bombardment ceased, and I brought the men back to their stations. F. now came from his job at Battalion HQ and asked if I wanted to request our guns to retaliate. It seemed to me completely futile. They could shell the empty German trenches, no doubt, but I preferred to get the men rested and ready for whatever the morrow might bring.

It brought rain, and then, just before midday, as I was going round suppressing fires that smoked too much, I was astonished to find myself confronted with four civilians in tweed suits and bowlers, following a red-tabbed GSO. I asked him who he was and what he was doing, and he replied that Corps ought to have told me that. I referred the party to F., who apparently had been warned that a deputation of munition-makers would be allowed to see round, to get some idea what the trenches were like, and go home to preach the gospel of work. St Jean was not the trenches by 1,000 yards, but it was within bullet-range, and I dare say they saw and heard enough. They were very quiet and kept together. Unfortunately the war was not at its liveliest that morning. It was no use pointing to a mess of bricks and burnt clothing and shards of all sorts and saying, 'Fifteen of my men were killed there last night.' Nor was it impressive to point to a small hole in the parapet and explain that it had been a dug-out for two, but that a whizz-bang had knocked the beam that supported its 2 feet of sand-bags through the chest of my best corporal. There was only the endless hiss and scream of machine gun enfilading and ricochet, and occasional shrapnel bursts over the road. They may have complained of the waste, for S.A.A. lay all over the place, where it dropped from the men's equipment as they did their jobs. One of B.'s platoon put down a brazier on the floor of a dug-out, and was rewarded by five loud pops. A full clip had been lying there and ignited by the heat – harmlessly, of course. And where the CT called Garden Street joined the keep, a Lewis gunner had been hit and had dropped a box of unbelted and unclipped cartridges such as he required. The corner was a very dangerous one, any number of people were hit there, until eventually poor G. of C Company, who had been given the job of 'OC Garden Street' with a special series of parties to mend-up that incipient drain, was killed there. I certainly did not encourage any of my men to pick the stuff up, even in the hope that it could have been cleaned and rendered fit for use. Or the same munitioneers may have caught sight of the abandoned gun positions on the by-road that led from the west end of St Jean Street to Potije Chateau. I don't know if these dated from before the reverse of April 15th, but there were smashed-up limbers and rings of cordite lying all over the place. What they did see was a set of grotesquely accoutred individuals, cooking food, smoking, reading or gossiping, a few doing odd jobs with wire or bags, such as could be done in daylight, and one or two, with rifles in their hands, peering out at various well-protected places enemyward. There was a good deal of noise and a comprehensive stink, and everything was wet. In any case, during the following years we did not lack munitions.

It was during this tour that we got another lesson. C., the machine gunner, was a merry fellow. When A. and I occasionally treated each other to bits of 'One Gerrard,' or other fashionable vocal music, he would ask:

'Do you chaps always sing in your bath?'
'This isn't a bath, it's a trench!'
'What's the difference?'

Or:

'Are you chaps Lollards?'
'What's a Lollard?'
'I don't know, but you sound as if you were it, defending its young!'

He could imitate animals, give burlesque renderings of regimental personalities, and even others. His 'Lord Kitchener on a Ration Party' was funnier than many a 'turn' I have paid to see, and his 'Mayor of Poperinghe getting Married' showed a real insight into national characteristics. But on this evening he was dull and depressed, and we only gradually got out of him that one of his section, in the reserve post by the church, while cleaning a rifle had put a bullet between his own toes. C., who liked his job and his men, swore that it was a real accident. Had it not been, it would have amounted to a crime: 'self-inflicted wound,' which, next to being found asleep or drunk on guard, or wandering without arms, was as grave a charge as anything up to thorough desertion. C., however, had bandaged the man, and it remained to get him a new pair of boots quietly from Q.M. stores. We might not go out for days yet, and even so, we were Brigade reserve and would be kept close to the Canal. The difficulty was solved by taking the right size of boots off a casualty, and I believe no one else knew of the incident.

Eventually we did go out, as F. had truly said, only a mile or so, to Machine-Gun Farm on the Ypres-Brielen road. It was a beautiful starlit night, and we got away without further casualties, which was lucky, considering our depleted numbers. The farm itself was a stout brick structure, about 300 years old, consisting of a courtyard, enclosed by two-storey buildings of great solidity on three sides, and on the fourth by a large double gate which gave on to a cobbled entry, and thus led to a bridge over a deep wide moat that surrounded the whole. On the outer side of the bridge was a barbican tower of sorts. The place had long been evacuated and was shelled, but had resisted pretty well. Gunners had dug-outs of immense strength in the cellars; we slept under protection of the inch-thick pantiles. The following day was Sunday, and as the weather had clouded over, we held morning service in the big barn. I can't say I liked it. It seemed a ghastly travesty. If the Germans could have seen us, they would have shelled us. Had we caught them in such a mass, we should have done the same; not that either event would have materially altered the course of the War. I took my place and saw that the occasion was decorously observed. I supposed it was part of discipline, and one felt bound by one's duty as an officer. In the afternoon we censored an enormous sack of letters. It was not difficult; few officers in the infantry, not to mention other ranks, knew enough to say anything informative; but, once more, one obeyed orders. What else was there to do?

In the evening we paraded working arties and marched them up to the line we had held four weeks previously. I had one which was detailed to work on some badly shelled and flooded bit of reserve line, where our first battalion headquarters had been. The enemy had grown nervous again, or disliked our successors more than us (or, dare one hope, that those successors' machine gun and bombing retaliation was less effective?). Anyhow, they would not let the place alone. By some miracle – probably the difference caused by varying atmospheric pressure between registering in daytime and firing at night – we did not lose a man. But the laborious digging was knocked about, and I had to keep men strung out as thinly as possible (men like to get together to talk and there is mutual support and encouragement in it, not to mention the man-and-mate habit of skilled labour). Even so, I, the RE Corporal in charge, and some of the party were knocked off the bags into a filthy hole. However, at midnight I was able to fall in and march back a full complement.

Another diversion at Machine-Gun Farm was the Find-your-own-Route game. I suspect it had its origin in the fact that someone discovered that our men would take off their equipment to dig. There were orders and commotions about it, and I remember one indignant telephone message from Brigade: 'Do you know you are the only reserve troops we have within an hour's march? What would happen if we were surprised?' I said I didn't know. I regarded surprise as about as likely as sudden Peace, but didn't say so. However, orders were orders, and rather than have men crimed, we saw to it. Now, following on from this, here came the regulation that officers were to make themselves acquainted with the shortest route to the Canal bank. It was also part of the growing nervousness on our side as to a renewed gas attack.

Accordingly A. and I set off in the morning, and were joined by two platoon commanders from C Company. We found a route certainly, but I doubt that, even had we been able to memorise it and find it again in the dark, we could have got the men along it, encumbered as they were. The rich meadows were just now flooded, and this rendered them as slippery as ice. We ran into several gun positions, and were requested to go wide of them and not give them away to enemy observation and shelling. I did not reply: 'That's what you're here for!' We also discovered a cottage in which two aged and incredibly decrepit women were still living, partly, I think, because they had nowhere to go and no means of carrying their few belongings, partly from sheer lack of imagination and initiative, partly because they made what probably represented a fortune by selling coffee to neighbouring gunners. They sold some to us. Why they had not been evacuated by our own people, or the civil authority, as the population of Vlamertinghe, miles to rearward, had, I can't think.

This, in fact, was the main impression of that walk. The Salient was, I believe, the first sector in which the continual 'strafe' – big black stuff was bursting over and around Ypres all the time – had made the war-zone proper, that is, the desert inhabited only by combatants, nearly 10 miles wide. We wandered about Ypres for a bit – its extraordinary resistance to destruction struck a sort of awe into the most callous – and were viewed with great suspicion by the Town Major, a heroic soul who lived there and had frequently to be replaced by another like himself. However, our orders covered us.

We next went into the line on the higher ground near Potije Wood. Here the trenches for some hundreds of yards were dry and fairly well built, and no-man's-land was much narrower and interrupted by a belt of trees, in among the roots of which we kept a man lying out all day from before dawn until after dusk to listen and look if he could. He never saw or heard anything worthwhile, but from his description I grew all the more certain that our enemies only patrolled their front line and did not live in it. And soon convincing evidence came. A knob or mound in the enemy's support line was discovered from an air photo, and our 9.2 guns were instructed to demolish it. Even F. admitted what the result would be, and putting all men except the necessary sentries under such cover as existed, he and I scrambled down into the morass on our right, due east of the wood, where our front line ceased entirely, having been heavily shelled and flooded, and thus relapsing into a 'cemetery' where poor decomposing bodies were lightly covered, or floated, offending even our trench-hardened noses. We could see very little, and before many shots had been fired from our side, wop, wop, wop, came the retaliation right in our fire-bays. Nor was that all. We were apparently enfiladed from Hooge, and the men who tried to drag their wounded comrades out of burst-in dug-outs or from flattened parapets were hit by bullets apparently descending perpendicularly behind our defences. F. and I were busy enough for half an hour or so, as it was impossible to evacuate wounded by daylight. Finally F. said he had had enough of it and wired for counter-retaliation. I never enjoyed anything so much in my life. The whole field armament of the division was let loose on the German reserve line, and bodies, stakes, wire, sand-bags, fascines and concrete went hurtling up in the air to the height of 20 or 30 feet, about 500 yards behind their front line, as near as we could tell. And this silenced them for the time. Why, I can't think, as in neither case were the guns the objective; but I suppose they were beginning then to nurse their infantry reserves for Verdun. And trench mentality cannot be better exemplified than by the fact that a decent member of the middle classes, such as I hope I am, actually enjoyed the spectacle.

I now began to learn the rhythm of the war in this sector. This sort of incident gingered up the artillery on both sides. Rationing and the evacuation of wounded became difficult. Nervousness increased certainly on the enemy's part, judging by the quantity of star-shells he used. It led up, sooner or later, to a minor operation on the one part or the other, and then quiet supervened; as no advantage was to be gained there, even by the gigantic effort of 1917, how much less, then, by our inter-battalion scrapping. We went out after four days this time, as the whole Brigade went back into Divisional Rest. 'Pop', or Poperinghe, to which we went, seemed like Heaven. We were billeted in a deserted convent. I have since tried to recapture the sensation of sleeping on the stone floor of a nun's cell, and waking in the morning to see the blue smoke of our cookers rise against the last gloriously russet leaves of a great chestnut tree in the garden. Once more we were soldiers; guards were set and parades ordered. Then there was the finding of a football field, and a good deal of eating and drinking. The first night there was neither whisky, wine nor beer (no Expeditionary Force canteen had been established), but someone procured a bottle of crème de Cacao and we drank that and water. Alcohol was a necessity, and we had long finished the ration rum.

The second night neither A. nor I had any parade, and went to the 'Follies', a perriot entertainment enlivened by two ladies in the caste. I believe that originally they were local girls, but their places were taken by male impersonators, and the names, Lanoline and Vaseline, with which they had been christened, gave way to Ack Emma and Pip Emma. I have heard 'The End of a Perfect Day' and 'Old Roger Rum' sung since that time without being able to account for the delight I then experienced, except that we were Divisional reserve and were liable, as many a Divisional reserve before and since, to be called out of the hall and pushed into the train for Ypres. The worst that happened on this occasion was that the tenor came on with his make-up half wiped off, and asked us to evacuate the building quickly and quietly, as the enemy were shelling the town and making the Town Major nervous. This caused pandemonium, as we did not think the reason sufficient, and the funny man took the opportunity to run from the back of the hall shouting, 'Do you want to buy a dug-out?'

Graver work was on foot next morning, however, when we officers were all summoned to a château in the rue de Fumes, to attend an officers' conference, I forget on what subject. But in the middle of it I was taken aside by the Colonel and told to report at Brigade Headquarters, rue de Proven, to take up the duties of Intelligence Officer. This gave rise to the usual witticisms, but I hastily 'poshed up', removed my Webb equipment, put on a Sam Browne belt, and a new cap and the riding breeches C. unkindly said belonged to the Underground Artillery.

I found the Brigadier and Brigade Major in a substantially furnished living-room of a house in the rue de Proven, was asked some questions and given my orders, which were to start next day with the Brigade Machine-Gun Officer to take over the sector into which the Brigade was shortly going. My companion K. and I accordingly set off the following day in the G.S. waggon that carried valises, and arrived at the Canal bank, but not the Canal bank that I knew. It was a stretch of the embankment nearer Ypres, and contained several line dug-outs, in which it was possible to stand upright, and which were lined with canvas and provided with wooden bedsteads with 'mattresses' of fencing-wire. Several beautiful old chairs diversified the S.A.A. boxes on which I was accustomed to sit. Thus the General and the Brigade Major (sharing with the Staff Captain) had a dug-out each, K. and I another, while a fourth was at once mess and office. In the thickness of the embankment a tunnel had been cut, giving access to the waterside, and in this the signallers worked and slept. Brigade Signals Officer had a small dug-out of the more usual kind near it.

The thing which I found so exciting was the large map, or, rather, set of maps, on the mess-office wall. Few infantrymen of that period had seen anything like it. There was the whole front (a much shorter affair than it subsequently became) with trenches marked, gun positions shown, areas of Corps, Divisions, and Brigades outlined, and the allotments of artillery and other support to first line troops indicated. I learned for the first time the size and weight of the guns supporting the very sectors I had held, and noted the many recent alterations and additions that had been made since the early 'offensives' when the entire ammunition supply had been shot away and the batteries rationed. There was even then, in the light of subsequent ideas upon the subject, the puniest armament of divisional and corps medium and heavy guns, while the concentrated weight of 'Army Troops' artillery that was massed for the later offensives was not indicated at all. I don't suppose it then existed. As regards the trenches shown, some existed in theory and had never been dug at all, some had been shelled flat, some flooded and fallen in, some had suffered a mixture of the last two fates. That much I could correct straight away. The more comprehensive side of the job, I saw, was to get to know the other units of the Brigade, each of which was to be provided with a battalion Intelligence Officer, with a corporal and section. I should have to 'do' for my own battalion as well as carrying on the Brigade duties. I got a line inserted in Brigade Orders, calling for a return of names, etc., for this organisation, and went to 'bed' directly after mess, as it was no good trying to do anything while the whole sector was swarming with fatigues and arties. I knew that this would be quiet by midnight or a little after, arranged accordingly and went to my 'kip'. It was dark, of course, and I was used to undressing without a candle, but discovered by sound that K. was already in 'bed'. I had missed him at mess, but assumed he had had to make an early start on his round. I made some remark and the reply was a groan. I then took my torch to look at him, and eventually got the admission that he was ill. It seems an anticlimax now, but those who did not know him and were not of our particular set, cannot imagine how deeply he felt the disgrace of being sick in the line. Against his wishes, and because of his extreme weakness, I got a doctor, who soon diagnosed appendicitis. How on earth he stood the jolting journey in the wagon I cannot think. The sequel is that after going home and being operated on, he went to the mounted MGC and was killed in Palestine, the natural fate of a better man and braver soldier than ever I was.

I still reckoned on four hours' sleep, but had hardly gone off before trench-instinct made me sit up and reach for my boots. At first it was only a great increase in rifle and MG fire, but suddenly the whole divisional artillery let loose salvo after salvo, and on the top of that the heavies joined in. Before they had fired twice I was in the office, where the Brigade Major was already at the telephone. He had the greatest possible difficulty in making himself heard in the din, but apparently located the trouble in the sector that had been held by my battalion on their first tour. He told me to get to divisional reserve and have them 'standing-to' in readiness, but by the time I was back from Signals the danger, such as it may have been, was over. It was a magnificent demonstration of that most important axiom of modern warfare: 'Never obey orders. They are already superseded.' The rule was that infantry units were not to communicate direct with gunners. The proper procedure was for the sub-command to inform battalion headquarters, these to request Brigade for artillery support, Brigade to speak to the appropriate gunner authority. Then, I knew quite well, would have followed the usual interchange: 'Have they advanced from their trenches?' 'How do you know?' 'On what front?' etc., and by the time some small detachment of wretched infantry in a water-logged gully had been massacred, some decision would have been taken. As it was, it appeared that a bright platoon commander in the –shires, finding himself confronted by a big raid or bombing party of the enemy, signalled SOS so violently that a sleepy signaller at battalion Signals had scared Brigade Signals into putting it straight through to the artillery. The result was that the attackers were immediately and effectively caught. Rifle and MG fire must have found many of them in the open, their trenches received the fire of our 18-pounders, while dug-outs, gun-pits, dumps and tramways, of which they had many – anything, in fact, that could be spotted by air photo – had the benefit of 4.7, 6 inch, and 9.2. The response was feeble and desultory, a few big shells bursting along the embankment of the Canal or among the gun positions. This seems to mark a sort of turning-point in the shift of initiative that was the characteristic of the transition from 1915 to 1916, the beginning of giving as good as we got, which, for some time to come, camouflaged for many an infantryman the fact that he went west in any case. I also caught a faint glimpse of the glory of war, and why the more secure persons are willing to wage it. From the safety of the embankment the sight was magnificent. The Brigade front was lit to a tawny red by the incessant discharges, shells flickered all over the ridges held by the enemy, and there was a majestic sonority in the deep-throated clangour of the guns behind. I did think of my battalion subjected to just such treatment, in the reverse direction, a week or two before. Anti-climax soon supervened. Nothing happened. Some scores of casualties, but the end no nearer save by the effluxion of time.

The next day was gloriously fine, and the banks of the Canal shone with the pale gold of the poplars. The cover they afforded was, however, deceptive, as I found when I took a number of NCOs to the western side to give them instruction in reading the compass and taking bearings. Wherever we went, whatever we did, large bursts of shrapnel followed us, so that eventually it was impossible to teach anything. Nor could I discover whether we were seen from Boesinghe or from beyond the Menin road. We had to be content with such training as could be carried out under cover. In the afternoon I saw the Colonel of my battalion appear at Brigade HQ, and was soon sent for. It seemed that B. had gone to an appointment at GHQ in the new Camouflage Department. He had some special knowledge, I forget what it was, of the work. I had seen the circular, but it meant nothing to me. His definite seconding from the battalion left F. with only one subordinate in the company. The Colonel wanted me back, so there was nothing for it but to hand over the job, such as it was, to one of the other battalion Intelligence Officers. Nor was it possible to discover which was the most use, or to recommend him if one had so discovered. The appointment had to be governed by the arrival of reinforcements which would permit of a CO releasing an officer for the duty. As a matter of fact, I only went to the other side of the Canal, and to superintending working parties. I was lucky, for shortly afterwards the entire squad was wiped out.

Occasionally I went across the bridge to Mess with Brigade by invitation. The General preferred having his in his bunk, but the Staff Captain, C., who had come from my battalion to do Brigade machine guns, the Signals Officer, and the new Intelligence Officer formed a cheery crowd, in that reasonably safe and fairly dry spot. C. insisted that there were oysters in the Canal, and when we defied him to produce them, said he was short of bait. As there did not appear to be much use in indenting for this, Intelligence suggested cutting up the Padre, very small, and throwing him in. Nor should it be for one moment supposed that this was said out of disrespect to this officer of his cloth. Had he not been a thoroughly good and brave chap, and emphatically one of us, his name would not have been taken so lightly.

What strikes me, however, in looking back at the Brigade Mess of that date, was the useful comparison which it forms with the later organisation of the War.

The formation of (nominally) 4,000 officers and men was self-contained and practically stationary. True, it had no jurisdiction over other arms or services, but it retained its allotment of Divisional Cyclists, with scarlet shoulder-straps, controlled its own Signals, as well as the activities above mentioned. It remained in the same Division, Corps and Army, and in practice went in and out of the same trenches. It was not until the Somme that my battalion changed neighbours. Not that one got to know other units in the Brigade. The trench warfare of the period was carried on by small detached units, companies split into platoons and parties, who seldom saw their own battalion headquarters, not to mention others.

These duties took us further south, nearer the Menin road. The trenches here were drier and better built, and had need to be, in view of rifle, grenade and Minenwerfer bombardment which they received, owing to the narrower no-man's-land. On the other hand, M.G. and rifle fire were practically ineffective and one moved with more ease than in the shoulder-high breast-works of the northern part of the Salient.

Here I begin to lose the thread of these memories. I kept no diary, and can only say that while the impressions of the first few weeks are fairly consecutive, there begins at the point I have now reached an increasing blur in the images I have retained. It was partly that the various incidents that succeeded were no longer novel but were mere repetitions of previous occurrences, partly the fact that I was trying to do two jobs at once, and partly that about this time – though why then and not before, I don't know – that the MO coming into the dug-out that served for Company HQ to make some arrangement, instead of giving me the usual greeting, took my wrist in one hand and with the other stuck a thermometer into my mouth. I think C. was there. I remember someone saying that I really preferred the old-fashioned tobacco. The MO said nothing to me, but I may have been thick in the head. I certainly disliked the dug-out, which was on a level with the Yperlé stream that ran behind and lower than the Canal, so much so that I did not sleep even during the short periods when I was not on duty, but watched the roof of the place, under the impression that there were rats in it, which was nothing surprising, as one of B.'s last experiences before he left us was to find one asleep on his feet. At another time I got the idea that the top was slowly sinking in on us. This again would not have been wonderful, but it struck me, for some reason, as additionally horrid by the light of the candle that we had to keep burning in case of some sudden call.

I am clearer about the next time I saw the MO The Brigade Intelligence Officer and I had occasion to go in broad daylight from St Jean by means of the ordinary road ditch, for the road here, on the eastern side of the St Jean undulation, was in plain sight of the enemy, from Hooge, for a couple of miles. Our idea was to take over an old OP the artillery had abandoned. It lay half-way down the slope, between our support and front line, and consisted in a tiny thatched summer house (in a little road-side garden belonging to some *rentier*) of which the bottom had been knocked away, and the conical top had settled down intact between some thick bushes. Among the roots of these a hole had been dug and we could squat in there and survey miles of wet upheaval, stakes and wire reflected in oozy pools, rotting sand-bags and blasted trees. I don't know what we expected to see, but we didn't see it. There was absolutely no movement behind the masses of German wire, and although it was interesting to observe our shell-bursts over the fold after fold of vaguely upturned earth, it became evident to me then that nothing of the nature of the bombardment of which we were capable would lay that labyrinth open to capture. I suppose we corrected the maps as far as possible, but what I remember best is seeing our doctor walking calmly down the middle of the road we had just avoided. I shouted to him to get into the ditch, but he replied that he must go to A Company in the fire-bays, where some badly wounded needed him. He passed on out of sight, and why he was never hit I can't imagine. The whole place skipped with bullets, and shrapnel was continuous, though, I thought, too high. He wasn't hit. I saw him later, in his dressing station, about some of our casualties. But that simple walk of his was a far braver thing than most historic heroics, and would undoubtedly, in any other war, have won him the VC. I have seen pictures of men gaining that rare distinction by doing exactly what he did.

It must have been about this time that all units in the sector were engaged in digging the Great Drain. It had been borne in on the consciousness of highly-placed people that it was useless for units to continue to pump or canalise the same lot of water from their own bit of trench to their neighbours, and a comprehensive scheme was set on foot to put the lot into the Canal. It was scientifically planned by REs and we all worked at it. It was, of course, soon spotted by the enemy, who mistook it for some recondite effort towards an offensive movement, and shelled it with big stuff. Thus, in the intermittent dark, trying to see where my party were flinging their shovelfuls of pea-soup-like 'earth,' I found myself involved in an upheaval like the last day. It took me seconds, I suppose – but apparently minutes – to move first one limb and then the other, and found that the left side of me was jammed in a wooden A-frame that had been closed up around me, like a pair of tongs. The terror of the moment, however, was its absolute loneliness. While trying to wrench myself free, the next flare went up, and although I was in the midst of a large army, there was not a soul in sight. I had a passing impression of being the last left alive in the whole Salient. This passed rapidly, of course, and I shouted for the NCO to get the men together and go on digging, especially as it was obvious that many of the party must have been buried. It seemed a long while before I heard an answering hail, and the party began to collect. Some had been flung many yards and appeared dazed. Some had simply taken the nearest cover. I forgot how many casualties there were. It took me several minutes to get free, and eventually an injury materialised that troubled me for years.

Another feature of the period was the stimulus given to the policy of raids. Those of us who had been there all the autumn knew what that meant, but we were addressed by the General on the subject, and there came to us an officer in semi-naval uniform, with some new and curious dodges for wire-cutting. These were large clockwork devices, like dumb-waiters designed by Heath Robinson, with a charge of gun-cotton, detonated by a trigger that was intended to catch on the enemy's wire as the machine ticked across the ground. After some abortive attempts to follow this up with raiding parties, this officer and a hundred of the Royals, next to us, disappeared altogether. I don't know if it was ever discovered what happened to them, but the raiding policy was less prominent after that, and company commanders were forbidden to take part. Raiders were promised artillery protection, of course, but as gunners subsequently explained to me, it was very difficult to be sure, with the variations of temperature and density, whether these night-barrages would do what was intended.

Yet from time to time we did make prisoners. I remember C Company being very proud of two Germans who walked, unarmed, into their lines. This enabled us to know what units were opposite us, and might have justified the raids even, had they not been so costly.

At that time I felt little bad result from being buried in the Great Drain, but the incident had a serious consequence. Just before it I had been sent to get pay for the company from the Field Cashier at Proven. Then we were suddenly sent up for the extra digging on the drain, and before we could pay out, I was buried. When we got back to the Canal bank, my clothes were in tatters and the notes – 1,000 francs, I think – missing. This necessitated a Court of Inquiry in a dug-out, and I was solemnly asked to produce the tunic and show the state of it. I replied that I had sent it to be mended. I don't know whether this went against me, but I never heard any more of the occurrence. I didn't much care, being by this time queer in the head. Soon after this F. gave me a chit and told me to report to the M.O. at Essex Farm. I can't say I connected the affair with myself particularly, but when I got to that shelled skeleton of a house, a doctor asked me some questions, took my temperature and put me on an ambulance. I lay that night on a stretcher on the stone floor of Trois Tours Chateau, I think. The CO took a good deal of interest in my wrists, which were very swollen from the rubbing of wet sleeves, but which looked funny, I suppose. Also I was in a filthy state, made worse by having had to tear up my sponge to clean my pistol. I was left alone with an officer who had several MG bullets through the thick of the leg, and another who was stuck fast with rheumatism (I think), so that when they lifted him he came up all in one piece as though he had no joints. He could speak, though, while the other was collapsed. I wanted to know, I remember, what the noise was. I could distinguish the regular sounds of the front, but between those and me was another roaring, rattling sound, and I could not make out if it were outside me or inside my head. He assured me that it was outside on the road, and was made by tractors taking up a new 8-inch battery, the first of this calibre, I recollect. For some reason this seemed to exonerate me from worrying, and I next remember hospital train, casualty clearing station, and finally Base Hospital at Boulogne. Once I was washed and fed and had rested in bed for a few nights, I soon threw off any symptoms I showed, and should speedily have been released for duty, but there were just then, I believe, the first paratyphoid and tetanus scares. Anyhow, they took some blood from my arm and analysed it. I suppose it passed the test, for, after a short convalescence in a French 'home' on the coast, I was discharged and returned to Depot. The main impression left on my mind is the extreme efficiency of the medical service. I saw casualties of all sorts brought into that Base Hospital, and the other medical units through which I arrived at it. In the initial stages, dressing station, aid post and clearing station, casualties frequently arrived looking like lumps of mud more than human beings. But they were washed and dealt with so that in a few hours they were sitting up and talking to one. Hospitals (like everything else) were then more general and less specialised than they subsequently became, for I remember all round me officers, and in the next ward other ranks, with every variety of gunshot wound, one case of pneumonia, one boy who had twenty odd pieces of shrapnel in him: they were always taking him off to the operating theatre, no light task as there was no lift in the building. He seemed to groan and cry all the time until he died. There were also gas cases, an officer with a nervous affection of the heart, and a case of delirium tremens, though how this last had managed to get enough stuff to bring about such a result has always been a mystery. He must have been employed at base or somewhere out of range. It was difficult enough in the parts where I had been to get any quantity of strong drink sufficient to disguise the chlorine in the water. I remember his wild talk about a negro and a black retriever dog that sat on his bed suddenly ceasing as the orderly ushered in a lady dressed in most beautiful furs, who had apparently been hurriedly summoned from England. She stood perfectly silent, looking at him, until with one shriek he buried his head beneath the bedclothes. I never knew what happened to him.

* * *

When I next saw the battalion it was in Poperinghe, preparing to go into the line. The whole brigade had been out to rest, reinforcements had come up, the depleted platoons were made up to strength, the battalion Mess was full of strangers. Among them was I., who came from the Honourable Artillery Company. He had a great tale of how his celebrated battalion arrived at Westoutre in 1914 and was brigaded with the old First Division. In an estaminet two members of the renowned regiment were discussing whether they had paid their subscriptions. A private of the –shires overheard and shouted: 'Hi, mates, here's a bloke in the Honourable b–––y Artillery what's been and paid to come to this b–––y country!' (Loud and prolonged cheers.)

On the whole the impression was favourable. Among the original 'K' enlistments had been men of all ages and conditions, who had joined from excellent motives, but had, in the enthusiasm of early days, not been sufficiently sorted out. The reinforcement were much more uniform in physique and age, and among the new officers we felt the benefit of the now innumerable promotions from the ranks. There were none, I think, who had no previous trench experience. One of the first people I met was the Major. He shook me by the hand. 'Good-bye, Mottram, I'm going home!' It came as a great shock. The removal of that figure with the South African and other ribbons, years of experience, and soldierly bearing, made one feel so exposed. I don't know if he had any personal reasons, but I believe that this was the time at which the order appeared that battalion commanders were not to be over 45 years of age, and seconds-in-command were limited to forty-two. He survived the War, but died at what seemed to me an early age for so robust a man, and I think his life was shortened by the horrid changes that had overtaken warfare, rendering the 'soldier' that he had been, and the 'fighting' he was prepared to do, completely obsolete. Among the 'other ranks' the matter was simpler. The RSM and the Police Sergeant simply walked into the orderly room, very correctly dressed, and presented their papers, showing them time-expired. After this, I doubt if there were a dozen regular soldiers left in the battalion.

We marched up, and I think that was the last time I (and possibly anyone else) ever saw a battalion in column set off from its billets and retain its formation until well through the artillery positions. We must have been obvious enough to enemy aircraft, but were not molested, and as we broke up into smaller and smaller parties, and took over the line from our predecessors, I began to have definitely what I can only call the nineteen-sixteen feeling. The machine gun and artillery fire against us was certainly not so sustained or deadly as it had been. This may well be the case, as the enemy were concentrating every available unit before Verdun, and may have actually depleted the forces opposing us, and were therefore anxious to be left alone as much as possible. Or the German command may about this time have renounced the Salient as a bad job. Certainly our people were in better heart, far more heavily armed as regards artillery, particularly in the medium calibres of howitzers. (When I say this, I am not relying on figures, which are not in my possession, but merely recording the personal sensations of an infantry officer, who, holding the same trenches at intervals for months, now began to feel much better supported.) But there was a new spirit of organisation abroad. It showed itself in the smallest detail of routine. The relief of the outgoing battalion was carried out, as I have said, piecemeal. I actually got my two platoons into their designated trench next Potije Wood with only two casualties. Mills grenades were now plentiful, and we received about this time our first issue of steel shrapnel helmets and box respirators. I think there were twenty of each for the battalion, and they went, of course, to stretcher-bearers and bombers. And yet further the new spirit became manifest. The machine gunners were now hardly part of the battalion, but worked almost entirely from Brigade; and there was already being formed an entirely new arm – the Trench Mortar. It is true that we had had experiments previously with small brass engines which we disliked, because, while not a match for the Minenwerfer of the enemy, they were sufficiently cumbrous and noisy to attract those most painstaking and nervous men, the German gunners, and while our infantry derived but little protection from these early forms of mortar, they caused the whole position for hundreds of yards to be plastered with shells. We were therefore most favourably impressed by the Stokes mortar, a device like a gigantic pencil-holder, a cylinder closed at one end, on the interior of which was a spike. The cartridge was allowed to slide in from the mouth, or open end, until the gun-cotton charge at its base was detonated by the spike, the shell being thrown high in the air and, falling flat in or upon the enemy works, bounced a few feet and exploded, giving a far-reaching shrapnel effect. The weapon was mounted on a simple tripod, was easily handled, offered no mark; owing to the high angle of fire, the ground took the recoil, if any, and the discharge of the loosely-fitting shell gave a pop rather than a bang, and being directed upwards, must have been very hard for the enemy to locate. Numbers of men had volunteered for this arm, or for the 'toffee-apple' and other varieties of mortar, and there also appeared orders for a roll of men willing to transfer to 'heavy MG Corps' and other specialities, the very names of which meant nothing. In fact, it was being recognised that the infantryman with his rifle and bayonet, fed even with grenades, was little else than that which the enemy had always described him as, fodder for cannon.

Another welcome change was the new flood of supplies especially those relating to the incessant building necessitated by trench warfare. The most important were the new frame dug-outs. Instead of shallow pent-houses of sandbags that fell down if they were not blown flat, we had now wooden frames roughly 6 by 3 by 2 feet high, which formed a solid basis on which sand-bags could be piled, with some chance of their staying. Then we had a fresh and efficient equipment of Vermorel sprayers (machines like blight eradicators, which squirted a compound that neutralised the chlorine gas), fans, and other devices. The trenches were better sited. It had, apparently, been decided to abandon the bit of front trench that ran north-east of Potiji Wood, which was blown flat and flooded, to replace it with a new trench that lay in a tiny but sufficient fold in the land north of and through the wood itself. It must have been very well concealed naturally, and it is difficult now to believe that most of the trees in the wood, a spinney of approximately 500 yards in each direction, were still standing. Anyhow, I remember that, at the north-west corner of the wood, there was an angle of brick wall with the framework, even some of the glass powdering down on the mummified grapes of a vinery, and, most surprising of all, a summer-house of 'rustic work', perhaps 20 feet high, stood erect. It is true that a 5.9 had gone clean through the trunk of it, but an artillery observer was secreted under the thatch, and his signallers in the brick basement. I made friends with him at once, and was allowed to crawl up into his nest, keeping flat against the wall, pore over his maps and have a squint through his glass at the masses of German wire.

It was a very fine vantage point. From it could be seen the whole field that had been fought over so intensely in the second battle of Ypres. I had read of the exploits of those half-dozen divisions that had been annihilated in establishing the very line of which I now held a bit, after the first gas attack. Even in the short space of time the conditions had changed almost out of recognition. Right up to the end of June, 1915, the defence of the Salient, frequently broken, had been conducted by counter-attacks carried out by hurriedly-summoned reinforcements of a battalion or less, here or there. Detailed accounts of what happened were even then to hand, and having read these, and looking at the very spots named in them, I marvelled at the alteration that had come about in so short a time. The now well-known incidents of field-guns brought up to fire at a range of 200 yards, of generals walking up to uncut wire, ordering the attackers to lie down, and then (presumably) walking back to the signallers and calling for further artillery preparation, had already become almost incredible, as were the British offensives at

Neuve Chapelle or Richebourg, with their puny resources and easy mark afforded by the German mass formation then in use. The difference was two-fold, physical and moral. As to the first, the landscape had completely changed. Then, natural cover, trees and hedges, buildings and embankments were all standing, but the artificial obstacles, regular connected trench-lines, always three and sometimes many more times deep, did not exist. This links up with the change in 'moral' or human outlook. The men of the dozen divisions of the second battle of Ypres were all heroes, not merely in effort but in the atmosphere through which they moved. They were mostly killed before they had time to discover how cold and wet and futile the War was. In fact, their war wasn't. Their trenches were too few and shallow to form a gigantic waterworks draining the whole countryside.

It mattered extremely, in those days, what a single platoon (or not infrequently a squadron of dismounted cavalry) did. Survivors to whom I have talked were quite unconscious of the tremendous fate that hung upon the use of their individual rifles, often do not seem to know what was happening, and even today could not find the spot to which they were rushed, in the nick of time, never having seen it on the map.

I caught but a glimpse of that period of the combat, in the early weeks of my time. But, virtually, Loos ended, and Verdun and the Somme put clean out of sight, that phase of the War. The gallantries of those early days would have been criminal lunacy a year later. By the end of 1915 it was possible to lose a whole platoon in raiding the German trenches, or even in doing nothing whatever, without affecting the War in the slightest, except to slow-up, very temporarily, our initiative. Before I had been long in front of Ypres, field-guns did not move by daylight within 5 miles, not to mention 200 yards, of their targets. We had acquired and used gas, and were even making a respectable competition in grenade and machine gun and trench-mortar tactics. Generals no longer walked up to the wire. But it is impossible to divide the War strictly into periods. The situation was even stranger than that. In between and contemporary with those early battlefields, from below the southern limit of the Salient, by 'Plugstreet', all-round the town of Armentières to Laventie, lay an extraordinary sector where the line did not budge for over three years. I do not mean that men were not being killed there all the time, or that the usual precautions were not necessary in clear weather, but the situation there was so extraordinary that I must deal with it separately. And lest I have made some mistake about the trend of the War, I have looked up Sir Arthur Conan Doyle's Campaign in *France and Flanders*. I find that, writing in early 1917 about the events of 1915, he says, speaking of '– – –, an artillery attack,' 'Such an attack probably represents the fixed type of the future, where the guns will make an area of country impossible for human life and the function of the infantry will simply be to move forward afterwards and to occupy ... It was not a contest between men and men, but rather between men and metal, in which our battalions were faced by a deserted and motionless landscape, from which came the ceaseless downpour of shells ...'

Such is the almost prophetic conclusion (strengthened, no doubt, by observation of the Somme battle) of an experienced and weighty writer whose knowledge goes back to the Boer War. His words describe, better than any I shall ever find, a change that began to daunt the soldier of 1916. The men of 1915 laid down their lives to hold some place of which they did not know the name. A year later, their successors knew the sector all too well. It was the place where the line had twice been pushed back a couple of miles, and where, in order to maintain the trenches in which we British were besieged, over half the battalion, including all their friends and fellow-enlistments, had been lost. Thus, queer as it may sound, I believe men welcomed the chance they got in the gas attack of December 1915, or the effort a month or so later on a narrow front to regain a trench which, if I remember, was called 'Willow Walk' and was, in my humble opinion, anyhow untenable. These little-known affairs of which I or anyone else saw little or nothing, did give an opportunity to the rank and file of shooting at something, though not, I think, at mass formations. The former disclosed the inefficiency of the calico PH helmet, for there were many gas casualties, and whole companies were vomiting and helpless. That may have been the last time wave gas was used. It might have been as serious in its consequences as the battle of the previous April, on almost identical ground, had not the breeze shifted to the disadvantage of the Germans at the crucial moment. The other affair cost many valuable lives, and produced a negligible result.

It is a pity that the painters of battle pictures cannot paint one of that typical minor offensive. The men crouching under a sloppy parapet, while for twenty-four hours great masses of metal were flung over their heads against the objective. Then the 'charge' – the slow and difficult crawl forward to find the enemy trench, that had been so carefully blown to pieces that it could not be identified; the attempt to make some sort of cover, and the inevitable counter-bombardment that wiped out the attackers, until a few famished scarecrows crawled back with the news to their starting-point. Officially, of course, soldiers never retire except by express order; frequently, however, in a modern battle any sort of order fails to reach them. It is not only that all soldiers, except a few inverted eccentricities, are afraid. They are. One of the few worthy traits of soldiering is the conquest, not the avoidance, of Fear. I remember, in the middle of one of these affairs, conducting a relief, and finding young X. of B Company going somewhere or other with a party. The kid (he was eighteen, I think) was sobbing, and as we passed in the CT he grabbed my arm, crying: 'Oh, Mottram, isn't it awful!' I told my sergeant to carry on, and walked a few yards with him, to point out how necessary it was that he should control himself before the men. The Colonel sent him home, but eventually he came out again and did well, I heard.

Coupled, then, with better organisation and equipment, the first rumours of the preparations for the Somme provided a very strong stimulus to the imagination. We were on the Canal bank when they first reached us, watching the slow demolition of Nordhof Farm. The big solid old place, companion to Machine-gun Farm, had withstood the new methods of war for a twelvemonth, but apparently the Germans now had made up their minds to destroy it. Corps Artillery, whose H.Q. had billeted there, had, I believe, already moved away, for by this time, except infantry reserves of small formations and guns in action, no one lived east of Vlamertinghe. The enemy artillery took all day, using (necessarily) very big howitzers. The row was regular and incessant, great columns of white dust from the plaster, and pink dust from the brickwork, rising high in the air. We had to put police on to prevent our men hunting for nose-caps when they ought to have been asleep, preparing for the night's digging. Even so, we got a remarkable collection, some 'noses' being constructed of what appeared to be the material of which telegraph insulators were made, on a metal frame, a fact on which we founded a good many theories. The evidences of preparation on our own side were even more pronounced. The personnel of the battalion was changing rapidly. Officers and men were constantly volunteering for balloons or flying, machine gun corps, or trench mortars.

All that was comprehensible and reasonable enough, although I and others had strong sentiments about sticking to the battalion. But about this time came queerer and queerer circulars, demanding the most extraordinary qualifications – all sorts of engineers, draughtsmen and mechanics went to special branches, and then there was a call for officers speaking Portuguese that we mistrusted, as it was taken to mean joining the East African Expeditionary Force, instead of which it was an endeavour to provide Liaison Officers for the Portuguese Army that joined us and was wiped out at Laventie in 1918; and another for those speaking French, coupled with some other ability which I have forgotten. I went down on this last list, under the impression that we were going into the Somme next to, or overlapping the French, and would require to be able to keep touch with them. Bolder spirits said it was because we were going right through, this time, into untouched country where the civil population had never seen British troops, and that I should get a sort of 'advance party' job for the brigade. I didn't mind which it was; there was a sort of etiquette still in the battalion that made us volunteer for anything that looked like being useful. The 'wangle' had not yet descended to us.

We next went into the new GHQ trench that had been dug in the rear of the Potiji position, to compensate, I suppose, for the obliterated bit of the front line. I don't know who gave the line that name, the only reason I discovered was the straightness of it, which made C. say that some chap at Montreuil had seen a map by accident and drawn a line on it. But the siting had a curious effect; the Germans, of course, found it in a photograph and took a dislike to it and shelled the portion next the Thourout road to bits. But further south their usually exact fire seemed to go just over the top by a few yards, so that one was safe close under the parapet, while the latrines were dangerous. Thus, at night, one had to climb on to the parapet and walk along it, as it was the only bit of firm foothold across what was otherwise a morass in which wading was deep and the depth of mud below unplumbed. This was partly owing to the nature of the soil, which made the top of the St Jean undulation hold water that would have run away a few yards down the slope on either side. However, by management, my command had relatively few casualties there, and these were mainly wounds in the lower part of the body, owing to the exposed means of access. These were difficult to handle, being much more noisy and convulsive than men hit in the head just over the sand-bags. One thing I remember well, and that is that after the regular carrying parties were gone and the spell of digging and revetting finished (for we now had a fair supply of timber, and regular workshops had been installed far back by Division REs), my last job was to go round before the shovels were gathered in and see that every scrap of new work, wood or bags, was liberally plastered with liquid mud from the trench bottom or rear. Anyone who has studied the sharp definition that contrasts in colour will give in a good air photo will realise why. Anyhow, it was a fairly lucky tour for us, and C.'s regular machine gun work every night seemed to do something to make the enemy keep his head down. This was as well, for we still had only wooden pickets, not the corkscrew iron of the Germans, and the noise made by working-parties in support lines was almost impossible to suppress, as it could be suppressed in the front line. Yet the showers of sparks from bullets striking on the wire that the men were using, and the constant searching with shrapnel, were certainly less frequent than they had been.

On one of these nights, Captain R., who had been promoted Major, came round 'visiting' in place of the Colonel. I was taking my turn off, in a cucumber-frame dug-out, and he crawled in beside me and we had a long discussion over a sketch-map I had made of the sector, and the possibility and advisability of trying to drain and rebuild the useless portion of the support line. The thing that sticks in my mind, though, is the way his sentences trailed off, as if he were thinking of something else and was just going to tell me what it was. I waited sometimes for a perceptible interval, hoping that he would tell me what was on his mind, not only from 'manners' to a superior officer but because I liked and respected him. He never got it out, however, and I have wondered since if he knew he was going to be killed. It didn't take much arithmetic to calculate what the chances of survival of any of us were, officers of the battalion averaging about six weeks' life, I think, at that time. But it seemed to me that it was rather a premonition than any logical view of his case that made him fall so silent. He had just over three months to live, and I never saw him again, except on parade.

For my luck just then asserted itself. I forget what trivial job I was doing in that yellow-and-black half-light, when a runner came to summon me to Company Headquarters. I left my sergeant in charge and walked along the top of the parapet to the Company Headquarters dug-out. F. told me to report to Divisional Headquarters in Poperinghe and C. stood me a drink. I never saw either of them again. F. was killed, of course, and C. wounded and sent elsewhere. I then walked to the Canal and had the luck to find some belated Brigade transport. I bagged the sergeant's horse, telling him he would find it tied up to the post outside the bath-house brewery in the Square at 'Pop', this being as much as I knew about the location of Divisional Headquarters. It was an interesting ride. I had never done anything like it without a body of men to look after, and with leisure to observe. The Spring night was not too cold, with a few stars, and all round was that extraordinary rumour of horse, foot and mechanical transport parties getting back to their camps and dossing down for the few hours left. At my back was the flicker, rumble and rattle of the endless trench warfare, all about me a double intermittent stream of traffic, walking stolidly up or hurrying and fidgeting down the road, and turning off to its myriad destinations. The animals splashed and grunted, the tractors and lorries vibrated and belched, the men were just in that state at which they smoked or sang fitfully and decreasingly, and went on, asleep, on foot or a-saddle. 'Pop' was dark, shuttered and still, but a shaded light faintly showed the door of the Mairie, and a policeman assured me that Headquarters were still there. I found Q. office and reported.

Here I had better explain that the structure of the Headquarters of a Division was then still what it had been in the early days of the War. A Major-General commanded and was attended by two aides-de-camp, of whom the senior was Camp Commandant. Under the General the work was divided, so that 'operations' or fighting was the business of three General Staff Officers known as GSO 1, 2 and 3, or the 'G' side, while the discipline and maintenance of the troops known as 'Q' side fell to the Assistant Adjutant and Quarter-Master-General, Deputy Assistant Quarter-Master-General and Deputy Assistant Adjutant and Quarter-Master-General. In addition to these 'soldiers', all of whom must necessarily have been combatant officers, there was already provision for an Assistant Provost Marshal, and for Assistant Directors of Medical Services (with a Deputy), of Veterinary Services and of Ordnance Services. The Commanders of the Artillery, ASC, and Engineers did not live with and rank as part of Divisional Headquarters, so that, although I did not know it, I was, with the exception of French and Belgian Liaison Officers, the first additional attachment to a body almost entirely of regular soldiers, commanding, in proper grades of delegation, a division still largely composed of regular troops. Only the DAAQMG and DADOS were territorial enlistments.

With a mind perfectly blank, I knocked on the door of the Salle des Mariages of the Mairie of 'Pop,' which had a large Q on a placard, and entering, completely blinded by the lamplight, came to attention in front of a table, at which was seated the AAQMG, a colonel by rank, an officer of Indian experience by his ribbons. I gave my name and regiment, and he gave me a good stare. I kept perfectly still, as neither I nor F. had the faintest idea why I had been ordered to report. The only thing I could think of was that the affair of the Court of Inquiry on the Company pay I had lost when buried, months before, had cropped up. But instead of placing me under arrest, he hunted among the papers on his table, and said: 'You say you can speak French?'

'Yes, sir!'

'Are you sure?'

'Yessir!'

'Look at the stuff on that table!' and as I went he added: 'It's a horrible business!'

The table in the corner was covered with a mass of papers, prominent among which were blue forms printed in French, backed up by *proces-verbal*, letters from very humble, and a few from very important personages, in Flemish or French. It amounted, in brief, to claims for compensation for depredations of the British Army in the Divisional Sector, drawn up under the French billeting law of 1877 and the corresponding Belgian enactments. It was an astounding mass of information on the habits of a population, the actual impact of modern War, and a satiric commentary on the superficial battle history of the previous year. It amused me, among other things, making me think of that incident in *Charles O'Malley* when the Iron Duke lectures the troops on the iniquity of plundering, and the cockerel in the Quartermaster's pocket crows after the third denial. And there was the imminent chance that I might find some necessitous foray of my own set down as '*degats occasionnes par les troupes britanniques*'. But the Colonel was waiting: 'Can you make it out?'

'Yes, sir, I think so!'

'Then you'd better take it completely off my hands.'

'Yes, sir. Now?'

'You can begin in the morning!'

* * *

I took the mass of papers that had so weighed on the AA and QMG and got to grips with it. Before I had digested and sorted into convenient piles, according to areas, the cases for investigation, there came the news that the whole division was going out into Corps reserve. After six months we were actually going to be relieved. The Guards were coming in and we were going right back into France, HQ remaining just north of Cassel, and the battered units in billets stretching away, some of them, as far as Calais; so I had to hurry. Far from finding the job 'horrible', it was, at last, something on which the mind could bite. It involved making oneself acquainted with the past and present history of the War, the movements of troops, the nature and conditions of local life, and the evolution of warfare during the first eighteen months. Luckily I was at home with French and Belgian currency and language.

The whole history of the matter appeared to be this. British troops had never fought on a friendly and densely populated soil. Not only African and Indian wars, but even the Crimean and the Peninsular, offered no parallel. Consequently there were no regulations, except such as were borrowed from our Allies, on which to base any policy as to the relations between our troops and the 'natives'. During the retreat from Mons all traces of British occupation disappeared. On the Marne and Aisne, it was early recognised that the perishable nature of the Entente would not survive the utterly new condition of things – the presence of an enormous army (the original Expeditionary Force was bigger than Wellington's or Raglan's armies) amid a modern civil state. The British came to deliver Belgium, but down in the centre of France the inhabitants looked askance at the trampled lands and houses that were hastily converted into barracks. The strong sense of property that is a French characteristic had already expressed itself in a law of 1877, under which any damage done by the annual manoeuvres of the French Army was legislated for. Naturally, in peace time, troops do not camp or bivouac except on waste land, and if they use public or private buildings and services, it is but for a few weeks. The War brushed all this aside. Apart from the scarcity of waste land in most of the districts over which the armies fought, other considerations became paramount. Troops had to be at certain places for reasons that had nothing to do with convenience, and the War soon outlasted the proper period of manoeuvres. No doubt officers and men meant well, but arriving from the battlefield in buildings from which the women, at least, had fled or been removed, the decent amenities of the home naturally vanished beneath their muddy boots and hasty meals. They moved on, in the morning, and the returning inhabitants found with dismay the state to which their homes had been reduced, and were even obliged to note the disappearance of certain articles as a result of the co-operation of their allies. Even in the initial weeks, the matter became so urgent that an ASC Captain whom I subsequently knew in a far more exalted rank, and a sergeant, were deputed to follow the track of the army, investigating and settling all such matters, guided by the French Law alluded to and the visible facts of the case, and obtaining receipts for the small sums paid out. The matter was bounded by wilful damage or theft on the one hand, which were matters of discipline and might even fall within the province of the APM, and, on the other, by *'Fait de Guerre'*, damage done by the enemy during his passage through the country, or by his shelling and bombing, or by any strictly military necessity such as flooding or destruction of objects likely to afford him ranging marks. This sounds a sufficient limitation to the legitimate claim, and so no doubt it was, since for the first months of the War the claims for compensation that were admitted as a reasonable public charge were settled by one officer and one NCO for a trifling sum. But very different developments followed the stabilisation of trench warfare in October, 1914. A permanent military population more than filled up the depletion of inhabitants caused by conscription and evacuation over a large area of France, and all surviving Belgium. The nearest parallel I can think of is reached by trying to imagine 2 or 3 million Frenchmen, of whom 1 per cent could speak English, living for four years in the counties of Cheshire, Lancashire and Cumberland, in order to repel an Icelandic invasion of Scotland. It was not that the British civilian-turned-soldier was a thief or detrimental. It was that modern civilised life cannot be squared with ancient war. The British, individually, were pathetically domesticated. How often have I not seen twenty or thirty of them packed into some little Flemish kitchen, treating the peasant women with elaborate Sunday-school politeness, doing odd jobs, generally giving rather than bartering their rations or presents from home in exchange for small favours, playing with the children or domestic animals, tittering slightly at anything not quite nice, and singing, not so often the vulgar music-hall numbers, as the more sentimental 'Christmas successes' from the pantomimes, 'The Roses Round the Door,' 'All the Little Pansy Faces,' as well as their own compositions, 'Mademoiselle of Armentières,' 'And the Same to You.' The more ribald entertainments, and the only sinister sign of those times, a song called 'Have You Seen the Corporal, I Know Where He Is!' were relegated to estaminets proper, though even in this matter it must be remembered that there were no sharp dividing lines. Every billet tended as time went on to become as much an estaminet as possible, to stick up its notice (written by the CQM's clerk in consideration of an extra drink of coffee or beer) 'Eggs, Fish, Chips, Tea, Stout.' Mainly it was the regular beer-houses that heard anything at all lubricious or violent, though often there, again, the one girl of the place could be seen revolving or cake-walking in the most sedate manner with figure after khaki figure, to the notes of a decrepit musical-box or fatigued gramophone. Venereal disease did not trouble us much in those forward areas. There was no opportunity as in the big bases and depots. In a word, the enormous British Army in France or Flanders must have been by far the most docile and decent disposition of troops ever made, just as it was the largest. Yet this did nothing to prevent constant and widespread damage. You cannot quarter troops by the million in a civilised population at a total cost of a few centimes per head per day. Things will wear up, smash, disappear. Outside, the case was worse. Where the farm was in Belgium, and held on the proprietary system common in England, substantial landlords had sometimes built good brick buildings floored with concrete. Otherwise, and increasingly as we spread south, the flimsy structures of peasant proprietors, mostly of timber centuries old, filled in with wattle and daub, fell down in all directions before the kicking of mules, the banging of doors, the hasty running-in by tired men of limbers or stores. Nor was it possible to make men take other than the most direct line from the corner allotted to their sections, across to the cookers, latrines or extemporised parade ground. Hedges were gapped, paths appeared through crops, gates were missing, pumps and drains succumbed to the impossible demands made on them. In the back areas, unknown to me at that time, was going on the most gigantic expropriation of some of the most tenacious people on earth. Camps and dumps, manoeuvre areas and aerodromes rapidly multiplying in number as well as size, were demanding square miles of the very ground the British troops had come to rescue or to defend. Had it been for a fortnight, or even a season, the inhabitants of those countries might have paid their useless rent, or even sacrificed the unexhausted manures, or forgone the profit of shop or warehouse. But when it came to years, their temper soured, and they had, in France at least, a solid legal foundation for complaint. Thus, even early in 1915, it had been necessary to found a Commission, sitting at Boulogne, under the presidency of a cavalry general, Morrison, who was subsequently killed while carrying out his duties, to deal with the totally novel situations that arose out of this unheard-of war. And among the first things I discovered on the table at Q. office was a book of instructions issued by this body for the guidance of harassed divisional staffs, on whom the entire administration in detail of the original Expeditionary Force depended, and of which I was now a member.

The fate of such divisional staffs may be imagined. They had already had eighteen months of unparalleled strain – that is to say, as much as the Crimean or Franco-Prussian Wars in length, and infinitely more in intensity. And just at this point, all sorts of new authorities were being created over their heads while they were still the standard formation asked to furnish reports, returns, and the circulation and enforcement of the, by then, bulky daily orders from GHQ. Small wonder that I heard the AAQMG declare in desperation, during my first week: 'The General wants me to go round the camps. Now, how can I?'

Indeed, looking at the deskful before him, how could he? This accounts for my presence in Q. office, and for the fact that a gunner officer who had previously been attached to Q. in my unnamed and unforeseen capacity of 'extra housemaid', having already been called up to the Commission aforesaid, the uninvestigated claims of nearly twelve months lay stacked on the table of which I now took charge. This again could not have occurred later in the War, but the then stationary divisions were landed with everything that happened within their sector.

The first papers I sorted out were those relating to the Belgian battlefield, practically contained in the Salient. It was urgent to get these settled before we went out, and leave a clean slate behind. A year after, I or another would have side-tracked the awkward-looking mass of papers by some 'passed-to-you-please' that became the habit of later stages of the War. In those days of early '16, however, one still did one's job to the best of one's ability, and borrowing horses, still officially allotted, two to each Q. appointment, whose holders could by no possibility find time to ride them, or cadging lifts in cars, or simply jumping lorries, I set to work to disentangle what I soon found to be the whole back-door history of the Second Battle of Ypres. For no history can ever be written of the events of April and May, 1915, so graphic as that I discovered in the stilted phrases of the *proces-verbal*, and the illiterate, or in some cases lengthy and formal complaints, in that batch of claims for compensation. Indeed, they could hardly be so called, and stand distinct from most of the material I subsequently handled, partly on account of the nature of the battle, one of the last for a long period in which the element of surprise, although abortive, played a part; and partly from the fact that, being largely from Belgian nationals, they lacked the threat, veiled, if always in reserve, that lay behind French claims – of questions asked in the Chamber, and pressure brought to bear from very exalted quarters.

I knew, from older soldiers in the division, that Ypres, although shelled, had not been evacuated at the time of the battle. Restaurants flourished there, and certain civil amenities.

Yet of Ypres there was not a word. The silence was eloquent. The actual evidence came from the village of Vlamertinghe, roughly half-way between Ypres and 'Pop', its Chateau, and neighbouring one called 'Goldfish' and 'Trois Tours', and the surrounding farms. I had no difficulty in reconstructing the scene – for I had already had the experience of a sudden, but not prolonged bombardment of 'Pop', with the usual panic, the rush of the considerable population, carrying whatever they could lay hands on, out on to the surrounding roads, the scores of casualties in billets, the request from an elderly woman, dragging two children by the hands, to know, 'Monsieur, est-ce bombarde soon finish?'

At Ypres it must have come as suddenly and more completely, and no one ever got back to assess losses, which, in fact, were obliterated by shell-fire and became '*Faits de Guerre*'. A mile or two back the situation was far more complicated. The villagers of Vlamertinghe (and there were some decent residential houses, besides substantial trading establishments) fled. The cavalry division rushed up to support the broken line, probably found (as I have since) the doors open, food cooking, fowls in the yard and beds unmade. They thought themselves in clover. Directly the situation was stabilised, the cavalry went back, and there must have been an indeterminate period, before official evacuation by the Gendarmes, when the owners and occupiers were able to take stock of events that had taken place in their absence. I more than suspect that their feelings were aggravated by the fact that the place was, for a short time at least, Lord French's headquarters, with its messes and other opportunities for profitable trading, by which thrifty people could recoup themselves for the interruption, if not the total destruction, of their means of livelihood. Some of them had already come there as refugees from Ypres, or even, originally, beyond. Here then was a typical incident of the War behind the scenes. The civilians had suffered sufficiently, and common sense, apart from sentiment and our public professions, bade us protect the Allies we did not want to lose. On the other hand, it was fortunately impossible to get any evidence to crime men who had subsequently mostly been killed, anywhere between Langemark and Hooge. True, various thefts and misuses were attributed to 'the British cavalry', or, more definitely, to 'the Hussars' or 'the Lancers'. But I knew that to a civilian writing long afterwards, in a very natural state of mind, 'Hussar' was a khaki trooper without a lance, and 'Lancer' the same, with one. Then came the depredations of '*Les Noirs*', which meant indifferently French Moroccan troops who had fled before the unknown gas that they believed to be magic, and the Indian regiments of our own divisions. These details must all have been supplied by hearsay, and one could only hope that the food, cooked or clucking, the bedclothes, buckets, ladders and other domestic objects that are the soldier's dearest and most comprehensible desire, contributed something to the defence of the Salient. I could only go over the ground, verify ownership and location as far as possible, and pack the whole off to the Commission with a report. The owners had long gone to Calais, Nice or Cheltenham, and what subsequent settlement may have been made with them I do not know. Only one thing was certain – that no further or more exact information could be obtained. I only just completed this investigation before the division went out.

CHAPTER TEN

STORM OVER ALBERT

By Guy Chapman

Up to the beginning of July, 1916 – that is, during our first eleven months – the war for us had been purely stationary; and warfare a matter of learning the job. There had been no fighting save a few encounters of patrols. All we had learned had been to try to keep our trenches healthy, and to suffer shell and trench mortar fire, if not with equanimity, at least with a cynical humour. Our wastage had not been high. In consequence, our spirits were not yet damped. Actually we knew very little; and if the battalion did not expect a walk-over, it still had the illusions bred of propaganda and the picture papers.

We marched out of Bailleulval with the band playing 'The Girl I left Behind Me'. We had garrisoned it for time enough to permit the traditional tune; though for the life of me I can recall no young face at the windows. As we followed a field track we were amused by the sight of a German 5.9 sniping lorries on the Doullens-Arras road. The companies sang; and even the Lewis gunners towing their baby carriages did not seem depressed. This gaiety could not last. About 2 miles from our destination the sky opened, and water fell on us in one jet. In a trice the road was flooded; a stream, calf-high, rushed down the track. We crawled into Humbercourt as helpless as moths with sodden wings.

* * *

The transport came in next day and we received a brigade order to move to Albert. There was no news of the battalion except a rumour that they were in the line. Fairburn and I rode to Albert that afternoon, clattering in under the leaning Virgin, and found a house in the street that leads out to Bapaume. There were beds on the first floor. Said Fairburn, looking out on to the stinking, garbage-strewn cobbles, 'Well, this is a bit of all right.'

Whoop, crash! A shell banged into the yard of the factory across the road. Planks and pieces of timber whirled in the air, clapping down on the stones. The clerks were arranging the front room for my office. My batman put his head in and said: 'There's Turnbull from No. 3 wants to see you, sir – and Mr Leader's dead.'

My mind shot out to the cheerful, comradely Leader. We had scarcely considered him last night; his grin, we felt sure, would bear him through all tribulations. Red-headed Turnbull, his creamy skin pale beneath his freckles, his eyes shadowed with grief and fear, slipped into the room. His uniform was plastered with clay, and he had no rifle. 'It was after the attack, sir. They was bumping our line cruel hard with 5.9s. Captain Nelson and Mr Leader was standing side by side. The Captain bent down to do up his puttee. A shell burst on the parapet above them. It missed the Captain, but it knocked Mr Leader's brains out. Yes, sir, we buried him last night, back of the parados. The Captain was wounded, too. The Adjutant sent me down to see about Mr Leader's kit, getting it home – and there's a note for you.'

Cuth's note said they had attacked and had taken all their objectives with comparatively few casualties, Leader killed, Nelson, Bliss, P.E. Lewis, and Morgan wounded. The battalion would reach Tara Hill during the early hours of next morning.

When I found them, the whole battalion, except the cooks and the half-dozen officers who had been left out, was asleep. They lay stretched on the hillside, their uniforms daubed with chalk, their faces and hands brown with mud, their hair tangled and their unshaved cheeks bloodless, the colour of dirty parchment, just as they had fallen in attitudes of complete exhaustion. Every now and then a figure moaned or beat the air with his hand. I found Cuthbertson engaged in an elaborate toilet. Even he who was ever the mirror of fashion was unkempt.

'We went up that night,' he said, 'and got orders to attack at half-past eight in the morning, to the right of and above La Boisselle. We went over. There was a lot of bombing up one of the communication trenches. That was where P.E. got his: but we got our line all right. We caught a lot of Boche there. Then we got astride the Bapaume road, where we had a marvellous view of the attack on our left. We could see the Boche in Ovillers packing up to go, but he was too far off for us to hit. We settled down in the line, and then they started shelling us. That was where poor old Leader was killed and the others wounded. The men stuck it very well; but – oh, my God! – that – ! I got him to go round the line once; he ran at full speed, keeping his head down, and then retired to his dug-out. About three o'clock that night, I'd just turned in when I saw him get up. He carefully put on his gas-mask, his belt, his revolver, map case, compass, and field glasses. I was so surprised that I asked him if he was going round the line. "Oh, no, no," he said, "I'm only just going to the water-closet." We *must* get rid of him. Little old Ardagh is furious with him. He was up in the line all day, running about looking at shells.'

While he talked there was a sudden stir. A few men rose, others woke and joined them, collecting in a mob round a khaki figure with a camera. Pickelhaubes (*sic*), German helmets, Teutonic forage caps, leaf-shaped bayonets, automatics, were produced from haversacks. The faces which ten minutes earlier had seemed those of dying men were now alight with excited amusement. 'Come on, come an' have your picture took,' echoed from man to man; and amid much cheering, the official press was obliged with a sitting.

I sat down with Blake and Sidney Adler, near the crest of the slope. From here we looked down over the clustered red huddle of Albert. The front line was perhaps 3,000 yards forward, yet the slope was thick with the infantry of four or five divisions. The enemy could not see over the crest without balloon or aeroplane observation, and no balloon could stay in the sky. Our aeroplanes were now strong enough to see to that. In between the lumps of infantry British 18-pounders and French 75s, tucked into shallow emplacements, were cracking and banging. A 60-pounder at the side of the road stirred the dust into whorls at each discharge; horses passing by shied and fled up the hill. There was a dressing-station by our side to which Ford ambulances came and went unceasingly and unhurriedly. Once or twice German shells fired blindly exploded on the road.

In the morning sun every figure, every stunted tree, was illuminated with a clarity of outline as in a Manet picture. The round white rumps of men seated on latrines facing the town added points of light to the drab tints of the worn grass, the baked leaves and the dusty, creamy track. The crowd shifted and heaved. But for the guns spitting and flashing and the half-naked men, it might have been Parliament Hill on an August Bank Holiday. Notre-Dame-des-Brebières clung tenaciously by her toes to the ruddy campanile. She was not yet to fall. Blake's face was slack and haggard, but not from weariness.

He greeted me moodily, and then sat silent, abstracted in some distant perplexity.

'What's the matter, Terence?' I asked.

'Oh, I don't know ... Nothing ... At least ... Look here, we took a lot of prisoners in those trenches yesterday morning. Just as we got into their line, an officer came out of a dugout. He'd got one hand above his head, and a pair of field-glasses in the other. He held the glasses out to S–, you know, that ex-sailor with the Messina earthquake medal – and said, 'Here you are, sergeant, I surrender.' S– said, 'Thank you, sir,' and took the glasses with his left hand. At the same moment he tucked the butt of his rifle under his arm and shot the officer straight through the head. What the hell ought I to do?'

He tore a withered blade of grass out of the ground, and chewed it angrily, his eyes roving over the barren landscape. I thought hard for a minute.

'I don't see that you can do anything,' I answered slowly. 'What can you do? Besides, I don't see that S–'s really to blame. He must have been half mad with excitement by the time he got into that trench. I don't suppose he ever thought what he was doing. If you start a man killing, you can't turn him off again like an engine. After all, he is a good man. He was probably half off his head.'

'It wasn't only him. Another did exactly the same thing.'

'Anyhow, it's too late to do anything now. I suppose you ought to have shot both on the spot. The best thing now is to forget it.'

'I dare say you're right.'

He got up and moved stiffly away. I turned to Adler, who was carefully powdering his feet. He was bubbling over with cheerfulness. Late on the previous night, Nos 3 and 4 had been pushed forward suddenly to take a line of trenches vaguely spoken of as lying a few hundred yards ahead. Either because the actual objective had been blotted out and the trench they eventually reached was past the one against which the attack was directed, or because our artillery was firing short, the gutter in which they eventually settled was being whipped by English shrapnel. They stood it for two hours, and then after messages had failed to stop the gunfire they were ordered to come back to the starting-point. They brought back the dead and wounded through a storm of low-burst shrapnel, quick flame and hailing bullets.

There was already a change in the battalion. In the first place, there had come to the men, now that they were awakened and had shaken out of them their first drugged nervous slumber, a new confidence, almost a jauntiness. They had come through their first battle successfully; they were all right. Secondly, between those who had been in the show and those who had not, there was a gulf fixed. It may have been due to a certain delicacy on the part of the latter; but the gulf existed.

There was enough to occupy one in Albert with the constant stream of messengers coming to and fro, the melancholy business of the casualty lists, next-of-kin, sorting out these humble parcels of the personal effects of the dead, the creased, greasy letters, addressed to No. 6494 Private Smith, On Active Service, BEF, the knick-knacks and trifles. There were letters to be returned. One addressed to Leader in a sloping French hand I put on one side. I had seen these before. I had to tear the envelope to discover the address and saw the first passionate lines. Strange that my ugly, stolid little friend should inspire such. I thought of him looking at me over a mug of hot milk and rum at stand-to in the dead of winter, and with a grin of his terrier mouth croaking, 'Chin-chin. Happy days.' I stumbled an hour over the appropriate letter.

Three nights later the battalion went up again, this time in support. By now we knew that our division had been split up, and the infantry loaned right and left. Our whole brigade replaced four broken battalions of the Fifth Fusiliers in the 34th Division, whose general was described as a fire-eater. The area was hotting up. The enemy had succeeded in getting observation over the ridge and had seen enough to justify him in shelling both sides of the road freely. One of our officers had been very slightly wounded in the hand. From the dressing station he was carried away on an ebb tide of wounded and before we knew of his wound was in England. Adler fell into a trench while leading a carrying party and broke his collar bone. Our street in Albert was becoming uncommonly nasty. German 5.9s would scream down out of the hot sky, smashing among the flimsy brick houses. The water main, cut by a shell, burst into a dusky fountain 100 yards from our door. Fairburn shook his head and decided that the stores would be more conveniently situated with the transport. I missed his company and felt unhappy at night alone in my cock-loft when the shells came over.

The sordid street never slept. The noise of wheels was ceaseless. Up and down, all day and all night, passed lorries, limbers, GS wagons, ammunition columns, ambulances. At the sides marched weary infantrymen stupefied with battle, dragging their feet as they came out to rest. Over it hovered and sank stagnant dust from road, broken brick, dried paint, stirred into lifeless movement by the wheels, only to fall back. Through it all the yellow smell of garbage, and beyond the guns thud-thudding, bruising the tired air. The 2nd SWB, short sturdy Welsh miners, occupied houses all round us. One platoon was billeted on the first floor next door. They sang choruses in fine deep voices; the tone was beautiful, but they sang all day and half the night, and at that one song. It had a refrain which sounded like 'Hop along, sister Mary, hop along.'

I also suffered another disillusionment. The bed on which I camped was, I discovered too late, infested. I was lousy. Hordes of minor parasites ran about my body, in and out of the seams of my breeches. In vain I attempted to hunt out the tribe by hand. It required a Briareus[1] to deal with the plague in this fashion. I surrendered and hoped I might one day see my kit again.

In the meantime the battalion near Contalmaison Wood was enduring pertinacious shelling and constant casualties. Each morning a list came down with a fervent appeal from Cuth to send up every man who returned from leave or a course. The big guard of half a company under Amberton had already come back. So, too, had Ned Kelly, a Punch-faced elderly subaltern with a row of ribbons from previous wars. His words were a sharp chirrup, precise as a thrush's. Borrowing a steel hat and a gas-mask he went up the line with a mackintosh over his arm and a little swagger cane, as cheerful as if he were going to a city dinner. He reached the battalion in time to join in one of the ghastly mistakes which break soldiers' hearts. A big attack on Pozières had been ordered. One of our battalions had already made an effort against this stronghold. The few who got as far as the orchards had been killed by machine guns. Today the Rifle Brigade were to take part in a big encircling assault at 11.00am, and the 13th were to support them. At the last moment the plan was cancelled; but the message reached neither battalion. So at zero they started with their flanks in the air and no protecting artillery. At once every German gun covering that section was concentrated on them. The Rifle Brigade struggled forward in the teeth of the storm, half-way to their objective. By that time their colonel and their second-in-command had been wounded, and all four company commanders killed. The attack withered away and stopped in a sunken road. Behind them the 13th moved forward 100 yards, and seeing the catastrophe in front, lay down. For an hour they endured a barrage in the open: then the news of the cancelling of the attack reached them, and Major Ardagh, who led, ordered them to fall back to their jumping-off line. The casualties were heavy. Williamson was severely wounded, and Blake, while both the sergeants whose conduct in the earlier attack had made him bite his nails, were dead. That afternoon I received a further urgent call for men from the adjutant. While I was reading it, Leader's Turnbull reported. His expression was worn and anxious.

'What am I to do, sir?'

'I'm afraid you must report to the company, Turnbull ... I'm sorry. Every available man has got to go. I'd like to keep you. But you see ...'

A docile resignation crept into his face. 'I suppose so, sir.'

At that instant there was a terrific explosion immediately overhead. Turnbull yelped and crouched. The hanging lamp over the table hovered for an instant and then crashed down. Bits of hard substance went banging into the floor, and about

---

1. Greek myth: a giant with a hundred arms and fifty heads who aided Zeus and the Olympians against the Titans.

the walls. There was a yell from the street, followed by shouts of 'Stretcher bearers, stret-cher bear-ers.' The passage was filled with dust and the stairs choked with débris. I ran out into the street. The shell had hit the roof exactly at the junction of the two houses. Screams and groans were echoing from next door. SWB stretcher bearers ran up the street. From the wreckage of the upper storey they pulled out two-and-twenty Welshmen, unconscious, pale and shocked. The orderly room emerged from the basement with self-conscious grins. My batman led me upstairs to look at the damage. Both rooms were wrecked and the contents of my pack tossed hither and thither among the fallen plaster. A pair of scissors had been neatly cut in two. I reflected on the prescience which had induced Fairburn to seek more pastoral surroundings. It was his hour for a nap, and the shell would have burst over his head. In the turmoil, Turnbull had disappeared.

I slept on the floor of the office that night. Next morning's runner from the line grinned when he saw me. 'We was laughing up there,' he said, 'to hear orderly room 'ad been done in.' I glanced down the casualty reports. One name stood out above all the others: 'No ... Pte. Turnbull, 3 Coy. SIW.'

On the night of 20th July, the battalion was relieved. That afternoon I removed the orderly room to the transport lines. My first action was to strip, walk naked into the middle of a small patch of standing corn, and drop my garments among the wheat. No doubt by the time the harvester found them they would be clean. Next morning we trudged solemnly back to Bresle. On the way an ambulance passed us. In it was one man with a bandaged foot. I caught his eye and waved a hand. Turnbull answered me with a melancholy grin as he was swept past the dusty, depleted companies. I have no doubt that those entirely efficient generals and staff officers on whose manner I should have modelled myself, would have reprehended so gross a failure in discipline. Yet I could not do otherwise. I had known Turnbull for a year. He had served – I might almost say, had shielded – an intimate friend through troubles and stresses. Perhaps with Leader's death something cracked in him. The loyalty to one man had been too concentrated, and with his end, it died, leaving him with no other creed. Into the vacuum rushed the need for escape. A bullet fired deliberately at the foot was the only way out. Perhaps those who called this man a coward will consider the desperation to which he was driven, to place his rifle against the foot, and drive through the bones and flesh the flames of the cordite and the smashing metal. Let me hope that the court-martial's sentence was light. Not that it matters, for, in truth, the real sentence had been inflicted long ere it sat.

CHAPTER ELEVEN

A CITY OF THE DEAD

By Charles Douie

The English language is reputed to present special difficulty to students on account of the variety of meanings which a single word may carry, and the constant changes which are always taking place. Terms of endearment become in the course of a few years terms of abuse, and earnest foreigners have been known to cause grave offence by the use of expressions which have the high authority of Shakespeare but have since fallen into desuetude. The process of change in the meaning of words was subject to considerable acceleration during the war. My first week spent in the trenches of La Boisselle may seem in retrospect to have been both noisy and precarious. For the purpose of official records, and in the common parlance of the trenches, it enjoyed the description of 'quiet'. The succeeding week spent in the town of Albert represented a period of 'rest.'

The precise significance of this word was borne in on my mind within a short space of time. After a week in the snow-bound trenches of La Boisselle, in the course of which I had had a few hours only of fitful sleep, I had fallen blissfully asleep in my billet in Albert. The hour of the night was late owing to the conditions under which the relief of the front-line trenches had been carried out. Shortly after dawn I became aware of a familiar figure bending over my bed, and when I had been sufficiently awakened I received orders to return at once to the La Boisselle mines on a carrying fatigue. In all the monotony of trench warfare there was no greater tedium than that of the carrying parties which were needed for the supply of material to the front-line trenches, and no greater patience and tact than that of the officers and non-commissioned officers of the Royal Engineers, on whose behalf the carrying parties for the most part worked. The infantry soldier regarded himself as a fighting man and could not be persuaded to take kindly to the role of pack animal. Soldiers who could be relied on to remain cheerful in the most exposed trenches in the front line became unwilling and resentful on fatigue. The daily lot of an officer in a field company of the Royal Engineers was to meet a body of over-tired infantry, nominally enjoying a period of rest, but in fact more busily employed than in the line, led by an embittered subaltern. In public the infantry reviled the sappers day and night; in private they extended an admiration, no greater than was due, to a body of men who never enjoyed a period of even nominal 'rest' out of the line, who endured many of the dangers and discomforts of the infantryman's life, yet were denied the occasional moment of exultation which was his compensation and reward.

The broad *route nationale* leading from Albert to La Boisselle had appeared in the small hours of the morning the friendliest of roads as I emerged on to it from the knee-deep mud of the communication trenches; as I returned at the head of my weary company I felt that I had never seen a road which I so much disliked, and my feelings, which were clearly shared by my men, were not rendered more amicable by the sight of a number of deep shell-holes of unmistakably recent origin. The sapper officer to whom I reported had no doubt learned, as part of his duties, the way to humour tired infantry, and we were at once on excellent terms. This state of affairs was due in part to the regard in which the mining company employed in the La Boisselle mines was held. The one occupation which the infantry admitted to be more hazardous and less enviable than their own was that of the men whose daily lot was to descend the mine shafts in and around the cemetery of La Boisselle. I descended a shaft on one occasion, and although assured by the officer on duty that there was no safer place on the Western Front, I ascended again with remarkable speed, preferring the hazards of an open-air life in the mine-craters to the narrow galleries, driven above and below the German galleries, where men lay always listening to the tap of enemy picks, and waiting for the silence which was ever the prelude to the blowing of mine or counter-mine. The men of my regiment, being drawn from an agricultural community, had a particular dislike for mining fatigues. The miners themselves, for the most part following their traditional occupation, never appeared happy until they reached the mines. Work during the war was not always well distributed. While watching my Dorsets passing in and out of mines, which had for them all the terrors of unfamiliarity, I recollected that some weeks before my company of Durham miners had been employed in cutting brushwood, an occupation which made them laugh so heartily and so long that it was carried on with little success.

 The day of rest drew on, and I found myself again at the crucifix on the eastern edge of Albert with visions of resuming my interrupted sleep. The vision faded as my company commander was observed to be coming up the road, and I learned that he had been charged by the brigade commander with the duty of plotting on the map the contour line of visibility from the village of La Boisselle. This occupation presented features of interest to anyone enjoying minor hazards. The routine was simple. We moved forward until we could see the German frontline, and in such an interval as the German snipers thought fit to afford took two bearings, one on the tower of Albert Church, and one on the spire of Martinsart. A rapid retreat was followed by a brief appearance at another point, until the contour line had been completed.

 Life in the town of Albert presented certain amenities not commonly enjoyed by combatant troops. In days of peace it had been a small manufacturing town, destitute of any feature of historic interest, but clearly substantial and prosperous. Deserted now by its inhabitants, but still having many houses but little damaged by shellfire, it afforded billets with real beds, carpets, and armchairs in lieu of the lath-and-plaster barns, sodden camps or rat-ridden dug-outs which were usually allotted to infantry when they were withdrawn from the trench lines for a period in brigade or divisional reserve. The officers' mess for battalion headquarters and the two companies in Albert was in the White Chateau. I still retain in my mind recollections of this château as a place of singular comfort and admirable design, but I suspect that the surroundings from which I had come, and to which I was so soon to return, conferred on it by force of contrast a beauty which it never had. Perhaps also the White Château is invested in my memory with something of the splendour of those who came there for a few brief hours and passed on to the Somme battlefield, to La Boisselle and Fricourt, and as the summer wore on to Pozières and Contalmaison, and up that long road whose every yard is marked by our dead from the white chalk of the great crater of La Boisselle to the grim slopes of the Butte de Warlencourt. The White Château is gone; not a trace remains. It would not have been fitting that it should stand, in mockery of those who were its lords, though for a brief hour only, and now are dust. Did it stand, the laughter of men on whom the presence of death had no power to cast a shadow could not but linger, echoing in its walls, and the sound of that laughter would break the hearts of men who heard it once but will never hear it again.

The White Château was solidly built, and at this early period of the war not seriously damaged. Its fate was inevitable if heavy fighting commenced, as the trench lines were not far distant. The German gunners rightly surmised that its apparent comfort would inevitably lead to its use as a headquarters, and adopted the practice of sending over a few shells at those hours when it might be expected that a meal was in progress. The approach to the château from my billet at the dinner-hour always presented an interesting mathematical problem, in which the distance between two bits of cover and the interval between two rounds of battery fire formed respectively the known and the speculative elements. The first 100 yards presented occasional shelter where the walls of the houses had not been entirely obliterated; the last 150 yards were devoid of cover. The sudden whoop and roar of battery fire on this open stretch of road made my progress from time to time unusually rapid.

The château attracted the heavier guns. One night as we sat at dinner there was a deafening crash, and the mess became silent for a moment. A major, who was in command at this time, asserted amid general incredulity that one of our own guns was firing. Another, and louder, crash failed to convince him. A captain on the brigade staff had opened a book on the distance of the nearest shell-hole, and was offering, as I thought, unnecessarily short odds on the lowest distances. Another crash and the entry of a large piece of shell by the front door convinced the major at last, and the mess servants were sent down into a cellar. The mess sat on, waiting for further instructions. There was, in fact, little point in moving, as the shells were so heavy that no cover available was likely to be of use.

It was an odd experience. The heaviest shelling in the trench lines was familiar to every one; but it was strange to be sitting at ease round a table lit by candles, in a comfortable room hung with tapestry, and to expect momentarily the whole to disappear, as suddenly as Cinderella's palace on the stroke of midnight. I saw no outward concern on anyone's face, and for my own part, though a little uncomfortable, I felt singularly detached. I realised that the apprehension of danger is to a great degree dependent on physical conditions. In the darkness and solitude of the trenches, and after many days of continual noise and sleeplessness, the constant mastery of fear is difficult to maintain; in a lighted room in the company of friends, it is easy. Still the odds against a direct hit being scored were very short, and for a moment there was an uncomfortable silence. This was broken appropriately by the padre, who, in a manner devoid of all concern, commenced a story which, to my regret, I feel unable to place on record.

The château was in fact hit, and the room shook. But no one was damaged, and shortly afterwards a merry party was engaged in measuring the distance of an enormous shell-hole for the purpose of adjudicating the bets, at the same time calling on their heads the wrath of some neighbouring field-gunners, who asserted that their battery position was being revealed to the Germans by the swinging of my lantern.

Day and night we were shelled. The square by the cathedral was the most dangerous place, and here we lost some good men. Our transport was so repeatedly shelled, and had so many casualties, that it had to move back to Millencourt. Security, however, was not always conferred by moving out of the town, as we discovered in the course of a football match in a neighbouring field. The game was terminated, without definite result, owing to a battery opening fire with shrapnel. This disregard of the decencies on the part of the German Army was the subject of much unfavourable comment. On another occasion our brigade headquarters was hit and the signalling officer killed. My billet was not seriously damaged during my few days there, but on one occasion the noise and clatter of falling masonry were so loud that I supposed that the top story had gone. In fact, it was the house opposite. A man's breeches rose high in the air, and descended into the road, shortly followed by the man himself. He had just taken them off when the shell removed them. The humour of the situation entirely escaped him, and he expressed himself with some freedom, oblivious of the good fortune which had provided that his breeches, and not himself, had been blown through the roof. The night was more disturbed than the day, and often I used to stand at my bedroom window, which looked out on the church, watching the great shells bursting in the square and illuminating in a fitful and unreal light the ruins of this desolate and twilight city.

Indeed, Albert at night after the rising of the moon assumed something almost of beauty, and in thought I can still wander through its ghostly streets. I see the Millencourt-Albert road stretching before me grey amid the darkness of the surrounding countryside, until the line of tall trees marking the *route nationale* looms before me at the western entrance to the town. The road descends under a railway bridge. Below lies Albert in the valley of the Ancre. The cathedral rises shattered but magnificent against the background of moonlit sky. The tower is riven by shellfire. From its summit the image of the Virgin and Child has been torn from its pedestal, but has not yet fallen; the outstretched arms of the Virgin seem to offer the Child to the broken and suffering town beneath. The houses are rent by a thousand scars; yet as the moon sheds its radiance on them it confers something of calm and healing. The town is asleep, as many other cities, but this is a city of the dead.

There is a roar, as of an approaching train coming nearer and nearer. But no train has crossed this bridge for many a day. A moment later a sheet of lurid flame leaps from the cathedral square, and the thunder of the explosion echoes endlessly through the deserted streets. The bridge shakes, and some loose mortar falls.

I pass down a long street; in every ruined house my footfall echoes. Often the cellar and a heap of brick and plaster are all that remains. The moon reveals many strange sights, here the billiard-table piled with rubbish of some estaminet, here an unfinished meal, here a mattress blown through a shattered window. The many human touches to be seen all around increase the sense of desolation. For here is the reverse side of war, the evidences of the sudden flight of a defenceless people into homeless night. The ruined cathedral, battered indeed by innumerable shells, still conveys the impression of majesty, of the victory of eternal faith. But there is no glory in these poor ruined homes. They speak only of the suffering of the inarticulate multitude, of the cruelty of war.

At the corner of the street leading to the church lie the remains of a cycle factory. The roof has disappeared long ago, and a great mass of twisted girders and fallen masonry is piled in inextricable confusion below. Through the gaping holes in the walls the moon reveals thousands of rusted iron frames and gears. A wild cat strangely human in this scene of desolation is outlined on a jagged wall. Near at hand is the railway station. Rank grass grows everywhere, through a hundred crevices on the lifeless platforms and luxuriantly amid the rusted lines. Here, too, where once crowds jostled in changing scenes of animated life, reigns universal death.

I turn towards the cathedral and come to the square. Every house has been utterly destroyed. The very ruins have been swept away. The moon plays strange tricks of fancy through the great rents in the walls of the cathedral, illuminating here a fragment of stained glass, here a broken mosaic, here a Madonna, here the figure of a saint. A soldier stands on guard under the tower, accentuating the desolation of the scene. I cross the square to speak to him, and stand for a moment under the great gilt figure of the Madonna. Clouds pace across the sky over the summit, and by a strange illusion the tower appears to be moving and the Madonna to be descending ever lower. There is a whine rising into a scream, and four shells strike the tortured building. There is a clatter of falling masonry, and a cloud of dust rises from the ruins. Then all is quiet again, and the cathedral stands symbolic in ineffable majesty, eternal and serene.

I turn towards the ghostly whiteness of the château and then over a bridge on to the Bapaume road. A challenge rings out and echoes through the shattered houses. Pack-mules loaded with rations, and the creaking wagons of a long ammunition column pass by in never-ending procession. The houses become fewer, and at last the great trees of a wayside calvary mark the limit of the town. From a battery position on the slopes leading down to the Ancre the boom of a heavy gun sounds, and a shell passes screeching overhead. A sudden light leaps from a village far in the German lines. Men and horses pass ceaselessly over a rise in front, silhouetted momentarily against the sky. From horizon to horizon innumerable flares rise from the sleepless lines amid the interminable rattle of musketry and the vicious bark of light guns. Behind me lies a city of ghosts and shadows fast bound in the sleep of death.

Our few days of 'rest' while in brigade reserve in Albert came to an end, and I found myself late at night progressing slowly down the long communication trench known as St Andrew's Avenue towards the cemetery of La Boisselle. The moon had risen and illuminated the sides of the trench, and the faces of men of the outgoing regiment, haggard and worn, as they passed down. The usual blocks occurred from time to time, accompanied sometimes by recriminations and sometimes by the form of boisterous and good-humoured sarcasm which was the *argot* of the trenches. On reaching the battalion headquarters dug-outs I found that the direct route, by Dunfermline Avenue, was impassable owing to the heavy shelling, and was ordered to make a detour. This formed a pleasant augury for the succeeding week, which did not enjoy the description of 'quiet' even in the trench diary. Indeed, the events of the week, as detailed quite truly by the German Daily Wireless, brought the village of La Boisselle, afterwards to become so well known, before the world for the first occasion in its history. A hazardous enterprise was carried out in the vicinity of the village by my regiment with a distinguished valour which led to special mention in Sir Douglas Haig's dispatches, but unhappily met with no success. This enterprise was one of the earliest raids, but the technique of the raid had not at that time been developed, and the form which it assumed, and the forces employed, gave it a greater resemblance to a night attack on a small scale. It is perhaps worthy of description, as the raid, in a rather different form, became a common feature of trench warfare, particularly when the identification of the German regiments in the line was a matter of moment before a battle.

The days preceding the raid were distinguished by shellfire of an intensity which in itself might almost have expunged the word 'quiet' from the diary. Coming in one afternoon after taking the morning tour of duty in the mine craters, I found the headquarters dug-out isolated by a rifle-grenade and oil-can barrage. The trench was blown in all round and almost impassable. An old private in the Manchesters, who had come up on fatigue, lay horribly dead across the entrance. There was no 'cunningest pattern of excelling nature' here. An officer passing by was blown down the dug-out steps. Our telegraph wires were broken, and the men who attempted to mend them were brought in badly wounded and bathed in blood. At last a breathless orderly came safely through. His arrival was a tribute to his resolution, but a greater tribute to his good fortune. As I took his message, I thought that it must be of vital importance. It proved to be, in fact, a futile routine message about the proportion of blankets per man in the present state of the weather. A second message was more apposite and the occasion of some mirth. It detailed the times at which burials would take place in the various cemeteries in the neighbourhood.

There was a certain grim humour also in the arrival of the post from England. My orderly brought a letter to me late at night in an exposed corner of the front line. It proved to be a quaintly spelt missive from a very young cousin, full of gossip of home, concluding with the words – 'we often talk and think about you and wonder where you are.' The question received an immediate answer, as it coincided with the 'nightly strafe', and the lurid light from countless explosions along the trench lines made clear the ruins of the village and cemetery of La Boisselle.

The night of the raid came towards the end of our tour of the trenches. After several days and nights of considerable strain I found myself in command of A Company, as my company commander had been sent by the colonel for a month's rest at the Fourth Army School, after a year's continuous trench warfare from the Menin road to the Frise marshes. Throughout the afternoon experienced soldiers (among whom I was not numbered) could tell that news of our impending attack had reached the German Intelligence, as we were subjected to a harassing fire, and registration by new guns on our support and communication trenches took place. I was in a state of inexperienced optimism, and firmly believed that the Germans were wasting ammunition which they would need during the night. I expected that the mine, whose explosion was to be the signal for our attack, would blow the village of La Boisselle high into the air, and that the survivors, if there were any, would soon be prisoners in our hands. As the hour of attack approached I became less sanguine. The night was still in a degree which no night had been before. The broken posts and wire which marked the boundaries of 'No Man's Land' and the white chalk of the mine craters were agleam in the moonlight, and it was so clear that I could discern the ruins and broken tree stumps of the village. Yet no shot was fired while a hundred men crawled through our wire into shell-holes in front. Behind them the trenches were lined with men, for the 'stand-to-arms' had been passed down. The deathly silence did not augur well, and as the colonel passed down the line I noticed grave anxiety on his face. Then at last the silence was broken by a machine gun firing from the dim ruins of Ovillers and sweeping our parapets from end to end. Then again there was silence. Two minutes to go. One minute. A thought flickered for a moment in my mind that many now very much alive would within a brief minute be dead. The thought passed. Half a minute. Time. The mine exploded. It seemed to me a very small mine. The earth throbbed. Then again, but for one moment only, there was an unearthly stillness. This was succeeded by a weird sound like rustling leaves for a fraction of a second; then with the noise of a hurricane the shells passed, and the whole outline of the German positions was seared with the appalling lightning and thunder of our artillery. There were a thousand flashes, and a lurid light spread over the battlefield, the light seen only in that most dreadful spectacle, a night bombardment. The thunder of the guns was such that speech was impossible. But there was no time to observe the scene, as in an inferno of flashes and explosions the German counter-barrage broke on our lines.

The intensity of the counter-baggage showed beyond a doubt that the German batteries had been standing to their guns and that every detail of our attack was known. The craters and trenches of La Boisselle were evacuated and full of wire in which those of our men who got through the entanglements were at once caught and impaled. Of Germans there were none to be seen, until their bombers closed in from each side. From end to end of 'No Man's Land' a hell of machine gun fire was raging; the trenches were quite untenable.

The signal to retire was given. But our wounded were everywhere, and time and again the survivors went out to bring them in. It seemed incredible that anything could live in that barrage of gun and rifle-fire, with the German bombers in full counter-attack, yet our men would not be denied. Two men refused to leave friends who were dying; by some miracle they survived and brought back a wounded man. A young subaltern stayed behind to help a wounded man out of the German trench and in the act was killed on the wire.

Gradually the fire slackened, and only the rat-tat of the machine guns and the whine of innumerable bullets disturbed the stillness of the night. I could hear the German transport far behind their lines. I was very tired. For five nights in six I had had no rest. At last the 'stand-down' came. Yet there were still two hours to day.

Dawn came at last. The ruins of the village and the surrounding trench lines became distinct, and it was day. On the German wire there were dark specks, among them the dead subaltern and my faithful orderly. Behind me lay a city of the dead, beside me the ravished graves of the dead, before me men, my friends, who yesterday had been so full of life and now lay silent and unheeding in death. Anger and bitterness were in my heart against those who had wrought this destruction, an anger which could find no expression in words.

CHAPTER TWELVE

AT PASSCHENDAELE

By Ex-Private X

Everything at Passchendaele was unique. The arrangement of our equipments – 'battle order' it used to be called – was all different from that of former and future occasions. We had to go over with our packs on. This was because we had to carry with us three days' rations, it being impossible for supplies to be sent up. We wore our entrenching tools in front instead of behind, to protect a part of the anatomy which it would be indelicate to mention. When we attacked every man carried a spade stuck down his back between his pack and equipment, so that he could consolidate any position in which he happened to find himself. Moreover, each of us carried 180 rounds of extra ammunition hung round our necks and I, being a rifle-grenadier, had to carry twelve grenades in an extra haversack, perforated at the bottom to allow the rods to stick through.

A Mills grenade, if I remember rightly, weighs about 5lbs, 300 cartridges weigh a bit, and there was one's rifle and the usual accoutrements, so obviously one was not quite a featherweight. Yet, burdened like packhorses, we were expected to fight for our lives with the bayonet if the occasion arose. No wonder that Haig afterwards said that no troops in the whole history of war had ever fought under such conditions; and the square-headed Hindenburg smugly observed that 'the British Army broke its teeth on Passchendaele Ridge.' It may be added that we had to wade through mud of various depths and of consistencies varied between that of raw Bovril and weak cocoa.

We are to go over from tapes laid by the Engineers. The whole thing must be done with mathematical precision, for we are to follow a creeping barrage which is to play for four minutes only 100 yards in front of the first 'ripple' of our first 'wave'. I am in the second 'ripple' 50 yards behind the first. The first 'ripple' is to go over in extended order, four paces apart, the second 'ripple' is to start in artillery formation – sections in single file at a given distance apart – changing to extended order after having covered 200 yards. It is of the utmost importance that we should keep as close as possible to our own barrage and even risk becoming casualties from it. Well, if we know our own gunners we haven't much doubt about the risk!

The lance-corporal in charge of my section is a man named Edmonds, much junior in service but considerably older than I am, and quite rightly promoted over my head. He is a conscript, a teetotaller, a non-smoker, a non-swearer, a hater of smutty stories, but a damned fine fellow. He is the father of a family and the owner of a one-man business which has gone west. He has been dragged into the Army with a real grievance, and shows himself to be one of the stoutest-hearted fellows in the whole crowd.

The mentality of Edmonds, with his pluck and his queer Nonconformist conscience, is of some professional interest to me. He tells me that he hates stories relating to the deed of kind because he thinks there is 'something sacred' in it. This shows that he is a sensualist, although he hasn't the brains to see it, because when a man considers that something is sacred he does quite a lot of thinking about it. My bawdy talk, which annoys him very much, is just the scum on the surface of my mind, but having spoken I don't go on thinking.

Edmonds doesn't take his rum ration, which is all the better for the rest of us. But he disapproves of rum. He has our ration in an extra water-bottle, but won't issue it overnight because he says we may need it in the morning. In the morning he gets wounded – and so the poor dogs have none!

We do not move up to the tapes until midnight, but crouch fidgeting behind our breastwork. Plenty of stuff comes over. Jerry treats us to quite a lot of petrol shells – containing liquid fire – but they don't do much harm and, in fact, provide us with a really beautiful firework display. They remind Edmonds of the Crystal Palace in the days of his youth. He must have gone there often, for a firework show was about the only kind of entertainment which wasn't considered immoral in the quaint creed in which he was reared.

D Company, in reserve, come up and dig in just behind us, and immediately they start they are plastered with shells, for all the world as if Jerry can see them. Then things quieten down and the other fellows in my section, wanting something to occupy their minds and remembering that I am a professional writer, ask me to tell them stories.

'Not your usual ones,' says Edmonds, who does not want anything to upset his elaborate preparations to meet his Maker. So I tell them, in my poor way, two of the finest stories in the language – Quiller-Couch's 'The Roll Call of the Reef' and Barry Pain's 'A Lock of Hair'. The former is of course well-known and highly esteemed, but Barry Pain's tale deserves to be taken out of its present obscurity. It is to be found in one of his books called *Curiosities*.

At midnight we move up to the tapes amid heavy shellfire. Each section digs for itself a little pit in which to crouch. It is called intensive digging. Each man in turn digs like fury until he is fagged out and flops, the others meanwhile lying on their bellies and waiting their turn to seize the spade. In this way quite a big hole, like a small section of a trench, can be dug in a very few minutes.

All the while shells are screaming over our heads, throwing up great geysers of mud all around us and further mutilating the ruined landscape. Our better 'ole is about big enough to accommodate us when there is a cry for help. The section, which includes Dave Barney, has been buried by a shell. Dave has given up stretcher-bearing for the time being and is a rifleman or bomber – I forget which. We dig them out again, swear at them heartily, and get back to our own slot in the ground. Ten minutes later they are all blown up and buried again, with worse results than before. Dave is the only one of them left alive, and he is entirely unscathed but badly shaken and inclined to think that war is an over-rated pastime. I want some rest, and beg him not to make a hobby of getting himself buried. One could always say light-hearted and stupid things even when one was frightened to death.

We went back to our little slot in the wet earth and I crouched down and proceeded to sleep like a hog. It would have been rather amusing if everybody had slept as I did, for there wouldn't have been any attack. I don't think that even the barrage, terrific as it was, would have wakened me. And at the same time I was already the victim of tragedy.

While doing my share of intensive digging I heard an ominous snick behind me. When you are batting, and miss a ball, and hear that snick, you know that a bail has gone. In this instance I knew that it was my rear trousers button, the survivor of two. Only men with very strong chins, such as 'Sapper's' heroes, can keep their trousers up by will-power alone. My braces were now a useless and invisible decoration, and I had to improvise a belt out of pack straps. This was very unsatisfactory, since there were no loops on the trousers to keep the belt in its place.

I was not allowed to sleep peacefully through the attack. Edmonds woke me at about a quarter to six by sticking an elbow into my ribs and we went forward to the tape. Ghostly figures ranged up on either side of us, and a dead silence was broken by mutterings and whisperings and the snap! snap! snap! of men jerking their bayonets on to their rifles. When one is in imminent peril some impressions are confused while others burn their way into one's consciousness. The first pale fingers of dawn were in the sky, just beginning to show above the horizon. Having regard to what I imagined to be our front, I had supposed that the sun would rise somewhere on my right. But evidently it intended to rise in front of me and half-left. This was very mysterious, and I haven't solved the problem to this day. Two thoughts occupied my mind while I waited for zero – the sun was rising in the wrong place and my trousers were in danger of leaving me – from at least one angle – naked to mine enemies.

I salute the artillery. At ten minutes to six, hundreds, perhaps thousands, of guns behind us went off like one gun. All the inhabitants of hell seemed to have been let loose and to be screaming and raving in the sky overhead. The darkness just in front of us was rent and sundered. Blinding flashes in a long and accurate line blazed and vanished, and blazed and vanished, while the guns which had at first roared in unison now drummed and bellowed and thumped and crashed in their own time. Their din was half drowned by the variegated noises of the exploding shells. No maniac ever dreamed anything like it.

Matters didn't improve. The German was not asleep, and within a minute his own barrage had multiplied the inferno by two, while machine guns broke out with the rattling of a thousand typewriters. I stood dazed by the din and didn't notice that our own barrage had lifted until somebody shouted: 'Come on!'

I must say, without meaning to praise myself, that it was a good show. Nobody hesitated or looked back. I was simply a sheep and I went with the flock. We moved forward as if we were on the parade-ground.

But it didn't last long. With shell-holes and impassable morasses we had to pick our way. It was no use looking for 'dressing' to the section on the left or right, which was either in the same predicament or had already been blotted out. Led by Edmonds my section made a detour, turning a little to the left and heading for some higher and drier ground. Unfortunately most of the battalion were compelled to do this.

I was in the rear of the section, and, through no fault of my own, kept 10 yards behind the man in front of me. My burden of rifle-grenades pulled me lop-sided and I had to keep on hitching at my trousers. Edmonds kept on turning and waving me on, with the heroic gestures of a cavalry leader in the Napoleonic wars. I cursed him heartily, although he could not hear. Did the damned fool think I was funking it? No, my trousers were coming down.

My trousers seemed a positive curse to me, but I believe they were a blessing in disguise. They may have saved me from an extremity of terror. The human mind is not capable of concentrating on many things at once, and mine just then was principally concerned with my trousers. We fell into mud and writhed out again like wasps crawling out of plums, we passed a pill-box (which we thought was in British hands), we staggered between a few shell-blasted trees, passed another pill-box and came out on to a little plateau of about the size of a small suburban back garden. From there the ground sloped down to the bed of the Paddebeeke, but there was no stream left. It had been shelled into a bog. The Germans had left one long single plank bridge, and we should have known what was certain to happen if we attempted to cross it. But we went on to the edge of the plateau – and it was perhaps as well for us that we did – until Edmonds noticed that nobody else was standing up. Then he signalled to us to take cover. We flopped into a shell hole, lying around the lip, for there was about 6 feet of water in the middle.

We had already seen what had happened to the first 'ripple'. They had all made for that spot of higher and drier ground, and the Germans, having retired over it, knew exactly what must happen, and the sky rained shells upon it. Shrapnel was bursting not much more than face high, and the liquid mud from ground shells was going up in clouds and coming down in rain.

The first 'ripple' was blotted out. The dead and wounded were piled on each other's backs, and the second wave, coming up behind and being compelled to cluster like a flock of sheep, were knocked over in their tracks and lay in heaving mounds. The wounded tried to mark their places, so as to be found by stretcher-bearers, by sticking their bayonets into the ground, thus leaving their rifles upright with the butts pointing at the sky. There was a forest of rifles until they were uprooted by shell-bursts or knocked down by bullets like so many skittles.

The wounded who couldn't crawl into the dubious shelter of shell holes were all doomed. They had to lie where they were until a stray bullet found them or they were blown to pieces. Their heartrending cries pierced the incessant din of explosions. The stretcher bearers, such as still survived, could do nothing as yet.

Well, I found myself in a shell hole with the rest of the section, strangely intact. I had lost merely a bit of skin from the bridge of my nose. I had been stung by something a minute after we started to advance and, having applied the back of my hand, found blood on it. This was a close shave, but a miss was as good as a mile. But a tragedy worse than the precariousness of my trousers had befallen me. I had lost my rations.

While crossing the plateau it had seemed to me that somebody had given the pack on my back a good hard shove, and I had looked all round but there was nobody near. Then I was aware of things falling behind me. A piece of shell about the size of a dumb-bell had gone through my pack, and all my kit and food were dropping out. I didn't stop to pick anything up.

How my section had so far remained intact is a mystery which I shall never solve in this world. After a minute or two of stupor we discovered that we were all as thickly coated with mud from the shell-bursts as the icing on a Christmas cake. Our rifles were all clogged, and directly we tried to clean them more mud descended. If the Germans had counter-attacked we had nothing but our bayonets. In the whole battalion only one Lewis gun was got into action, and I don't think that more than half a dozen men in the three attacking companies were able to use their rifles during the first few hours.

We saw Germans rise out of the ground, and bolt like rabbits, and we had to let them bolt. They had been able to keep their rifles covered and clean, but we had bayonets on ours. Moreover their artillery knew just where we were, and our own gunners were now firing speculatively. We were getting the shells and the rain of mud and the German wasn't. Good soldier that he was, he soon took advantage of this, and we began to suffer from the most hellish sniping.

The mud which was our enemy was also our friend. But for the mud none of us could have survived. A shell burrowed some way before it exploded and that considerably decreased its killing power.

Edmonds decided that our shell hole was overcrowded, and told me to get into the next one. I didn't like exposing myself even for a second, but it was only like rolling out of one twin bed into another, and besides I wanted to get away from the awful man Rumbold who was quite likely, at any moment, to ask me if we were under fire. Half a dozen bullets spat at me in the one second it took to make the change.

There were two men in my new temporary abode, a fellow who was in the Bedfords – on our left – who had got himself lost, and a chap in my company, but not in my section, I knew his company by the red square on his shoulder.

This man lay with his rifle at his shoulder, in the attitude of one about to fire. I spoke to him and he didn't answer. Then I shoved him. Then I noticed that there was a jagged hole at the back of his tin hat and a thin trickle of blood down his neck. He had got it right through the head, and this – if I had needed it – was a warning to keep mine down. I addressed myself to the Bedford.

'Well,' I said, 'we're in a pretty nasty mess. Are we going to get out of it alive, do you think?' I did not say this lightly; I am trying to make it quite clear that I was no hero, and I was just then one of the most hot-and-bothered men in the universe.

The Bedford rolled his eyes.

'I put my trust in Almighty God,' he said.

The remark infuriated me. I prayed for myself – as I shall tell later – but I never 'trusted' in God in the sense that I expected as a right that He should do as I asked. To beg for something is one thing; to 'trust' you are going to get it is another. Thousands of us had to be killed, and it was damnably presumptuous of this fellow to say that he trusted in God to save his own wretched life.

I pointed to the shambles behind us where £500,000 worth of education was already beginning to rot.

'You bloody fool!' I said. 'Do you think some of those fellows didn't put their trust in God, too! He isn't up there just to look after you!'

The Bedford thought I was blasphemous – God knows I wasn't – and obviously didn't like my company, for he presently braved the hell which was raging outside the shell hole and went off to find his own people. I hope he did, but he was probably dead in less than a minute. Anyhow he would probably have been killed if he had stayed, for I don't think two men in the same shell-hole could have survived the narrow squeak which came to me immediately afterwards.

There was still a tornado of shells raging around us, and one must have landed in the same shell-hole with me. I didn't hear it come, and I didn't hear it burst, but I suddenly found myself in the air, all arms and legs. It seemed to me that I rose to about the height of St Paul's Cathedral, but probably I only went up about a couple of feet. The experience was not in the least rough, and I can't understand why it disturbed me so little. I think that by this time I was so mentally numb that even fear was atrophied. It was like being lifted by an unexpected wave when one is swimming in the sea. I landed on all fours in the shell-hole which Edmonds had told me to leave, sprawling across the backs of the rest of the section.

'And now,' I said firmly, 'I'm going to stop.'

Edmonds didn't demur, and I asked him what about some rum. The Nonconformist conscience prevailed, and he said that we might need it presently. Merciful heavens! didn't I need it now? We lit cigarettes and I began trying to think. I wondered if I could smile, and, still having control of my face muscles, found that I could.

After all, I was not very much afraid in that shell-hole, but I knew that I daren't move out of it. I dared not go out and try to do anything for the wounded – coward and hound that I was. After all, I wasn't a stretcher-bearer. A damned good excuse.

Nothing had stood up and lived on the space of ground between ourselves and the pill-box 150 yards away. I saw a stretcher-bearer, his face a mask of blood, bending over a living corpse. He shouted to somebody and beckoned, and on the instant he crumpled and fell and went to meet his God. To do the enemy justice, I don't suppose for one moment that he was recognised as a stretcher-bearer.

Another man, obviously off his head, wandered aimlessly for perhaps ninety seconds. Then his tin hat was tossed into the air like a spun coin, and down he went. You could always tell when a man was shot dead. A wounded man always tried to break his own fall. A dead man generally fell forward, his balance tending in that direction, and he bent simultaneously at the knees, waist, neck and ankles.

Several of our men, most of whom had first been wounded, were drowned in the mud and water. One very religious lad with pale blue watery eyes died the most appalling death. He was shot through the lower entrails, tumbled into the water of a deep shell-hole, and drowned by inches while the coldness of the water added further torture to his wound. Thank God I didn't see him. But our C of E chaplain – who went over the top with us, the fine chap! – was killed while trying to haul him out.

I don't subscribe to the creed of the Church of England. The cognoscenti of my Church – when they can be got to speak frankly – are dubious about the post-mortem fate of heretics and less than dubious about the fate of heretic clergy. But I am very sure, if I am to believe in anything at all, that our dear Padre is in one of the Many Mansions. I like to think of him feasting with Nelson and Drake, Philip Sidney, Richard of the Lion Heart, Grenville, Wolfe, and Don Johne of Austria. And perhaps when these have dallied a little over their wine they go to join the ladies – such ladies as Joan of Arc, Grace Darling, Florence Nightingale, and Edith Cavell. *Requiescat* – but he needs no prayer from a bad soldier and a worse sinner.

Edmonds and I held a sort of council of war. If we were counter-attacked in our present circumstances we hadn't the chance of mice against cats. My theory was that we ought to make a bolt for the pill-box behind us, clean our rifles once we were inside, and thus have a defensive position and a chance to fight for our lives if Jerry decided that the bit of ground we had won was worth re-taking.

Edmonds agreed with me, but was loth to retire. I daresay he thought that an extra 100 yards or so of mud was going to make a material difference to the result of the war. If he had had a Union Jack with him I think he would have stuck it in the ground as a kind of announcement that we were there. He wouldn't go back on his own initiative and at last told me to go and find company headquarters and get an order from Captain Medville.

Company headquarters was an shell-hole that Captain Medville might be in if he happened to be still alive. I didn't want to wander about in an area in which nobody had been seen to stand up for much more than a minute, so I told Edmonds I didn't know where to look. He saw by my eyes that I was afraid to go, and before I could summon a little more resolution and stop him, he went himself.

By a miracle or an accident he found Medville, who seemed to have agreed with my suggestion. Edmonds came lumbering back and waved us towards the pill-box, himself starting in that direction. But he hadn't gone 10 yards before he rolled over, clutching at one of his thighs. I saw him crawl into a shell-hole, and I am glad to be able to say that eventually he got back to safety.

That left me in command of the section.

II

I was the senior private, and I suppose by strict Army law the others were compelled to obey me. But not having the authority of even a single stripe, and knowing that whatever I decided was most likely to be wrong, I said that each of us ought to please himself as to what he did. I gave a brief harangue (without any 'hear, hears') and, of course, I don't remember exactly what I said, but the gist of it was this:

> Here we are, being shelled to Sodom and Gomorrah. If a small boy came over armed with a catapult he could pinch or murder the whole bloody lot of us. We've been directed to retire to the pill-box, but we haven't had an actual order. Once there we shall be fairly safe, but it's the getting there. I think now it's every man for himself, but what are you going to do?

The general opinion, after a long argument, was that we should make for the pill-box one at a time. The next question that had to be decided was who should go first. Having Lance-Corporal Edmonds's wound on my conscience, I said that I would. I don't know if the others attempted to follow me or not. I saw only one of them again, and that was, of course, the awful man Rumbold, who was unable to give a coherent account of what had happened. I dumped everything except my rifle, and the extra ammunition hanging round my neck, and made a dash for it.

I ran and ducked and dodged like an international three-quarter, slipping, falling, rising and plunging, and getting somehow over the mud and the dead bodies and between the shell-holes. It amuses me now to think that during this mad dash it was quite possible that not a single shot was fired at me. Probably the spectators in field grey were laughing too heartily to begin to take aim. It used to amuse us to see some poor devil of a German dodging about like a stoned rat, and their humour was at least as grim as ours.

The little concrete blockhouse was approached by a sort of slide leading to its only entrance. I skidded on the seat of my trousers down a muddy incline and into a pool of water which swam in an open doorway not much higher or wider than the entrance to a dog's kennel. I saw at once that the place was uninhabitable, so far as I was concerned. There was about 3 feet of water inside, and the dead bodies of the late German garrison were floating about. I did not then know that it was in German hands when we passed it in the morning, that we owed a great many of our casualties to the machine gun crew who were now safely dead, and that we had to thank our own C Company for a really magnificent deed of arms. Since I was not in C Company and wasn't even aware that this phase of the fight was going on, I can tell of it without being accused of boasting.

Thanks to our magnificent Staff – God bless them! – we had gone over from a jumping-off place which we knew nothing about. The two pill-boxes in front of us were supposed to have been vacated by the Germans. Nobody had orders to take them. C Company on our extreme left became painfully aware that one of them was in German hands but thought that the job of obliterating it belonged to the Bedfords – on their left – since they had had no orders. When the true state of affairs became known C Company went back and got that pill-box. It could only be got by being surrounded and by somebody heaving a few bombs through the kennel-like door. This was done. When C Company came out of the line it was twelve strong and led by a lance-corporal. The dead were found by a burial-party – from the RMLI, I think – in an accurate circle around that pill-box.

I was fairly safe in the half-fathom of water into which I had slid, but I could not stay there and I was feeling rather homeless. I scrambled up again and dodged round to the other side of the premises, where there was a certain amount of cover. To my surprise I found a sort of family gathering. All the wounded who had managed to crawl so far were congregated there, and I was delighted to find that three of my old friends had 'Blighty' ones.

One of them, a very old man of nearly 40 and a Boer War veteran, had been shot sideways through the seat of the trousers. He was in considerable pain, but responded quite happily to badinage. I told him that he couldn't possibly show his honourable scars to his lady friends and that he might find it difficult to convince the pretty nurses that he was facing the right direction when the bullet found him. I pulled his leg to buck him up, not to annoy him, and the brave fellow, who was lying on his stomach, laughed quite happily. I hate to record that his wound turned septic, and that he died very shortly afterwards in a CCS.

Tim's Irish pal, who attributed all his misfortunes to the machinations of Protestants, had a bloody bandage around one arm instead of a sleeve. He couldn't very well blame the followers of that strange but business-like bookseller, Mr Kensit, for what had happened to him, but I believe that even to this day he is sure that it was a Lutheran Prussian who shot him.

The boy with the almond eyes, who used to put me to bed in England when the bed revolved or miraculously multiplied itself, had one through the shoulder, and seemed not to be in very much pain. They were all waiting to be carried away, or for nightfall and the chance of crawling out on their own legs.

Captain Medville had evidently thought that my suggestion to make for the ill-box was a pretty sound one, for I found him already there. He had been wounded in the process of arriving, but not badly enough to necessitate his going down the line. He was calm but looked very worried and was, I suppose, being baffled by the problem of how to get together what remained of his company. I asked him what I should do and where I should go, and he told me to go and join D Company, which had been in reserve to the other three companies and was now strung out in a long line of shell-holes on either side of the rear pill-box. This was obviously to be our line of defence in the event of Jerry seeking to regain his lost ground.

D Company was lucky. It had lost only about half its men. I faded away in the direction indicated and found a D Company sergeant who was pained because I hadn't shaved. He told me to get into a shell-hole – any one would do – clean my rifle and shoot anyone who couldn't properly pronounce the consonant 'W'. Like a fool, I got into a shell-hole just in front of the pill-box.

It was now about two in the afternoon. Time is supposed to drag when one is in misery. This is generally so, but to me the past eight hours seemed to have gone in one. I settled down alone in my shell-hole, and proceeded to have my 'bad time', which, thank God, nobody witnessed.

The Germans started a really appalling bombardment, quite as bad as the one we had endured in the early hours of the morning. Shells fell around me like acorns dropping from a tree, and the shock of every explosion was like a punch over the solar plexus. I had been through a great deal already, and now I felt that I couldn't bear it. I crouched shivering and whimpering in my extremity, and cried out on God. I don't think it was altogether funk; I think my wits were being blasted out of me. I didn't realise at the time that the Germans were shelling the pill-box, and that I, being just in front, was getting the exclusive attention of a few batteries of field artillery.

I crouched, moaning, 'Oh, Christ, make it stop! Oh, Jesus, make it stop! It *must* stop, because I can't bear it any more. I can't bear it!'

It was the only time in my life when, so far as I can be sure, I had a direct answer to prayer. I don't mean that the shelling stopped: that would have proved nothing to me, and besides the shelling hadn't. I may never again enter a branch of my infallible Church, and try to follow the Mass and go to Confession and Holy Communion. I can't quite believe in a lot of it. I wish I could, for I should be a better and a happier man. But I do believe in God, and I do know that God, the Father of us all, hears us and answers with a Father's gentleness when we cry out to Him in our last extremity.

I begged God to spare me for my mother's sake, while all the while I knew that I was only praying for the preservation of my own dirty hide. I made Him promises of the saintly life I would lead if I got through – promises which I didn't keep and He knew that I wasn't going to keep them. But He was merciful, and His mercy came to me like a sudden shaft of sunlight. It happened all in a moment – a sudden change to peace and calm and perfect confidence. It was like a miracle, and perhaps it was one. All in a moment I was changed from a raving, gibbering idiot to a calm and serene man, utterly fearless for the time being, and quite confident that I was safe. A 5.9 crashed down not more than 5 yards away, drenching me with mud, but I did not mind it. I knew that God was going to save me.

This, having regard to what I had said to the Bedford a few hours since, may seem paradoxical. But I only 'trusted' God after He seemed to have spoken to me. I did not say in effect: 'Well, I've prayed to You, and now it's up to you to get me out of this. Fair's fair.' Believers and unbelievers may make what they like out of this. Snuffy little short-sighted doctors who attribute every malaise and cure of the mind to sex would probably give me some quite astounding explanation. I only know that if an angel had come and taken me by the hand I could not have been more assured of my present safety.

I don't mean that I was never afterwards afraid. I merely knew that just for the present I was safe. Physically I was still wretched enough, starving, mud-drenched and tortured by lice. My improvised belt kept slipping, and every time I moved, lying on the incline of the shell-hole, my trousers, slack at the waist, scooped up mud which ran down cold along my belly and thighs.

Strangely enough I thought of a girl I had loved as finely as I knew how, some two or three years since. Wisely, she had not cared for me, and was now married to another man. I had stopped loving her, but I revered her, as I still do. I felt that if she saw me now, filthy and verminous, as I was, she could not but put her arms around me in compassion.

After this excursion into sticky sentiment, I thought I had better find some grub. There were plenty of fresh corpses lying about with food in their packs or haversacks. However, I hadn't to rob the dead, for I had no sooner started on my food-hunt when I found two D Company fellows in a shell-hole only a few yards away who had plenty to eat. The shelling had died down a bit, but I jumped into their shell-hole to dodge one which seemed to be coming uncomfortably close, and landed almost on top of them.

I didn't know them, but they were decent chaps who shared their food with me. Also they provided me with human society, which I needed more than food and drink. They seemed to think they had had a pretty rough time, and were horrified when I told them that I didn't think there were fifty officers and men left out of the three companies which had made the attack. Mine was a pretty good guess. When we eventually mustered we numbered forty-nine. My company (A) was eighteen strong, including two officers, there were nineteen of B, and twelve of C.

Just before nightfall I saw Lloyd threading his way towards us, and hailed him. Lloyd was a signaller in my company, a little rosy-cheeked Welsh boy aged about 19 who had joined the Army straight from school. I asked him what had become of the rest of the company, and he told me that, so far as he knew, we were the only two who had not become casualties; and he looked at me out of the haggard eyes of an old man.

Lloyd and I both decided that it would be a good idea to spend the night in the pill-box a stone's throw away if it happened to be dry enough inside. It would be safer in there, and there would be shelter of a sort from the rather threatening weather. Since there were no shells coming over at the moment we went and prospected. It was beautifully dry inside, but a number of wounded had crawled there, and the place stank of blood worse than a slaughter-house. Still, we should have put up with that, but the loathly person Goatly (the ex-village schoolmaster officer) was in possession, and meant to spend the night there himself, so he turned us out, although there was plenty of room. I hated this vulgar and domineering person, but I heard that he had behaved with the utmost gallantry, so all is now forgiven. He didn't worry us much longer, for he got a series of soft jobs and became, I believe, a chronic 'town major'. If he reads these lines in the intervals between teaching the Third Standard long division and how to control its water there is not the least chance that he will recognise himself, so he will not require my blood in a bottle. I salute him as the bravest cad with whom I ever had to be associated.

Lloyd and I began by camping in a shell-hole. I think it was the one in which I had had my 'sticky time'. We fired questions at each other, trying to get news, but neither of us seemed to know much. Then Lloyd answered unconsciously the question I had been afraid to ask. He told me that Dave had been killed.

That was the last straw. I was still pretty badly rattled, and I began to cry like a baby. A damned funny sight I must have looked. Oh, Dave, are you really gone? Shall we have no more meals and drinks together? Shan't I ever hear you sing *Songs of Araby* again? No more women for you? No more love – as you understand love since that wife of yours was taken from you? Did God at the last moment stretch out His hand to you and re-unite you with her? Or are you wallowing somewhere in a worse hell than this? Whatever the change, you have gone somewhere else, and here am I, a filthy oaf, with the tears running down my dirty cheeks because of you.

Owing to the conditions something like 70 per cent of the casualties could be marked down as killed. Lloyd and I knew that it must be so. Nearly everybody that we knew and liked seemed to have gone west.

We did not find the slope of the shell-hole conducive to slumber, so we decided to sleep in the open if we could find a dry spot. We found a corrugated iron arch called a 'baby elephant,' and used for the support of shallow funk-holes and dug-outs. We crawled under this, and with no protection against the cold of a night which ushered in the month of November, except the clothes in which we lay – without even our overcoats – we slept like hogs until a red sun winked in our eyes and finally woke us.

Only twice did these mud-sodden, overgrown Babes in the Wood wake during the night. Once we were roused by the screams of a wounded man who was being carried to the pill-box. He kept shrieking, 'Oh, God! Oh, Christ!' – the same words over and over again. We were sorry for him, of course, but for our own sakes we wished he wouldn't do it. On the second occasion Lloyd nudged me and complained of the cold and asked me to lie closer.

The pill-box presented a queer sight in the morning. We went in to see if we could do anything for the wounded and found others trying to improvise a breakfast for them. Medville was feeding his own batman like a baby. The poor fellow had been badly hit and he died shortly afterwards. There was still that terrible stink of raw blood which smote our nostrils pretty hard as we came in from the fresh air.

The regimental Aid Post was a mile or so back, and it took time to get the wounded there. Our MO – whom I didn't particularly like – had worked like a slave, and when we passed the shelter on our way out that night there was a pyramid of shorn limbs standing outside. He had been busy with the casualties of other units besides our own, and had been rather a mark for stretcher-bearers because of the dimensions of the Red Cross Flag which floated above.

There were quite a lot of field guns near that Aid Post. Query: were the guns too near the Aid Post or was the Aid Post too near the guns?

Lloyd and I began to think rather wistfully about breakfast, but we hadn't so much as a crumb between us or a drop of water. I don't know what had happened to Lloyd's rations. However, he had a Tommy Cooker and a tin of coffee cubes, so we decided to risk making coffee with shell-hole water. Lloyd went out with our mess-tins to find the cleanest looking shell-hole, and came back with them full, and quaking like one about to vomit. He had found half a well-preserved Highlander lying just outside the shell-hole from which he had drawn the water, and had had a good look at him and wished he hadn't. He kept on saying: 'I wish I hadn't looked at that damned Scotsman.' It wasn't until after we had drunk the coffee that the horrid thought occurred to us that the other half of the

Highlander might be in the shell-hole from which Lloyd had drawn the water. This was probably not so, for we suffered no after effects.

Soon after we had had our coffee Lloyd was sent for. There was a job of some sort for him. I remained in lonely glory for some hours. A few shells came over, and during this period a terrible scarecrow came running and dodging towards me. The face seemed to me to consist entirely of gold-rimmed spectacles and teeth. It was the awful man Rumbold.

I kept my head down, but with the unerring instinct of the bore, who has scented his victim from afar, he came straight to me, flopped down beside me and said cheerfully: 'Hullo, is that you?'

I didn't tell him it wasn't, because he wouldn't have believed me, and he would have stayed all the same.

He didn't seem to know where he had been during the past twenty-four hours, what he had been doing, or what had happened to anybody else. Indeed, he was magnificently unconcerned with these things. Suddenly and quite chattily he asked me: 'I say, X, what do you think of Lloyd George?'

Now how could I tell him what I thought of Lloyd George? I didn't want to use such language. I might be killed at any moment and I wanted to die in a state of grace.

I suggested that there was another shell-hole over there which looked awfully comfortable, but of course I couldn't get rid of him. He stuck to me closer than a brother until we were relieved at night by a battalion of marines.

We learned during the day that the Canadians on our right, advancing at the same time as ourselves on the higher and drier ground, had taken their objectives. Subsequently we were told 'unofficially' that we were not expected to get very far through the swamp and that we were merely being used to draw fire while the Canadians did the job. Well, it wasn't the last time that I was used as cannon-fodder.

The papers were loud in praise of the Canadians, but had practically nothing to say about us – except in the casualty lists. Officially we were told that we were 'too brave', and had gone too far. But Sir Arthur Conan Doyle in his *History of the War* dismissed us with the remark that we 'seemed to find some difficulty in getting forward'. The difficulty consisted mainly of being killed in heaps.

Now, I love Sir Arthur Conan Doyle without ever having met him. His stories delighted my youth, and he sent a charming letter to me – a practically unknown man – complimenting me on one of mine. But he should have left the war alone. I should go to him if I wanted a really authentic photograph of a fairy or a trunk call through to one of my sleeping ancestors. But he should have left the war to the soldiers. You cannot write about the war by merely reading newspaper reports and looking at maps.

The remnants of us crawled out dead-beat along the eternal duckboard track. Some of us would have collapsed if we hadn't met a water-cart on the way. We got to Irish Farm and were greeted by a really hearty air-raid – as if we hadn't been through enough already.

When it was over and we started looking for the tents allotted to us I was struck by the kindness of the fellows who had remained behind. Our QMS, whom I had always found rather military, met us and carried my rifle for me.

'You've had a hell of a time,' he said with a catch in his voice.

'Pretty bad,' I agreed, 'but it might have been worse.'

'Worse!' he gasped.

'Yes,' I said. 'We didn't see any of the bloody Staff.'

That at least made him laugh.

CHAPTER THIRTEEN

AT A SAP-HEAD

By David Phillips

A fellow named Kendall and I palled up the day after he joined our company. We were in a sugar factory at the time, where we were to spend the night before going into the line. I had found two planks and trestles, and thought, in my ignorance, to make a bed where the rats would not disturb me, and while I surveyed the available floor space the slinking form of a large rat, just discernible in the dimming light, made me turn sharply round. My planks struck Kendall's and in trying to save them, he received the full weight of one on his foot.

'Clumsy swine!' he shouted, and hopped in a threatening attitude towards me. As I put up my lists, I appraised his ability. He was lean and lanky. I decided to punch him in the stomach and upper-cut him as he crumpled but the platoon-sergeant intervened and warned us both for guard from two to four o'clock the following morning.

Kendall spat copiously after the retiring sergeant.

'Stop that!' I said in mock seriousness, 'or I'll have you up for dumb insolence.'

Kendall laughed outright.

'Well, if we've got to go on guard together we may as well kip together.' He had two planks but no trestles, so we jammed the four planks together on my trestles, and next morning on guard we got to know each other better.

Looking back, I am vaguely conscious that the human associations of those War years live more vividly in my memory than the horror and unspeakable realities of war, much as they tormented me.

Kendal and I did many duties together after that and we grew in each other's regard. Of course we never voiced it – at 20 years of age one does not, nor, I suppose, at 60. I don't know. But how else can I explain why he cursed me more abusively than my fellows? Or that my references to his mode of travel along the trenches as being due to chronic 'wind-up' caused him to smile and make dumb signs with his fingers, yet when others said so he would rise in a flash to silence them with his clenched lists.

One night when Kendall and I, together with two others, were over the parados busily digging, the enemy's machine guns traversed in our direction. It was soon after nine o'clock when 'Jerry' started to strafe us pretty generally along the line with 'minnies', 'coal-boxes', 'flying pigs', 'toffee apples', aerial torpedoes, 'flying fishes', 'pip-squeaks', – a very mixed assortment from his stock, to be recognised by whichever of their names you knew them.

Soon we heard the cry: 'Stretcher bearers!' Again and again it was repeated as we crouched lower in our now deepening pit.

'Down Sap 26 – shouldn't wonder,' Kendall said, rising and plying his spade once more. '"D" Company's getting it good and heavy. Damned if I don't think we are better off out here over the –.' A 'pip-squeak' exploded nearby and the sprayed earth tinkled on our steel helmets. The next minute our captain dropped into the pit. We stopped working and wondered what he wanted. He said to me, 'A 'minnie' has dropped plum into the middle of the support bay of Sap 26 and wiped all four of them out, poor chaps, and the two men at the sap-head have been sent down with shell-shock. I want you and someone else to man the sap-head and hang out as long as you possibly can, because the company is short of men and I can't spare any to remain in support. If you get into trouble you must send up a couple of Verey lights and make your way back to the front line. Now, who'll you take with you?'

'Me, sir!' Kendall answered quickly.

'Right! You others must come to the front line. This job must wait.'

We gathered our tools together and prepared to make our way back to the front line.

'Sergeant Popple and I will come with you as far as the support bay. Wait for us at the entrance to the sap.'

Arrived at the entrance, we waited for the captain and Sergeant Popple. They soon came up, bringing the Verey light pistol with them.

'All O.K.?' the captain asked.

We nodded.

'Then lead the way – you'll find it's knee deep in mud. Halt at the support bay, or where the bay was before the 'minnie' dropped. We're sure to struggle out going through the mud.'

For the first few yards of the sap – a roughly hewn trench leading forwards from our front line – the going was good and the desultory shelling ceased. Then the mud became thicker, almost knee high, and footholds none too easy. And the squelching as each foot was lifted out of the mud seemed deafening in contrast with the piercing quiet that had descended on our sector.

I floundered into a hole, loin high in the mud. ''Ware hole,' I whispered over my shoulder to Kendall and heard him pass the warning on to the captain, who in turn passed it on to Sergeant Popple. And in a few moments more I heard the captain's muffled curses as he floundered as I had done. At last we arrived at the 'minnie' hole, where the support bay had been.

'Jerry could hear us a mile off,' Kendall whispered.

'How much farther to the sap-head?' the captain asked.

'Another 60 feet or so,' I replied.

'All right. We'll give you ten minutes by my watch, and unless you signal us before that we'll return to the front line. I'll have you relieved as soon as I can, but it won't be before morning. Don't make yourselves objectionable, because I can't spare any men to support you. Good luck!'

The mud was not so deep at the sap-head. Kendall made himself comfortable on the small fire-step close to the supply of Mills' bombs, having first put a couple handy beside him. He looked at his watch: 'Five minutes to ten,' he whispered. 'They'll be back in the front line by now. Say, Jerry's only a few yards away, isn't he?'

'Yes,' I answered. 'No need to whisper, but don't shout. Jerry's sap-head is about 25 yards from here. Sometimes, when it's quiet, you can hear him knock a tin over. I believe they've got a little dug-out at their sap-head.'

'Seems damn silly, doesn't it,' Kendall remarked. 'Couple of Jerries, or so, 25 yards over there and us over here, sitting on our backsides doing nothing.'

'Shift farther up, then I can sit down and help you. When Jerry sends a couple of bombs over after he's had his supper we'll send one over just to let him know we're still awake.'

'We shan't have had any supper though. Have you anything to eat?' Kendall asked.

'No. Have you?'

'Not a thing, only these hard biscuits.'

Apart from two small explosions nearby and our reply, the night was comparatively quiet. But a continuous booming as of distant thunder came from the direction of the Somme.

Kendall noted it.

'Worse places than this, I suppose,' he said.

'Yes. Still you might have had a soft look-out job in the front line. What did you want to come down here for, anyway? Always thought you were windy.' I bantered.

'So I am,' he confessed; 'windy as hell.'

'So am I.'

'Then why did the captain call on –'

'Shut up! I haven't told him yet.'

Kendall became reminiscent as a rat scuttled up the bank to the side of us.

'Funny, that night in the sugar factory. Lord, how I cursed that sergeant sticking us on guard together! And here we are – snug as a couple of bugs in a rug.'

'Not so strange after all. Perhaps, if we knew Jerry better, there'd be none of this,' I ventured.

'Perhaps so. Yes. And here we sit, and over there Jerry sits, lousy as hell – platoons of 'em in column of route marching all over you: drink that's one part water and four parts chloride of lime and brought up from the well at Ecurie in 2-gallon petrol tins; a bath every eighteen days and a shave when you're lucky enough to find a puddle that hasn't been stirred for an hour or so. What the devil made you join up?'

'The papers talked me into it – and vanity, I suppose,' I answered.

And so we talked through the night, gathering our greatcoats around us in the chill of the morning before dawn. A night crammed full of self-revelation –

interesting as nothing else – of intimacies conveyed half-banteringly, yet with a veneer of cynicism!

And at dawn we eyed each other, a little shamefacedly perhaps, with a new interest and greater understanding.

'Gets colder between stand-to and stand-down,' Kendall remarked. He jumped down from the fire-step, where he had been looking towards the German lines. 'The sun'll get stronger presently. Keep an eye on that poppy' – it grew on the edge of the trench – 'watch it open. That'll help the time to pass.'

'Blimy (*sic.*)!' he continued. 'We've done eight hours already. Must report to the union when we get back.'

Sergeant Popple crawled warily up to the sap-head, carrying two hunks of bread, two small pieces of bacon, and a dixie of cold tea. We welcomed him as uproariously as the proximity of the two sap-heads allowed.

'Well, Pop,' Kendall said, 'how are things?'

'Lost a lot of men in the bombardment last night – Jerry's got our range to an inch. Davies gone, poor fellow, and Wellshead; Ashton blown to pieces; and Wheeler, poor kid. Only 17 too! Got out here by bluffing his age and now a shell's taken his head clean off while he was standing on the fire-step. Goodness knows how many have had "Blighty ones".' Sergeant Popple looked grave as he stood with bended back, biting the ends of his grey moustache, the mud dripping from his puttees.

We ate the breakfast he had brought, filled our water bottles with the cold tea that was over, and asked him when he thought we would be relieved.

'Can't say,' he replied. 'Won't be before this afternoon, anyway. And cookie's got a touch of nerves, so I'll bring you along some grub when I get the chance. Captain wants you to keep a sharp-look-out from this sap-head, and you're not to leave it on any account.'

'Right-o! Pop. Kiss the captain for me,' Kendall answered, and we watched Sergeant Popple down the sap, his back bent low, and carrying the empty dixie.

'Some say, "Good old Pop?"' I ventured.

'Some don't so say,' Kendall replied with gusto.

The afternoon turned in an hour from sunshine to rain. A wind sprang up, a regular gale, and from over the German lines heavy clouds rolled disgorging torrential rains. Dinnertime had long since passed and Sergeant Popple had not brought us any. We were hungry as we stood in the lee of the firing-plate, which, sand-bagged on the other side except for the peep-hole, formed the sap-head. So we munched the few scraps of hard biscuits that were left and took draughts from our cold tea.

At six o'clock we tossed for sleeping. Kendall won, and tucking himself well into the corner of the fire-step, with his waterproof sheet pegged to the sand-bags so that his head and body were completely covered, he tried to sleep. I heard him muttering to himself every now and then; he cursed the conditions, the rain, the lice and, above all, the relieving party that had not arrived. But it was evident he would not be able to sleep. He was already wet through from the thighs downwards as I was.

'Thank your lucky stars you're not out here,' I said, as I heard the scratching of his lighter and knew, although I could not see, that he was going to light a cigarette. He did not reply, but started cursing again.

The rain came down still heavier and the wind swept it across the open, washing the trunk of the tree on our right – such a tree; dead, shell-torn, barkless!

Night came. We continued to take turns at resting on the fire-step; one resting, the other standing at the far corner and looking out over the lines into the darkness, which was relieved now and again by a fizzing Verey light. At midnight our artillery made a show and the Germans replied vigorously. In No Man's Land, as we were, it was comparatively safe, though the shells screeching overhead in both directions were particularly nerve-racking in our exhausted state.

Kendall cursed the relieving party again and again for not coming. All that night he cursed them venomously; for no one had been to see us, to bring food, and our biscuits and cold tea were long since finished. We no longer attempted to rest. Drenched to the skin and painfully in need of sleep, we propped ourselves up on the fire-step or in the trench, now a quagmire. And Kendall's obsession, the relieving party, soon made it impossible for him to stay on the look-out. And as for me, every stake in No Man's Land turned into a stalking German after a momentary stare, and I would have to look away and blink before the Germans would revert to stakes once more.

After stand-to on the following morning we were relieved. Dog-tired and hungry, we returned to the front line, where only the minimum of sentries were on duty owing to the shortage of men. We were given hot tea, bread, and bacon, and we went down a dug-out to sleep.

Soon – it seemed about five minutes afterwards – we were roused again and placed on sentry duty in the front line. Perhaps our periscope was a little too high, for Jerry paid some invidious attention, so with the dirt showering all about us we lowered it for a while.

After two hours Corporal Simpson brought two men to relieve us. I was looking through the periscope at the time and Kendall, who sat cleaning his rifle, was the first to see them.

'What do you want?' Kendall asked the Corporal.

'Brought the relief, of course,' the corporal replied.

'Relief! We don't want a b– relief. We've held this position for thirty-four hours twenty-seven minutes. Clear out or I'll plug you!'

Tired as I was, it was some seconds before I realised that this was no ordinary banter, that Kendall still imagined we were holding the sap-head. I turned round towards him.

'Clear out, you b–!' Kendall shouted, and with a quick movement slid the bolt of his rifle back and forced a bullet into the breach.

I fell on him, pinning his shoulders to the ground, and, with Corporal Simpson and the assistance of the two men, barely managed to restrain him. And as I sprawled across his chest I looked into his staring, glassy eyes and realised he was mad – stark, staring mad!

CHAPTER FOURTEEN

A PADRE IN SALONIKA

By Henry C. Day

While the infantry and engineers were hard at work constructing roads and fortifying hills round Salonika, my old 2nd South Midland Mounted Brigade, the Notts and Derbys – now known as the 7th Mounted – were engaged in patrolling the front beyond the marches of the 'Bird Cage'.

On arriving in the country I was immediately posted to them, and attached by the Brigade to the headquarters of the Derby Yeomanry, with whom I began my military experiences shortly after the commencement of the war. There was no delay on my part; I started next morning to join the regiment at Langaza, where headquarters and 'A' Squadron were under canvas.

Army could give me transport only as far as the old rest camp at Karassi. But before I had been there half an hour, to my great relief and delight, a convoy arrived from the regiment, who straightway escorted me to my destination. Lieutenant R.H. Humphries and Trooper King were of the party, and between them they arranged the loan of a horse for me, while my baggage travelled on the half-limber brought for the purpose.

Reaching camp in good time on the Saturday evening, I was able to arrange overnight for the service which took place early the next morning in a large field tent, and was splendidly attended.

Sunday afternoon and next day were given to renewing and making acquaintances. There were several changes in the regiment – Lieutenant-Colonel G.A. Strutt was now the O.C., with Major the Honourable Dudley Carleton as his Second-in-Command, and Captain F.B. Swanwick Adjutant. Colonel Strutt and Captain Swanwick I had met in England and in the Dardanelles. The Major was a new acquaintance, who, however, soon became as good a friend to me as the rest. Captain R.M. Wilson was still our MO.

I was looking out for a batman, when Trooper J.H. Tugby, of 'A' Squadron Transport, came to my tent on Tuesday evening, and volunteered his services. He was a Catholic from Yorkshire, and his father carried on a large building business in Swinton, where he was well known and respected. He was only 18 and had joined up under the Derby Scheme. Though a stranger to me, everything in the youth's appearance and manner – he was well set up, of fair complexion, and frank and straightforward – at once appealed to me. He wanted to be my servant because he was a Catholic – would I have him? Of course, I would, if I could get him.

First I approached the Transport Officer, who reluctantly gave his consent. Tugby, he said, was the smartest boy of his lot, but if I required him, I must have him. The Orderly Room did the rest, and the next morning Trooper Tugby reported to me for duty. We soon became pals, and we have remained fast friends ever since. He continued to be my servant until the end of the war. He has since married and is the proud father of a young family.

Our camp, well off the road, and by the side of a little stream that ran into the lake a mile or two to the east, was conveniently near to the town of Langaza. This was quite a fair-sized place, and contained a few decent farmhouses on the outskirts, where there were also a number of rather large trees. The streets, of course, were without pavements, and consisted, as usual, of mud, holes and stones. In addition there were some half-dozen petrol gas lamps. Most of the houses were dirty and dilapidated.

The better class of houses conformed to the prevailing type of farm cottages throughout the country. This type of dwelling was a two-storied house, the lower rooms of which were merely earth-floored stables, and were commonly used for storing the farm tools, and the winter supply of corn and fuel. Outside, a wooden staircase led up to a veranda, off which were the two or three living-rooms of the family. Each room was provided with a fireplace, a couch or bed, and some scanty furniture of the roughest sort.

In the Turkish and Bulgar houses, which we always preferred for billeting, the beds as a rule were spotlessly clean. There was also a profusion of whitewash, and plenty of evidence of scrubbing and cleaning. The children in the villages appeared to be well kept and sufficiently nourished and healthy. On the other hand, public sanitation was woefully lacking, the houses being without baths or water-closets or even cesspools. There was no water supply, and what was required for household purposes had to be fetched in jars or buckets from wells or streams, never far distant.

I do not remember visiting the church of Langaza, but I recall making a journey, months afterwards, with a non-Catholic officer to inspect a very old and interesting parish church in the neighbouring village of Baldza.

The outside of the building was plain, but the simple piety of the interior impressed us both. There were neither chairs nor benches in the nave, which was divided up the centre by a roped-off path, to separate the men from the women. In the sanctuary, which was entirely shut off from the rest of the church by a wide screen, lavishly decked with ikons, were a number of stalls and lecterns. Sacred pictures on wood also adorned the walls of the aisles.

Before leaving, we lit candles in honour of the Patron, St George, and, on our way out, the very unwashed sacristan gave us each a rose from the garden. Just beyond the village we passed the priest on his way back to the presbytery. He did not seem to notice us, but we observed him closely as he rode by on his donkey, followed by a boy who ran behind, and alternately coaxed and belaboured the beast with a stick.

The priest was a middle-aged and lean man, with a full beard and long lank hair, much greased and tied up in a knot at the back. Add to these adornments a shabby high stove-hat of the conventional type, and a long greenish-black robe, carelessly tucked up, and you have a picture of a typical orthodox country pastor. I saw many such priests on the roads afterwards. They did not appear to me altogether presentable, and I sometimes wondered if our eminently respectable Anglican clergy would be quite as keen on reunion with the Eastern Churches if they had lived for a time in the Orient, and seen their desired confrères at close quarters.

Donkeys were common objects in Macedonia, and entered much into the life of the countryside. A young donkey could be purchased for three or four drachmae, and, when grown up, he was available for almost any and every sort of transport. Often you might see in the distance what appeared to be a small haystack walking along on its own; but when the moving mass drew near, closer inspection would discover a donkey in the midst of it all.

There were other and more serious settings in which this lowly animal of the people revived memories for ever sacred in the history of the race. More than once I saw on the road a group straight from the Bible – a donkey bearing a woman and a child, and led by a man. It was the Flight into Egypt to the life – the same donkey, the same pack-saddle, and the same manner of dress, now as then.

There were other customs also which recalled life as described in the Bible, as, for example, the primitive methods of harvesting. Both in Palestine and Egypt threshing and winnowing from time immemorial have been accomplished in the open, according to this method which is still pursued. A round beaten space in the fields, preferably on an eminence, so as to be exposed to the free sweep of air currents, provides the floor on which the sheaves are first spread in a wide circle. Over them four or five oxen, harnessed to a heavy oblong board, roughened on its underside by having sharp stones or nails inserted, are driven round and round until a sufficient loosening of the grain is effected. Additional weight to that of the driver is supplied by heavy stones placed on top.

The first time I saw the counterpart of this in Macedonia was on a journey from Janes to Causica, with my friend, Captain A.O. Morris, of the 90th Anti-Aircraft Section, Royal Artillery. He was taking me in his car to visit one of his gun positions.

It was a bright sunny morning, and as we approached the village of Hadji Junus, we were surprised by the sound of an indescribable din caused by shouts and cries mingled with peals of laughter. This medley of human expression in an apparently deserted Greek village mystified us at first, but on reaching the centre of the village, our puzzlement was solved. There a strange sight was revealed. Travelling round and round the circumference of a circle of hard earth, about 30 feet in diameter, appeared a large wooden sledge drawn by a tiny donkey and an ox, harnessed tandem. Seated or standing on the sledge were the driver, a Greek peasant, his wife, and the numerous members of his family – a good round dozen in all! They were shouting and singing whilst the younger members banged tins at intervals.

What was it all about? Were these folk taking part in some family game, or was it a serious business? On stopping to inquire the cause of the commotion, we received a full explanation. The rotund, good-natured peasant, grinning all over his face, explained that he was threshing corn, and that the weight of himself and his family helped to loosen the grain from the husks. When this was accomplished, he added, the next process was that of winnowing. The bruised husks were gathered from the threshing floor, and a favourable day awaited with a suitable wind. Then, willing hands would cast the chaff and grain into the air from shovels and sieves, and the chaff being lighter was carried away by the wind, whilst the grain fell to the ground, to be collected, stored and eventually ground into meal by the womenfolk, and made into the coarse brown bread of the country.

The native population, here as elsewhere in Macedonia, apart from a sprinkling of Bulgars, consisted chiefly of Greeks and Turks. The proportion of the two nationalities was equally distributed, so that it was quite the usual thing to find a village divided by its main street into two distinct parts, of which one would be Turkish, and the other Greek, with a small Bulgar element – the Turkish side being invariably distinguished from the Greek by an appearance of markedly greater cleanliness and tidiness. There was little fusion between the two parties. In fact, law and order, such as they were in that country, was the single unifying principle; it was represented in the person of a so-called Greek gendarme, usually a retired comitadji or brigand of notoriety, who, by reason of his past exploits, commanded a measure of respect from all.

The Greeks were much divided in their loyalties. The King's party, nominally our friends, were really pro-German, and constantly intrigued against us. The party of M. Venizelos, on the other hand, were equally pro-British, and consequently were anxious to enter actively into the war on the side of the Allies, which, after the revolution at the end of July, they did. The remaining party of the Army was an uncertain quantity to the end, and of its politics and feelings we knew little or nothing.

Of all the native inhabitants, the Turks proved to be the most reliable. If a Turk entertained you – and he appeared to be always willing to do so, even though your nation was at war with his – you knew that you were perfectly safe. This was one reason why our patrols, when they were obliged to stay out at night at any village, sought hospitality at the principal Turkish house, where it was invariably accorded with the best grace, and the greatest generosity possible in the circumstances.

In physique and general appearance, the Turks and Bulgars – some of them really fine-looking men – had the advantage over the Greeks, who were usually both smaller and less presentable.

The market, which gave Langaza its chief claim to distinction and attracted visitors from miles around, was held weekly in a wide and long corridor that ran through the centre of the town. Here, vegetables and fruits, wines and spirits, and all sorts of merchandise of reliable quality, could be obtained at a far cheaper cost than in Salonika. It was, in fact, a sort of Covent Garden for all Southern Macedonia, and since it was also in part a social gathering, residents and visitors alike would come in their gala attire, and avail themselves of these occasions to display their finest and most gorgeous raiment, the men appearing in wonderful red, green and yellow sashes and shirts, and the women in correspondingly bright head-dresses and pinafores.

Within a mile of the town, in connection with one of the thermal springs for which the neighbourhood was famous, was a fine old octagonal Roman bath. This building was solidly constructed of stone, and covered by a domed roof, perforated by large holes for the purpose of light and ventilation. The basin of the bath was of marble, and through it ran a stream of sulphur water which was really hot, but not so hot as to be unpleasant. The place appeared to be free and open to all at any time. There were many such baths in the country, and I never missed an opportunity of patronising them. The Langaza bath accommodated forty or fifty swimmers at a time, and it used to be crowded with officers and men every day, in the mornings and evenings. But neither there, nor in any of the other baths, do I remember ever encountering native bathers. Whether they abstained on our account, or on principle, we never knew; but it was all to our advantage that they did so.

Game in the neighbourhood of our camp was extraordinarily abundant. Great flocks of geese and wild duck, and swarms of snipe, inhabited the vicinity of the lake, while quantities of partridges, as well as a number of brown hares, were to be met on the foothills. Grouse alone were absent. I remember Colonel Strutt and Major Carleton used to disappear from the camp towards evening, armed with guns that were not rifles, and that the headquarters mess was invariably supplied with better fare than mere army rations.

Everyone who spent any time about Langaza will recall the frogs, big and little, old and young, fat and lean! The old fat frogs lay in the streams off the roadsides all day sunning themselves; and, when we passed, they would blow out their cheeks into big bubbles, and say:

Wah! Tchah, tchah, tchah!

This was all right; but it was a different matter when, as in the play of Aristophanes, countless thousands 'raised their full choir shout', and sang through the night:

Brekekekex, ko-ax, ko-ax;
Brekekekex, ko-ax, ko-ax!

Then the uproar was such as to awaken light sleepers, and it was even known to have caused alarms of Zepp raids. In the circumstances, it was not surprising that other croakers were to be found amongst ourselves, who, like Dionysus of old, mocked and cursed 'the children of the lake and fountain':

Brekekekex, ko-ax, ko-ax;
Brekekekex, ko-ax, ko-ax!
Hang you and your ko-axing too,
There's nothing but ko-axing with you!

Yet this was not all the truth. The Langaza frogs were not ordinary frogs – they were of the edible sort, and had extraordinary fat hind legs. These succulent members, cooked to a turn and served on toast, provided a favourite delicacy at our mess. When this bonne-bouche appeared on the table of an evening, the offences of the previous night were invariably forgiven and forgotten.

Our Brigade, which was made up of the Derbyshire Yeomanry, the South Notts Hussars, and the Sherwood Foresters, had been given the task, with other Yeomanry detachments, of patrolling and reconnoitring the whole of the British zone, comprising a breadth of well over 100 miles, and a depth of at least 25 miles. North of this line was the neutral area occupied by the Greek Army, with headquarters at Seres.

To cover so extensive a front, the regiments and squadrons were necessarily widely separated. Thus the 'B' Squadron, the nearest to us at the time, was 18 miles east of Langaza, at a place called Langavuk, while 'D' Squadron was another 27 miles farther on at Stavros.

During my first ten days, I contented myself with visiting the few scattered troops of the Derbyshires in the neighbourhood, and also a camp of the South Notts at Guvesne. Then, on the 16th, I started off with my batman for Langavuk, to spend a few days with Major A.A. Shuttleworth's Squadron. I found them encamped in a sort of ravine or nullah, while in other nullahs nearby were an RFA Battery, a Field Ambulance, and three infantry battalions of the Royal Irish, the Leinsters, and the Royal Irish Fusiliers.

All these units belonged to the 27th Division, who had their headquarters also at Langavuk. The infantry, apart from their officers, were nearly all Catholics. There were three RC Chaplains in the place – Fathers Reardon, Bowes, CSSR, and Rusher.

Father Reardon was attached to the 81st Field Ambulance, and Fathers Bowes and Rusher to the Royal Irish Fusiliers and the Leinsters. The Royal Irish had no Padre of their own, and thereby hangs a tale.

The next day, Friday the 17th, was the Feast of St Patrick, and the Irish units held sports in the afternoon, which I attended. On Sunday the 19th I said Mass in my tent for the Yeomanry, and on the following Tuesday, at Father Bowes' request, I held a voluntary service for the Royal Irish. Having heard Confessions in their camp the previous evening, the early morning Mass and Communion were both well attended.

The same afternoon I lunched at the headquarters of the Royal Irish Fusiliers, where I first made acquaintance with Lieutenant McCarthy O'Leary, the Adjutant. He was a son of Colonel McCarthy O'Leary, the hero of Spion Kop, whom I had met years before.

The OC of the battalion, Lieutenant-Colonel Orpen Palmer, invited me to dine on the following Thursday. This invitation I gladly accepted, but I was obliged to decline later, on account of a telephone message from the Brigade, instructing me to proceed to Stavros the same day. The message further instructed Major Shuttleworth to supply bivouac sheets for myself and my servant, as well as a pack-horse.

The pack-horse was duly provided, but there was no pack-saddle with it. The extra animal, as one might have expected, was anything but the pick of the

Squadron mounts. He was just a common stocky chestnut pony, with a hard mouth, and short unpleasant pace and temper. On account of his appearance and character we called him 'Red Ginger', and he fully lived up to his name. He was the sort of animal no one would have cared to ride, and none could have been found to fall in love with him. Tugby, I fancy, from the beginning took a distinct aversion to him. However, there he was, and we had to make the best of him. With a pack-saddle, if such could be got, he might be really useful, in spite of appearances. There was also the consideration that he enhanced our importance; with transport of our own, we seemed to become a sort of self-contained cavalry unit – in fact, a more or less independent half-section.

Before leaving on Thursday morning for Savros, I had occasion to visit Colonel Vaughan, the AAG of the 27th Division. Of course he knew nothing of Chaplains' pack horses or pack-saddles, but he kindly suggested that the Division would be glad of my services, if I cared to take on the Royal Irish Regiment. At the same time he mentioned that the Yeomanry were about to move to the front, and that the infantry would follow on later. In the circumstances, I thanked him, but explained that, for the present at least, I felt I ought to remain with my old mounted Brigade, especially if they were likely to be involved in any immediate fighting.

I had only four days with 'D' Squadron at Stavros, but they have left very pleasant recollections. The place is amongst the most beautiful in Macedonia, and I was fortunate enough to see it at the best time of the year. It is situated at the mouth of a river which joins Lake Beshik with the sea. On either side of the gorge through which the river flows are foot-hills and wooded ravines, bounded on north and south by high mountains and plateaux. Our camp was near the river bank, pitched on a slope of land from which water seemed to ooze perpetually. There appeared to be springs and rivulets everywhere.

The camp, in consequence, was pretty well water-logged, and even the floor of the headquarters mess was not without puddles. But these minor inconveniences were more than compensated for by the happy comradeship which prevailed in the Squadron. Captain D'Arcy Clark was our OC, and with him were Lieutenants A.R. Willan, W.D. Blatch, J. Rogers, A.G. Burdett, W.M.B. Fielding, and C.A. Branfill. A more congenial and cheery set of young officers one could not have desired to meet.

The country was rugged and mountainous, so horses required some time to become used to it. The Squadron horses were by now well trained, and almost as sure-footed as the native donkeys, or our own imported mules. As my grey mare from the Brigade, a fine old hunter, was regarded as insufficiently familiar with the terrain, I was provided by Captain Clark with one of his own ponies; and Lance-Corporal A. Webster, the Captain's groom and orderly, was deputed to look after myself and my mount.

I remember that my first day was spent riding with Captain Clark round our trenches to the north of the camp, along Brown Hill and Four Tree Hill, and back by the 83rd Brigade Head-quarters. We dined in the evening with Captain

Stavely, RN, on board HMS *Endymion*. I had never dined on a British man-of-war before and I quite enjoyed the experience, which was subsequently repeated on two or three occasions, when, on visiting Salonika, I was entertained by Colonel John Noble on board HMS *Lord Nelson*, the *Exmouth* and the *Agamemnon*.

The Colonel belonged to the Royal Marines, and was the brother of a school companion and lifelong friend of mine, Robert E. Noble, now a puisne-judge[1] in the British West Indies. Colonel Noble returned to England later on, and died at Woolwich in consequence of war service. He was a highly esteemed and extremely popular officer.

The next day was Saturday, and I rode out again in the morning with Captain Clark and Lieutenant Rogers, to visit Maslar Troop.

Our way lay farther over the mountains, and the track in places was exceedingly precipitous. At one point it took the form of a passage, about the length of a cricket pitch, along a ledge little more than a foot wide, with a wall of cliff on one side and a sheer fall to a mountain torrent 20 or 30 feet below. It recalled to me the passage of the *mauvais pas* in Switzerland between the Rhone and Rhine Glaciers, which I had made many years before. Then I did actually slip over the precipice, and recovered my footing only by chance, which I still regard as coming near to the miraculous. This time the skill and responsibility rested with the horse. I looked straight ahead, dropped the reins on his neck, and gave him full freedom. I remember feeling the animal's flanks trembling in a quite unmistakable and alarming manner. We got across all right, however, but like the 'wise men' in the Gospel, we were careful to return another way.

In the afternoon I visited the Naval Division, which was stationed a mile or two up the valley, to arrange for some of the units to attend my service the following morning in the Yeomanry camp. Punctually to time, Major Edwards arrived the next morning with a large contingent, and conducted the music of our Sunday service, which was held in the open, and concluded with the National Anthem.

Orders had arrived by Saturday for 'D' Squadron to proceed on the following Thursday to Langavuk, in order to replace a Surrey Yeomanry Squadron as Divisional Cavalry. It was also known that the Brigade had moved on towards Kukus. I now realised that I must prepare to get on the road, and obtain a pack-saddle by some means.

Our Quartermaster-Sergeant, Sergeant-Major Warner, had done all he could, and had sent an indent to Army Ordnance at Salonika. But all was in vain. GHQ simply refused to recognise a pack-saddle as being 'authorised equipment' for an Army Chaplain; when it was explained that I actually had a pack-horse, even the existence of the pack-horse was ignored. It was not 'on the strength', consequently I was not entitled to its saddle, and that was the official end of the matter.

The only way out of the difficulty was to order a Greek pack-saddle, which at the best is a clumsy wooden contrivance. For this purpose I started off again on

1. A regular member of a court other than the court's chief judge or chief justice, or any *ex officio* member of the court.

Monday morning, this time by a safe track, for the village of Maslar which I had previously visited, where a reliable Greek harness-maker happened to reside. The bargain was struck, and the saddle was promised to be delivered on Thursday morning at a point on the road a few miles from our camp on the way between Stavros and Langavuk.

The Greek, faithful to his word, met me with the saddle at the place and time appointed, and fixed it on the back of 'Red Ginger'. Then we proceeded on our journey independently of the Squadron, and reached Langavuk late in the afternoon of Thursday. Here I decided to wait over Sunday, for the sake of providing service on that day for the troops in the neighbourhood.

On the following Monday morning, April 6th, we – that is, Tugby and myself – started off on our lone trek to rejoin the Brigade. The first day's journey led us over the hills by way of Jerakaru, Dogandzi, Hortiach, and Eurenjik to the rest camp at Karassi close by Salonika. From Dogandzi the road became a mule track, and continued as such for some miles along the slope of the hills overlooking the lake and plain of Langaza.

Here, while we stopped to admire the scenery, 'Red Ginger' gave us the slip, and for the next quarter of an hour the beauty of the landscape no longer interested us.

Our pack-horse, with his pack all awry, was galloping off towards the lakes, while we two, scarcely less awry, and looking more like American cowboys than members of the British Army, in slouch hats and shirt sleeves, were scouring round in different directions in order to circumvent and arrest him.

We had not seen a soldier or a native since we started, but at this embarrassing moment who should appear on the horizon but a General and his staff. It might have been the GOC and his entourage, but it turned out to be Brigadier-General Nichol of the 10th Division, with his ADC and an orderly.

Fortunately we caught 'Red Ginger' shortly after this untoward apparition, and the General and his staff moved away without saying anything – as far as we knew. The rest of the journey was accomplished without any further regrettable incident, and we arrived in time for dinner in the evening at the rest camp.

I devoted the next day and the morning of the following Wednesday to shopping with my servant in Salonika. A parting purchase was a fine bivouac tent, which I obtained for fifty drachmae from a Greek tent-maker in a poor quarter of the town. On the completion of the purchase, the Greek, with the assistance of a few bystanders, obligingly made up the canvas and poles of the tent into a convenient package, and fixed it on to our pack-saddle with the rest of our luggage. The party of natives was profuse in civility, and demonstrative in professions of loyalty to M. Venizelos and the cause of the Allies. Everything seemed propitious, and we parted in the most amicable manner.

But, alas for the fickleness of fortune! Scarcely had we proceeded 200 yards, when we discovered to our amazement that the carefully-secured package had vanished. Where had the whole caboodle gone? We returned immediately to question our friends – but they, too, had disappeared, except the Greek, who shrugged his shoulders ominously, and gesticulated suspicions of his erstwhile assistants. The place, he declared, was infested with rogues, and it was hard for an honest man to live and conduct business in such a vagabond neighbourhood. At first he appeared simply desolated and dumbfounded at the news of our misfortune, but his sympathy soon took on a practical form, and expressed itself in an earnest desire to make good the loss. Would I accept another and better tent as a gift in return for the bare cost of the material – sixty drachmae?

It was difficult to withstand such sympathy and generosity. Besides, I was bent on having a bivouac at all costs, and there was no longer time to make further search in the shops, most of which I had already explored in the course of the morning. Accordingly I smothered resentment and suspicion, and consented to the bargain with the best grace I could. Then we moved off again, but this time we kept an alert eye on tent 'number two' until well out of the city.

We were now once more on our way to rejoin the Brigade, and after stopping at Karussi for lunch, we started along the Seres road for Kukus. The first stage of the journey ended at Guvesne, where we halted and stayed the night with 'B' Squadron of the Surrey Yeomanry. The next morning, leaving the main road, we continued our trek north-west, across the series of low wooded hills and plains which form part of the watershed of the Galico.

There were few villages on the way, and it was difficult to obtain precise information. However, we picked out the best tracks we could, and managed to reach Kukus before nightfall. The Brigade then directed us to the camp of the Derbyshires, which was pitched in the bed of the Spant River, a tributary of the Galico, at a point 2 miles north-east of the town.

This town of Kukus or Kilchis was the centre of a pre-war prosperous tobacco industry, and once a famous rendezvous for Greek and Bulgarian revolutionaries. It lay on the Guvesne-Janes road, at a point where that road is crossed by another running north to Snevce. Since both roads were principal traffic routes, and the town itself was the most important in the district, we often had occasion to visit it.

As far as I can remember, the Kukus of our time consisted chiefly of a long straggling street, with two attempts at side streets, running right and left at the main crossing. Behind an open space near the end of the town, and by the turning to the left, stood the French Convent School and the Catholic Church. These together formed a fairly good block of buildings. The only other large buildings were a few pretentious edifices on the western slopes of the hills above the principal street. Small native stores, cabarets and dwelling-houses lined either side of the main thoroughfare, and stood well back from the road, like some of the shops in Mile End. The walls of most of the houses were plastered with dung-cakes – a chief source of fuel in the neighbourhood – and festooned with tobacco leaves exposed to the sun to dry. This useful expedient for drying the leaves also gave a festive appearance to the place.

The cabarets were typical of the country, and I often enjoyed a simple meal, sitting alone or with a companion at a rough table, while peasants in the same room ate, smoked, and drank 'mastics'. Entertainment was provided in a bare kitchen on the ground floor, and one simply walked in and helped oneself to the various stews and dishes, which stood cooking on a wide stove at the farther end of the room. It was an excellent method, and overcame an all too common difficulty of having to choose food from unintelligible bills of fare when visiting hotels and restaurants.

In America, I rediscovered this simple Balkan principle in the elaborate system of cafeteria prevailing through all the large cities. Why cannot the idea be introduced into England? No prizes are offered for the best answer, but only a lucky chance of a fortune.

Of the disposition and number of the forces opposed to us, little was known except that they were reasonably near and made occasional cavalry sorties. A French Brigade of Chasseurs d'Afrique, on our left, also reported that there were bands of Comitadji in the neighbourhood.

On the following day, April 7th, the regiment was ordered to fill a gap between the Sherwoods and the French Chasseurs at Janes. Strangely enough, this order was cancelled at midnight from England, and superseded by another the next morning, directing our 'A' Squadron to reinforce the SRY in the neighbourhood of Irikli, 6 miles farther north.

Our position was now on the extreme east of the Brigade support line, which extended westward as far as the town of Kilindir on the Kilindir River. The advanced line, consisting of scattered outposts, occupied the high ground in front, called the Gola Ridge, after the village of Gola on its crest.

The French line, with headquarters at Hirsova, led among a further reach of low hills, between which the Kilinder River flowed north into the lake. These hills, and the river between them, which bore a close resemblance to a typical Scottish glen, separated our Gola Ridge from the mountains protecting Doiran town for the enemy.

The third stage of the war had now begun. This period (April–June, 1916) was marked by a gradual movement of the allied troops towards the Greek frontier, for the purpose of establishing a forward position, which could serve either for offence or defence, according to circumstances.

For the Yeomanry, whose duty was to keep in constant touch with the enemy during these operations, the three months were more than usually busy and exciting. They were also, I recall, days of extraordinarily quick changes and rapid movements. A whistle would sound to 'strike camp', and we were packed up, and away on our horses to another hillside or nullah, in anything from an hour to a couple of hours at the utmost. I shared to the full in these exciting changes, moving from camp to camp with the rest. In addition I had my duty movements from regiment to regiment, and from squadron to squadron.

Each morning our patrols would mount and start away early, sword on one side of saddle and rifle in its bucket on the other, to surprise and ambush the Uhlan cavalry, who, with spear and carbine, were equally active on their part in the pursuit of a similar enterprise.

Sometimes our parties remained out for two or three days; more often they returned the same evening. Frequently they brought back thrilling stories of adventure-encounters with spies, sharp skirmishes with the enemy, and hairbreadth escapes. Occasionally they met with reverses and casualties. For the most part, however, they were successful, and took prisoners. Invariably they gathered useful information.

The scene of these activities was a broad expanse of wooded hills and rolling plains, at the northern extremity of the Galico valley, where that plain flanks Lake Doiran on the south-east and at the point where the Greek, Bulgar and Serbian frontiers met.

This 'no-man's-land' of the Gola Ridge, with its steep slopes, secret ravines, and pleasant plain stretching south from the lake, afforded a happy hunting-ground for the British, French and German cavalry patrols. From its northern edge, where the ground fell gradually till it reached the level of Lake Doiran only 2 miles away, it also afforded a wonderful view of the surrounding country.

Half-way down the slope, nestling in a clump of trees, which continued in a line of thick wood for 1.5 miles towards the lake, 6 miles in length and almost oval in shape, appeared the deserted hamlet of Pataros. The sole occupants of the place at the time were a couple of Greek policemen, on whom we perforce relied for information of enemy patrols in the district. Later we discovered that their loyalty was somewhat divided – one being pro-British and the other pro-German.

Approximately 2 miles to the right along the ridge, and a mile below the village of Gola, was another village, called Sirlova; while beyond it, towards the eastern end of the lake, and well in the centre of the plain, lay the small town of Brest. All three places were held by the Bulgars.

On our left in the distance could be seen the Kilindir River, with the railway running from Kilinder through the Galico valley to Salonika. Surmounting this was yet another cluster of hills, which dropped abruptly down to the shore of the lake, and commanded a full view of Doiran station, 3 miles from the town. These hills, as we were soon to discover, were likewise occupied by the enemy.

Still farther on our left, and covering the approach to Doiran from the south, were the group of high mountains which, later on in the war, became all too well known to us under the familiar names of Petit Couronne, Grand Couronne, and the Pips. They are really spurs of the central mountain mass of the Beles or Belashitza range, which under different names extends from the western extremity of the lake, along the edge of the Butkova and Struma valleys to the sea.

Through the whole length of this solid mountain wall, which forms a natural barrier between Bulgaria and Macedonia, there is only one pass – at Demirrhissar, and this was securely guarded on the Greek side by the strong modern fortress of Rupel. Shortly after our arrival at Gola, however, the Greeks, at the instigation of King Constantine, treacherously surrendered the fortress to the Bulgars, giving them direct access to the Struma valley, and seriously endangering our positions.

On April 26th, a reconnaissance – for the purpose of discovering the position of enemy guns suspected to be in the hills above Doiran station – was carried out by two squadrons of the South Notts Hussars and a squadron of the Derbyshire Yeomanry.

I was with the South Notts at the time, near Irikli, and took the opportunity to accompany them. Our contingent, including 'B' and 'C' Squadrons and head-quarters, started off soon after breakfast, and reached the assembly point on the

Ridge, 8 miles away, early in the forenoon. On arriving we dismounted, picketed our horses amongst the trees beneath the brow of the hill out of sight, while we ourselves lay on the top to observe. After an hour of silent watching, signs of activity began, and parties commenced to mount and move off in different directions. I attached myself to a patrol led by Lieutenant Repton, which made straight for Pataros and the wood.

The Greek Police signal, a white flag, indicated that the wood was clear of the enemy. Nevertheless, we proceeded cautiously. Beyond the wood was a swollen stream, with a stone bridge in bad repair. While crossing this, we had to avoid several shell-holes.

On the other side of the bridge we were joined by Lieutenant Lawrence's troop, and with them formed up into three sections in extended line, keeping this formation, the whole line galloped straight for Doiran station, 2 miles over the plain. I rode with the centre section.

On reaching the station, we came under a fairly sharp fire from a nest of machine guns half-way up one of the hills. Pi-e-e-e-ing! Pi-e-e-e-ing! sang the bullets, some passing overhead, some dropping short, and some piercing the woodwork and corrugated iron of the railway station. It was like being exposed to the commencement of a heavy hailstorm. We immediately took cover. Lieutenant Repton, desirous of reconnoitring farther, rode off along the railway line in the direction of the firing. After he had gone a couple of hundred yards, I mounted and followed him.

Before long he was galloping back in hot haste. 'What's the matter?' I shouted. There was no answer. So I also turned and galloped back as fast as I could on his heels. The fact was we had come under fresh rifle fire at close range, and the sand was flying up in little spurts a few feet behind us.

On our return to the station we were surprised to find Major Fairburn's 'B' Squadron there. The presence of this squadron – which we had expected to remain in support, and only to advance in case of necessity – caused us some embarrassment. The large number of troops in the little station was likely to attract shell fire from Doiran, in addition to the machine gun and rifle fire to which we were already exposed.

Accordingly, orders were given to retire independently, and concentrate at a given point between the bridge and the wood. It was a fine sight, and would have made a splendid picture for the 'movies' to see Yeomanry with their heads and bodies leaning over their horses' necks flying across the plain. I was reminded of the scene once or twice later on in France, when, in the course of infantry engagement, cavalry patrols appeared suddenly in close proximity and were compelled to retire rapidly.

At the stream a choice had to be made between the passage of the bridge or the water. Remembering the holes in the bridge, and following the example of majority, I plunged straight into the water and got safely across. With the single exception of a trooper, who was swept away with his horse by the current, we all crossed safely. This accident, and the loss of one of the Derbyshire Yeomanry horses, shot by the enemy, were the only casualties that day.

Adventures of this sort were common enough at the time, and associated in my mind with one of them was the loss of my pack-horse.

I was returning alone, mounted for a change on 'Red Ginger', from another reconnaissance, marked by the capture of an Austrian Uhlan, complete with helmet and lance, when my horse got entangled with a telephone wire and bolted down a ravine. Slithering on a rock, he fell on his side, and pinned me beneath him. Then he got up and galloped off again, dragging me several yards. When I found him, he was badly gashed, and his head and forelegs were bleeding.

Remounting, I managed to get home, and after a twenty-four hour 'slack' I was fit again; but not so 'Red Ginger', who had to be destroyed a few weeks later. I never succeeded in wangling another pack-horse, though I made more than one endeavour to do so at Remounts. My case now rested on the possession of a 'pack-saddle', as before it had rested on the possession of a 'pack-horse'. But where had I obtained the 'pack-saddle'? If I had got it from the Army, it must be due to a mistake and should be returned forthwith to Ordnance. If it was private property, it was no concern of the Army and gave me no claim to the pack-horse. To solve the problem, and avoid complications, I sold the wretched saddle to a Greek for 5 drachmae.

The loss of my private transport happened to synchronise with the termination of the three months of movement, which, as I have already said, marked the third stage of the war.

CHAPTER FIFTEEN

IN RETREAT

By Herbert Read

We received the warning order just before dinner, and for a while talked excitedly round the mess fire, some scoffing at the idea of an imminent battle, others gravely saying that this time, at any rate, the warning was justified. Two deserters, with tales of massing guns and the night-movement of innumerable troops, had reached our lines the previous day. Of course, deserters usually had some such tale designed to tempt a captor's leniency, but this time it was likely to be the truth. What else could the enemy's long silence mean? To that question we had no answer. We went early to bed, expecting an early awakening. The harnessed horses stood in lowered shafts.

There was scarcely a wall standing in Fluquières: everywhere demolition and bombardment had reduced the village to irregular cairns of brick and plaster. Winding among these cairns were the cleared roadways. Men and horses rested in patched sheds and an occasional cellar. S. and I were in a small repaired stable, each with a bed-frame in a manger. I had livened the cleanly white-washed walls of the place with illustrations from a coloured magazine. That evening all save our trench-kit had been sent to the transport-wagons, and we were lying on the bare netting with only our trench coats thrown over us.

For some time I was too excited to sleep, and none too warm. But weariness did at length triumph, and when, a short while afterwards, I was roughly awakened, I had become unconscious enough to forget the continuity of things.

II

Yes, suddenly I was awake. A match was being applied to the candle stuck in the bed-frame above my head. With his excited face illumined in the near candle-light, an orderly bent over me and shook my shoulders. I heard confused shoutings, and the rumble of gunfire. I had hardly need to read the message-form held out to me: 'Man Battle Stations' – the code words I knew only too well, and all that they implied. I was shivering violently with the cold, but in the shaking candle-light I scribbled messages repeating the code to the company commanders, the transport officers, and to others. S. was moving on the other side of the wall that divided the mangers.

'We're in for it, my lad,' he yelled, above the increasing din. Just then there was the sudden shrieking rush of a descending shell and its riotous detonation very near. Our candles jumped out, and we were in darkness, with bricks and earth falling like a hail on the roof. My servant came in, and hastily helped me to gather my equipment together.

I fixed my revolver and ammunition securely, and set out to the orderly room, some 500 yards away. It was now about 5.00am and still dark. I picked my way along a path which led across the great heaps of rubble. Shells were falling in the village. I still shivered with cold. My electric torch was nearly exhausted, so that I kept falling as I went. When I reached the orderly room, which was in a restored cottage, I found everything in a great hubbub, orderlies coming and going, the sergeant-major shouting orders. Inside, the doctor was bandaging a wounded man.

I then joined the colonel, and with one or two orderlies and the sergeant-major we followed the companies along the back lane that led from Fluquières to Roupy, a distance of about 1.5 miles. The morning was cold and a heavy dew lay on the ground. As we walked the light of dawn began to reveal a thick wet mist.

III

At 6.50am I sent a message to the brigade, informing them that the battalion was in position. We had been shelled all along the way, and when we neared Roupy, the cross-roads seemed to be under a continuous barrage. Nevertheless, we got into position with very few casualties. Safe in the bowels of the headquarter dugout, we thought the worst was over, and began casually to eat the tongue-sandwiches and drink the tea provided by the mess-corporal.

The dugout was new and spacious, and odorous of the fresh chalky earth. It was about 30 feet deep, and partitioned into three sections, of which the middle one was occupied by the headquarter officers. Because it was new it was unfurnished, and we had to squat on the bare floor, grouped round a few candles.

For me that cavern is a telephonic nightmare. The instrument, a 'D III converted', was placed on the floor in a corner of the dugout. Two signallers sat with their legs straddling round it. At first the companies, then the neighbouring battalions, and, finally, the brigade, kept me there crouching on the floor, yelling till I was hoarse into the execrable instrument. When I was not speaking, the signallers were receiving or sending Morse messages.

Above the ground, the situation was disquieting. The thick mist of the early dawn persisted: a man 10 yards away could not be distinguished. The gunfire, tremendous in its intensity, continued hour after hour to pound into the invisible foreground. The earth vibrated almost hysterically. An occasional shell crashed near us, but after the first three hours (at 7.30am) the enemy's fire seemed to be concentrated on our front-line defences. No messages, telephonic or written, came to relieve our anxiety.

The gradual accumulation of our anxiety should be realised. Every minute seemed to add to its intensity. By 10.00am or so, our hearts were like taut drumskins beaten reverberantly by every little incident.

Then the skin smashed. Bodily action flickered like flame. The sense of duration was consumed away.

Shortly after 11.00am, a gun team galloped madly down the main road. Then two stragglers belonging to the Machine-Gun Corps were brought to headquarters. They informed us that the front line had been penetrated. Later, an officer from the front line battalion, with five or six men, came to us out of the mist. Most of the party were wounded, and as the officer's leg was being bandaged in the dugout, he told us his tale. He was haggard and incoherent, but the sequence was awfully clear to us. The enemy had attacked in great strength at 7.30am. They had apparently reached the observation line unobserved, and overpowered the few men there before a warning could be given or an escape made. Advancing under cover of a creeping barrage, they had approached the main line of defence. No fire met them there, or only fire directed vaguely into the fog. The fight at the main line had been short and bloody. Our men, dazed and quivering after three hours' hellish bombardment (I could see them cowering on the cold mist-wet earth), had been brave to the limits of heroism; but pitifully powerless. The ghastly job had been completed by 8.30am. About 9.00 fresh enemy battalions passed through their fellows and advanced towards the front-line redoubt (L'Epine de Dallon). Our artillery fire must have been useless by then, still falling on the old enemy front line. At any rate, the enemy quickly surrounded the redoubt, and then penetrated it. This officer himself had been captured, and later had made his escape in the mist. He thought it possible that the headquarters of his battalion were still holding out.

We were still questioning our informant when an excited voice yelled down the dugout shaft: 'Boches on the top of the dugout.' Our hearts thumped. There was no reason why the enemy shouldn't be on us. They might have been anywhere in that damned mist. We drew our revolvers and rushed to the shaft. We did not mean to be caught like rats in a hole.

I remember my emotion distinctly: a quiet despair. I knew I went up those stairs either to be shot or bayoneted as I emerged, or, perhaps, to be made prisoner and so plunge into a strange unknown existence.

Half-way up the stairs, and a voice cried down: 'It's all right, they're our fellows.' Some artillerymen in overcoats, straggling across the open, had looked sinister in the mist.

We turned to the dugout, the released tension leaving us exhausted.

Patrols from our front companies had been feeling outward all morning, at first without result. At 12.30 B. (commanding the left front company) reported:

> Machine gun and rifle-fire on left and right can be heard. Shelling very hard. Can see nothing. Patrols are being sent out.

At 1.00pm he reported:

> Boche are in quarry just in front of me. We are firing Lewis guns and rifles at him. He seems to be firing from our right flank too, with machine guns.

These and other messages all came by runner. The telephonic communications to the companies had broken down before noon, though I think we remained in touch with the brigade until late in the afternoon.

About midday the mist began to clear a little. At 1.00pm the enemy, having massed in the valley 500 yards immediately in front of us, attacked in mass strength. The fusillade that met them must have been terrific. They came on in good order, extending and manoeuvring with precision. At 1.20pm B. reported:

> No. 5 Platoon report enemy on wire in front. Artillery assistance is asked for. We are firing rifle grenades into them.

And again at 1.30pm:

> Boche attacking in strength with sections in front. Front troops are in valley in front. They are also heading to my left flank.

Between 1.30 and 1.40 the attack reached its greatest intensity. By 1.45 it had withered completely before the hail of our fire.

At 1.45pm B. reported:

> Boche running back like hell near Savy. They seem to be running from artillery as much as anything.

(Savy was 1.5 miles to our left front: it was on the slope that rose away from the valley in front of us where the enemy had massed his forces before his attack.)

For a moment we became elated. There was cause enough. The mist had lifted, and a pale sun shone. We had defeated a strong attack. We received a message from the Inniskillings on our right to say they still held their positions intact. And wider afield the coordination of the enemy's advance seemed to have broken down.

We made haste to distribute our reserve ammunition, to clear the dressing-station, and generally to make ourselves ready for the next happenings.

In reply to my inquiries B. sent this message, timed 2.15pm:

> It is very difficult to tell numbers of enemy. I can see the ground north to Savy, and saw them scattered. The line advancing had about 300 men to every 100 yards. We do not require SAA yet. Can you instruct Rose (code name for a company) to fire up Soup Valley, please? We will want Verey lights for the night. Will a supply be forthcoming? Can see no movement now. Boche is putting up white lights all along valley.

IV

The lull was not of long duration. Either we had been deceived by the movements near Savy, or the enemy had made a miraculously swift recovery. At 2.45pm I received another message from B.:

> Enemy movement at F.12 at 4.0, They appear to be carrying in wounded. Enemy also advancing across valley on left on F.5, in small parties. Estimated total strength seen, fifty men. Boche aeroplanes are flying about 300 feet above our lines, and have been for a short while past. There is still some machine gun fire in front. Is 'A' redoubt holding out?'

The aeroplanes were evidently making a preliminary reconnaissance, and I guessed the movement to be significant of a new attack.

On the mists clearing, the aeroplanes were able to sight position, and soon the artillery on both sides became active. Our own artillery, alas, fired short, smashing our already weakened defences. The Germans brought up their light field guns with great skill and rapidity. Several batteries were observed coming over the ridge at L'Epine de Dallon – only a few hours ago the headquarters of the battalion we were supporting. We now realised our position in earnest, and I sent a detailed account of the situation to the brigade.

Towards 4.00, the enemy shelling increased in intensity. The second attack was now imminent. B. sent the following message, timed 4.30pm:

> Boche is attacking on right about 400 strong, and is massing in the valley right in front of Roupy. We want some more SAA. During the Boche retreat the riflemen and Lewis guns did good work, killing many. Shelling very heavy.

The heavy shelling continued, and under cover of its intensity the enemy again massed in the valley in front of us. The men held on grimly. Thus B., timed 5.10pm:

> Line holding still with some casualties. Reports not in. Line heavily shelled. SAA received correct. Situation still the same. Touch is being kept with battalion on our right, and patrols go constantly. Our chloride of lime is missing and cannot be found. Machine guns very active.

And again at 5.40pm:

> The Boche is 50 yards or less from our line, and is also passing down the valley for another attack.

Then suddenly those massed men leapt from cover, and came on in their grey, regular formations. At headquarters we were only aware of the angry surge of rifle and machine gun fire, deadening even the detonations of shells. All this time I was spending tiring, exasperating hours at the telephone, striving to get in communication with brigade and artillery headquarters. Again and again the wire was broken, and again and again the linesmen went out into the mist to mend it. Then it got disconnected irreparably. We were isolated in that chaos. About 6.30pm B. sent the following momentous message:

> Boche got inside our wire on right and left. No. 5 Platoon are all either wiped out or prisoners. No. 7 Platoon took up position on left of keep, but Boche were in it when I left. They also were in trench on right of road left by C. Company, and we killed several on road near camouflage. I am now in redoubt with twenty-five men.

The climax had come. We had still one card to play – the counter-attack company. On receipt of B.'s message, the colonel decided to order C. to attack in accordance with the preconceived plan.

We only heard of this counter-attack from the mouths of a few survivors. It was one of the most heroic episodes in the retreat. The company gathered together in the shell-battered trench that they had occupied all day, and then took the open. No artillery covered their advance. It was hopeless, insane, suicidal. They had perhaps 150 yards to cover. They advanced at a jog-trot, lumbering on the uneven ground. One by one they fell before the fusillade that met them. C. had reached the enemy with about a dozen men. These leapt in among the Boches, and a hand-to-hand struggle ensued for a few minutes. C. was last seen cursing, pinned to the trench wall by a little mob of Germans, in one hand his empty smoking revolver.

V

It was now dusk, and with dusk came peace and silence. And at dusk this was our position: The front rim of the redoubt was in the enemy's possession. The counter-attack company had disappeared. The company keeps still held out with a few men in each. The inner ring of the redoubt was held by one company, and the remnants of three. B. had survived with one of his officers. But several officers in the three front companies had been either killed, wounded, or captured. There were probably 200 men still surviving in the battalion.

In the darkness the colonel and I walked up to the line. As we went along the road, the stillness was abruptly broken by the sounds of three or four shots, screams and curses. We flung ourselves on the roadside, our revolvers ready. We shouted, 'Who goes there?' English voices answered, and the sergeant-major went to investigate. Two German privates had walked into a sentry on the road, coming from behind us. No one could understand what they said, and they were sent back to brigade headquarters. And I don't remember that any one of us was perturbed by the incident, eerie though it was.

Just after 1.00 in the day we received long-awaited instructions from the brigade. The battalion in reserve was to deliver a counter-attack. The line of deployment was given, and the direction of attack. The battalion was to leave its position at 12.45, and the guns were to start a creeping barrage at 1.33am.

The whole thing was a ghastly failure. The night was black, and the battalion attacking was unfamiliar with the ground it had to cover. We waited hours for a sign of their approach. About 2.00am a stray officer came to us, having lost his company. Eventually, about 4.00am, one company did appear. It went forward in the darkness, but got dispersed and uncontrollable in the effort to deploy into attack formation. Dawn found us as dusk had found us, with the sole difference that some 200 men of the counter-attack battalion had found refuge in our redoubt, and in the keeps in front.

I think by then we were past hope or despair. We regarded all events with an indifference of weariness, knowing that with the dawn would come another attack. We distributed ammunition, reorganised our Lewis guns, and waited dully, without apprehension.

Again the morning was thickly misty. Our own artillery fire was desultory and useless. Under cover of the mist, the enemy massed in battle formation, and the third attack commenced about 7.00am. We only heard a babel in the mist. Now our artillery was firing short among our men in the redoubt. About 10.00am the enemy penetrated our left flank, presumably in the gap between us and the battalion on our left, which was still in position. Machine gun fire began to harass us from that direction, somewhere in the ruins of the village. We never heard from the battalion on our right, and a runner I sent there did not return. I think they must have withdrawn about 10.00am.

This new attack petered out. I fancy it was only half-hearted on the part of the enemy – probably only a demonstration to see if we intended to make a determined resistance, or to fight only a rearguard action. Finding the resistance determined enough, they evidently retired to prepare the real thing.

This fourth attack was delivered about midday. The mist still persisted thinly. One could perhaps see objects 50 yards away. I don't know what resistance the platoon-keeps offered. They were in a hopeless position, and would easily have been swamped in a massed attack.

Shortly after midday, the enemy came in direct contact with the inner ring of the redoubt.

We fired like maniacs. Every round of ammunition had been distributed. The Lewis guns jammed; rifle bolts grew stiff and unworkable with the expansion of heat.

In the lull before noon, the colonel and I had left the dug-out, in which we were beginning to feel like rats in a trap, and had found an old gun-pit about 250 yards farther back, and here we established our headquarters. An extraordinary thing happened. The gun-pit was dug out of the bank on the roadside. About 2.00pm one of our guns, evidently assuming that Roupy had been evacuated, began to pound the road between Roupy and Fluquiéres. One of these shells landed clean on the road edge of our pit. We were all hurled to the ground by the explosion, but, on recovering ourselves, found only one casualty: the colonel had received a nasty gash in the forearm. We then went 200 to 300 yards across the open, away from the road, and found a smaller overgrown pit. The colonel refused to regard his wound as serious; but he soon began to feel dizzy, and was compelled to go back to the dressing-station. I was then left in charge of the battalion.

It was now about 2.30pm. The attack still persisted in a guerrilla fashion. But the enemy was massing troops in the trenches already taken. At 4.00pm the intensity of the attack deepened suddenly. A new intention had come into the enemy's mind: he was directing his attack on the flanks of our position in an effort to close round us like pincers. On the left he made use of cover offered by the ruined village, and eventually brought machine guns to bear against us from our left rear. On the right he made use of the trenches evacuated by the Inniskillings.

In the height of this attack, while my heart was heavy with anxiety, I received a message from the brigade. Surely reinforcements were coming to our aid! Or was I at length given permission to withdraw? Neither: it was a rhetorical appeal to hold on to the last man. I rather bitterly resolved to obey the command.

Another hour passed. The enemy pressed on relentlessly with a determined, insidious energy, reckless of cost. Our position was now appallingly precarious. I therefore resolved to act independently, and do as perhaps I should have done hours earlier. I ordered B. to organise a withdrawal. This message despatched, I lay on my belly in the grass and watched through my field-glasses every minute trickling of the enemy's progress. Gradually they made their way round the rim of the redoubt, bombing along the traverses. And now we only held it as lips might touch the rim of a saucer. I could see the heads of my men, very dense and in a little space. And on either side, incredibly active, gathered the grey helmets of the Germans. It was like a long bowstring along the horizon, and our diminished forces the arrow to be shot into a void. A great many hostile machine guns had now been brought up, and the plain was sprayed with hissing bullets. They impinged and spluttered about the little pit in which I crouched.

I waited anxiously for B. to take the open. I saw men crawl out of the trenches, and lie flat on the parados, still firing at the enemy. Then, after a little while, the arrow was launched. I saw a piteous band of men rise from the ground, and run rapidly towards me. A great shout went up from the Germans: a cry of mingled triumph and horror. 'Halt Eenglisch!' they cried, and for a moment were too amazed to fire, as though aghast at the folly of men who could plunge into such a storm of death. But the first silent gasp of horror expended, then broke the crackling storm. I don't remember in the whole war an intenser taste of hell. My men came along, spreading rapidly to a line of some 200 yards length, but hunched here and there. On the left, by the main road, the enemy rushed out to cut them off. Bayonets clashed there. Along the line men were falling swiftly as the bullets hit them. Each second they fell, now one crumpling up, now two or three at once. I saw men stop to pick up their wounded mates, and as they carried them along, themselves get hit and fall with their inert burdens. Now they were near me, so I rushed out of my pit and ran with them to the line of trenches some 300 yards behind.

It seemed to take a long time to race across those few hundred yards. My heart beat nervously, and I felt infinitely weary. The bullets hissed about me, and I thought: then this is the moment of death. But I had no emotions. I remembered having read how in battle men are hit, and never feel the hurt till later, and I wondered if I had yet been hit. Then I reached the line. I stood petrified, enormously aghast. The trench had not been dug, and no reinforcements occupied it. It was as we had passed it on the morning of the 21st, the sods dug off the surface, leaving an immaculately patterned 'mock' trench. Approximately 100 yards on the right a machine gun corps had taken up a position, and was already covering our retreat. I looked about me wildly, running along the line and signalling to the men to drop as they reached the slender parapet of sods. But the whole basis of my previous tactics had been destroyed. I should never have ordered my men to cross that plain of death, but for the expectation that we were falling back to reinforce a new line. We found an empty mockery, and I was in despair. But I must steady the line. On the actual plain the men obeyed my signals, and crouched in the shallow trench. But even as they crouched, the bullets struck them. On the road, the straight white road leading to the western safety, there was something like a stampede. S. and the sergeant-major went and held it with pointed revolvers. But it was all useless – hopeless. On the right, I saw the enemy creeping round. They would soon enfilade us, and then our shallow defence would be a death-trap. I accordingly gave the signal to withdraw, bidding the two Lewis guns to cover us as long as possible. Once more we rose and scattered in retreat. It would be about 700 yards to the next trenches – the village line round Fluquières – and this we covered fairly well, sections occasionally halting to give covering fire. The enemy had not yet ventured from the redoubt, and our distance apart was now great enough to make his fire of little effect. And I think as we moved up the slope towards the village we must have been in 'dead' ground, so far as the enemy advancing on the right was concerned.

We reached Fluquières, which lay on the top of the slope, and found there some deep trenches on each side of the road at the entrance of the village. Farther to the left, I found certain London troops commanded by a major. One of my Lewis guns still remained intact, and this I placed to fire down the straight road to Roupy. The enemy had now left the redoubt and were advancing in line formation.

We were at Fluquières about an hour. The enemy evidently did not intend to rest content with his capture of the redoubt. It was just beginning to get dusk. Earlier we had noticed sporadic contact lights go up. But now they shot into the sky from all along the plain. Low-flying aeroplanes hovered over the advancing line, and their wireless messages soon put the German guns on to us. Big black high-explosive shells began to fall on our position, making our tired flesh shudder. I now began to be amazed at the advancing contact lights. They did not merely stretch in a line in front of us, they encircled us like a horseshoe, the points of which seemed (and actually were) miles behind us. On the right the enemy was enfilading us with machine gun fire.

I searched for the major commanding the troops on my left, but could not find him. By this time I was determined to act, and therefore gave the order to withdraw. The men filed through the village, gathering fresh ammunition from a dump at the cross-roads. From the village the road went up a slope leading to Aubigny. The enemy's fire soon followed us, and we proceeded along the ditches on each side of the road.

Three-quarters of the way up the slope I observed a trench running at right angles to the road on each side of it. I ordered the London men to go to the left, my own to the right, there to reorganise into companies. The twilight was now fairly deep, and I thought that with evening the enemy's advance would stay. The major I had seen in Fluquières now appeared again, and cursed me for giving the order to retire. I was too tired to argue, and even then a gust of machine gun fire swept above our heads. They were going to attack again. We could hear them moving in the semi-darkness. Something else we could hear too – the throb of a motor-cycle behind us. It was a despatch rider, and when he drew level to us, he stopped his machine and came towards me with a message. I opened it. It ordered all troops east of the Aubigny defences to retire through Ham.

I was glad. I believe I thought then that it was the end of our share in the battle. I went to the men, and assembled them in companies, and in close artillery formation we retired across country due west. We came to the Aubigny defences, manned by fresh troops, about a mile farther on, and then we gathered on the road again and marched wearily along. I remember coming to a water-tank, where we all drank our fill – our mouths were swollen with thirst. When we reached Ham, an officer met us and ordered us to proceed to Muille Villette, about 2 miles farther on, and there billet for the night. Ham, as we walked through its cobbled streets, seemed very hollow and deserted. The last time we had seen it, it had been a busy market-town, full of civilians. Now only a few sinister looters went about the empty houses with candles. We saw one fellow come out of a door with a lady's reticule and other things over his arm. We should have been justified in shooting him, but we were far too tired. We just noticed him stupidly.

The road seemed long, and our pace was slow, but at last we reached the village of Muille Villette. We found it full of artillerymen, and a few infantry. Every available shelter seemed to be occupied, but at length we got the men into a school. Our transport had been warned of our station for the night and turned up with bully-beef and biscuits. These we served out.

I had four officers left with me. We could not find a billet for ourselves, but finally begged for shelter in a barn occupied by artillerymen. They looked on us unsympathetically, not knowing our experiences. On a stove one of them was cooking a stew of potatoes and meat, and its savour made us lusting beasts. But the artillerymen ate the slop unconcernedly, while we lay down too utterly weary to sleep, languidly chewing bully-beef.

VI

It was after midnight when we came to Muille Villette; I suppose about 2.00am we fell into an uneasy sleep. At 4.00am we were awakened by the stirrings and shoutings of the artillerymen. I drew my long boots on my aching feet, and went out into the cold darkness. I found an officer of some kind. The enemy were reported to have attacked and penetrated the Aubigny defences, and to be now advancing on Ham. All the troops stationed in Muille Villette had received orders to withdraw.

We assembled the men, stupid with sleep. I knew that brigade headquarters were stationed at Golancourt, 1.5 miles along the road. I resolved to proceed there and ask for orders. We marched away while the dawn was breaking.

I found the brigade established in a deserted house. T., the brigade-major, was seated on a bed lacing his boots. No orders for the brigade had yet been received, so T. advised me to find billets for the men, where they could rest and get food. The companies then sought billets independently, and, what was more blessed than anything, we managed to get them hot tea. I went and had breakfast with the brigade staff. The tea revived me, and I remember how voracious I felt, and that I tried to hide this fact. The brigadier came into the room and seemed very pleased to see me: apparently he was very satisfied with our conduct, and especially with the frequent reports I had sent back. Till then I had only felt weariness and bafflement – even shame. But now I began to see that we were implicated in something immense – something beyond personal feelings and efforts.

The brigadier told me as much as he knew of the general situation. It was not much. The communications had apparently broken down. But it was enough to make me realise that more than a local attack was in progress: the whole of the Fifth Army was involved: but there were no limits to what *might* be happening.

I also learnt that Dury – where the divisional headquarters had been stationed – a village some 5 or 6 miles south-*west* of Roupy, had been captured about 2.00 on the afternoon of the 22nd, several hours before we had evacuated the redoubt. Only a miracle of chance had saved us from being cut off.

The brigade seemed to have difficulty in getting into touch with the division, or, at any rate, in obtaining orders from them. But at 10.00am I was told to march to Freniches and await orders there. We assembled in the village street and marched on again. The road was busy with retreating artillery and a few infantrymen. From behind us came the sounds of firing: the enemy were attacking Ham. We trudged on, passing villages whose inhabitants were only just taking steps to flee. They piled beds, chairs, and innumerable bolsters on little carts, some hand-pulled, some yoked to bony horses. They tied cows behind. There were old men, many old women, a few young women, but no young men. They and their like proceeded with us along the western road.

We had gone perhaps 5 miles when an orderly on horse-back overtook us with orders. We were to report to the –th Division at Freniches.

This we eventually did, and a fat staff colonel studied a map, and then told me to take my battalion to Esmery-Hallon, a village 4 miles due north, and there take up a defensive position. This was more than I expected. I explained that my men had been fighting continuously for forty-eight hours, and were beaten and spiritless. But I received no comfort: the situation demanded that every available man should be used to the bitter end. I hardly dared to face my men: but I think they were too tired to mind where they went. We turned off at a right angle, and slowly marched on. The road led through a beautiful patch of country, steeped in a calm, liquid sunshine. We tilted our bodies forward, and forced our weary muscles to act.

About 2 miles south of Esmery-Hallon, an officer (a lieutenant) appeared on a motor-cycle. He was in command of a scrap lot – transport men, cobblers, returned leave men, etc. He seemed to have the impression that the enemy were upon us, and wanted me to deploy and take up a position facing east. I explained that we were much too tired to do any such thing. He expostulated. Did I realise this, that, and the other? I explained that I had cause to realise such things better than he did. He raved. I told him finally that I didn't care a damn, but that I had orders to defend Esmery-Hallon, and thither I must go. He went off in a rage, seeming incredibly silly and fussy to us all.

Esmery-Hallon is a small village perched on a detached conical hill, overlooking the plain on all sides. The defence was simply arranged. Two companies of engineers were entrenched in front of the village. I sent a lookout on to the top of the church tower, and extended my men astraddle the hill on each side of the village, north and south. The men on the south found a ditch, which made an admirable trench. The men on the north extended over the ploughed land, and dug shallow pits for shelter. We had no machine guns or Lewis guns, but every man had a rifle and a decent amount of ammunition. I established my headquarters on the north side by a quarry, where I had a wide view of the plain.

The day was very still, and the distant rattle of machine gun fire carried to us. A few enemy shells fell ineffectively about the landscape. I got into touch with a major of the Inniskillings in command of 150 men on my right, and we co-ordinated defences on that wing. My left wing was in the air, so to speak – not a soul visible for miles.

When our dispositions were finally made, I returned to the quarry edge. My servant T. had already been away to search the village, and now came laden with samples of red wine and cider which he had found in a cellar. So I sent him back to the village with other men, telling them to search for food also. They soon returned with bottles of red wine and a large tin of army biscuits. Evidently there was any amount of wine, but I was afraid to distribute it among the men for fear lest on fasting stomachs it should make them drunk. So S. and I each took a wine-glass, and starting at different points, we began to go a round of the men. Each man lay curled up in his shallow pit, resting. To each we gave a glass of wine and a few biscuits. They took it thankfully. There was a lull in the distant fighting: I don't remember any noise of fire during that hour. The sun was warm and seemed to cast a golden peace on the scene. A feeling of unity with the men about me suddenly suffused my mind.

VII

It was nearly 2.00pm when we got settled. About this time I interrupted a message which gave me the useful information that the enemy had been seen in Ham at 10.00am. I guessed that the silence meant they were now consolidating along the Somme Canal. Later in the afternoon a cavalry patrol trotted up to our position. Officer, men, and horses all looked very debonair and well fed. The officer was very condescending towards me, but made a message of the information I gave him, thought it would not be worthwhile venturing further on to the plain, so rode away back, harness jingling, the sun shining on well-polished accoutrements.

About 5.00pm, I judged that we were to be left alone for the night, and made my plans accordingly. I sent the following message to B., who was in charge of the men on the right of the village:

> We hold on to our present positions unless otherwise ordered. When it is getting dark close your men in a little to form about 7 or 8 pickets. From these pickets send stand-patrols out about 150 yards, or to any good observation point within warning distance. Any show of resistance should drive off any enemy patrols. But as far as I can make out the Boche is still east of the canal. Should you be attacked by overwhelming numbers, withdraw fighting in a due westerly direction under your own arrangements. I should do the same in case of need. I suggest you come up to have a look at our position before dark.

But just after dark, I received orders to relieve the Royal Engineers in front of the village. I regretted this order, but had to obey it. We now found ourselves in freshly dug trenches on the flat of the plain, our view to the left and right obstructed by woods.

Included in the orders mentioned was a message to the effect that advance parties of the French would probably arrive that night, and the positions would be shown to them. This message filled us with wild hope; we became almost jaunty.

But the night was very cold, and heavily wet with dew. We improved the trenches, and stamped about, flapping our arms in an effort to keep warm. I sat with L., bravest and brightest of my runners, on a waterproof sheet beneath a tree in the centre of our position. We waited for the dawn: it was weird, phantasmagorical. Again the fateful mist. As it cleared a little, the woods near us hung faintly in the whiteness. At 8.00am we began to observe troops retreating in front of us. They came in little groups down the road, or straggled singly over the landscape. The mist gradually lifted. We heard machine gun fire fairly near, somewhere on the right. The stragglers informed us that the enemy had crossed the canal in the early dawn, and was advancing in considerable force. We waited patiently. At 9.00am the enemy came into touch with our fellows on the left, and here we rebutted him successfully. At 9.30 the troops on our right were reported to be withdrawing. About 10.00am, there happened one of those sudden episodes, which would be almost comic with their ludicrous *bouleversement* were they not so tragic in their results. Seemingly straight from the misty sky itself, but in reality from our own guns, descended round after round of shrapnel bursting terrifically just above our heads, and spraying leaden showers upon us. Simultaneously, from the woods on our right, there burst a fierce volley of machine gun fire, hissing and spluttering among us. We just turned and fled into the shelter of the village buildings. I shouted to my men to make for the position by the quarry. We scuttled through gardens and over walls. By the time we reached the quarry we had recovered our nerve. We extended and faced the enemy, who were advancing skilfully over the plain on our left. We on our part were a scrap lot composed of various units. We hastily reorganised into sections. Retreat was inevitable. Then followed a magnificent effort of discipline. A major took charge of the situation, and we began to retire with covering fire, section by section, in perfect alternation.

We were now on a wide expanse of plain, sloping gently westward. We stretched over this – a thin line of men, perhaps 1,000 yards long. We were approaching the Nesle-Noyon Canal. When within a few hundred yards of the canal, we closed inwards to cross a bridge (Ramecourt). At the other end of the bridge stood a staff officer, separating the men like sheep as they crossed, first a few to the left, then a few to the right. Here I got separated from the majority of my men, finding myself with only fifteen. We were told to proceed along the bank of the canal until we found an unoccupied space, and there dig in.

As we crossed the bridge, we saw for the first time the sky-blue helmets of French troops peeping above a parapet. I think our eyes glistened with expectation of relief.

We went perhaps half a mile along the bank of the canal, and there I halted my attenuated company. The sun was now blazing hotly above our heads. We dropped to the ground, utterly exhausted. Presently some of the men began spontaneously to dig. R., the only officer left with me, also took a pick and joined the men. I began to feel ashamed just then, for I would willingly have died. I took a spade (there was a dump of such things just by us) and began to shovel the earth loosened by R. I seemed to be lifting utterly impossible burdens. My flesh seemed to move uneasily through iron bands; my leaden lids drooped smartingly upon my eyes.

We dug about 3 feet deep, and then ceased, incapable of more. At the foot of the bank there was a small pool of water. The enemy was not now in sight, so we plunged our hot faces and hands into its weedy freshness, and took off our boots and socks, and bathed our aching feet.

In the evening, about 5.00pm, a few skirmishing patrols appeared on the horizon. But our artillery was now active and fairly accurate, and machine guns swept the plain. The patrols retired, without having advanced any distance. A large German aeroplane, with a red belly, floated persistently above our line. We fired hundreds of shots at it, but without effect. T., my servant, nearly blew my head off in his efforts.

We had gathered a lot of sun-scorched hemlock and bedded the bottom of our trenches; and when night came on we posted sentries, and huddled down to the bedding. The night was clear, and I gazed unblinkingly at the fierce stars above me, my aching flesh forbidding sleep. Later, I must have dozed in a wakeful stupor.

VIII

The next daybreak, that of the 25th, was less misty. Bread and bully-beef had come up during the night, and we fed to get warmth into our bodies. But the sun was soon up, and we began to feel almost cheerful once again. There was no immediate sign of the enemy, and I walked along to the bridge we had crossed the previous day to glean some information of our intentions; but the only plan seemed to be the obvious one of holding on to our positions. I noticed some engineers were there ready to blow up the bridge if need be.

About 8.00am we saw little groups of enemy cavalry appear on the horizon. Through my glasses I could see them consulting maps, pointing, trotting fussily about. Our artillery was planting some kind of scattered barrage on the plain, and an occasional near shot made the horsemen scamper. We watched them rather amusedly till 10.00am and then we saw signs of infantrymen. They came from the direction of Esmery-Hallon, and at first seemed in fairly dense formation. But they extended as they cut the skyline, and we soon perceived them advancing in open order. As they got nearer, they began to organise short rushes, a section at a time.

We were now well stocked with ammunition – there were piles of it laid about – and as soon as the advancing troops were within anything like range, we began to 'pot' them. In fact, the whole thing became like a rifle-gallery entertainment at a fair. But still they came on. Now we could see them quite plainly – could see their legs working like dancing bears, and their great square packs bobbing up and down as they ran. Occasionally one dropped.

Immediately in front of our trench, about 800 yards away, there was a little copse of perhaps fifty trees. This they reached about 11.00am and halted there. If only our flanks held out, I guessed they would never get farther, for between the copse and our rifles and Lewis guns there was not a shred of cover; and we were well entrenched, with a wide canal in front of us.

Of course, the artillery was busy all the while: not methodically, but thickly enough to give the day the appearance of a conventional battle. But then the unexpected (really we had no cause longer to regard it as unexpected), the fatal thing happened. A battery of ours shortened its range, and got our position exactly 'taped'. The shells fell thick and fast, right into our backs. We were, remember, dug in on the top of a bank, perhaps 15 feet high. All along this bank the shells plunged. Immediately on our right, not 50 yards away, a shell landed cleanly into a trench, and when the smoke cleared there remained nothing, absolutely nothing distinguishable, where a moment ago had been five or six men. We grovelled like frightened, cowed animals. Still the shells fell: and there was no means of stopping them. I glanced distractedly round; men on the right were running under cover of the bank away to the right. Other men on the left were retreating to the left. I resolved to get out of it. Immediately behind us, 50 yards away, was a large crescent-shaped mound, very steep, like a railway embankment, and perhaps 60 feet high. It occurred to me that from there we should command, and command as effectively as ever, the plain in front of us. I made my intentions known, and at a given signal we leapt down the bank, and across the intervening 50 yards. We were evidently in sight, for a hail of machine gun bullets made dusty splutters all round us as we ran. But we reached the mound without a casualty, and climbed safely on to it. There I found a few men already in occupation, commanded by a colonel, under whose orders I then placed myself.

The enemy's artillery fire now increased in volume. I saw a cow hit in a field behind us, and fall funnily with four rigid legs poking up at the sky.

At 3.30 we saw the French retiring on the right, about 1,000 yards away. They were not running, but did not seem to be performing any methodic withdrawal. We then fell into one of those awful states of doubt and indecision. What was happening? What should we do? There was angry, ominous rifle-fire on our immediate left. About 4.00pm there was a burst of machine gun fire on our immediate right. I noticed that the stray bullets were coming over our heads. This meant that the enemy were advancing from the right.

I then saw English troops withdrawing about 600 yards away on the right – evidently the troops that had been defending the bridge. I did not hear any explosion, and so far as I know the bridge remained intact.

At 4.15pm I saw the colonel with his men suddenly leave his position on my immediate left. Although I was within sight – within calling distance – he did not give me an order. I was now alone on the mound with my fifteen men.

I did not wait long. I resolved to act on my own initiative once more. We had now moved off the maps I possessed and might as well be in an unknown wilderness. I resolved to proceed due west, taking the sun as a guide. We moved down the back slope of the mound. At the foot we found a stream or off-flow from the canal, about 10 feet wide and apparently very deep. As we hesitated, looking for a convenient crossing, a machine gun a few hundred yards away opened fire on us. There were a good few trees about which must have obstructed the firer's view: the cut twigs, newly budded, fell into the water. We hesitated no longer: we plunged into the stream. The men had to toss their rifles across, many of which landed short and were lost. The sight of these frightened men plunging into the water effected one of those curious stirrings of the memory that call up some vivid scene of childhood: I saw distinctly the water-rats plunging at dusk into the mill-dam at Thornton-le-Dale, where I had lived as a boy of ten. The water sucked at my clothes as I met it, and filled my field-boots. They seemed weighted with lead now as I walked, and oozed for hours afterwards.

We came out facing a wide plain, climbing gently westward. Machine gun and rifle-fire still played about us. We could see a church steeple on the horizon due west, and I told the men to scatter and make for that steeple. Shrapnel was bursting in the sky, too high to be effective. We ran a little way, but soon got too tired. A., a faithful orderly, had stayed with me, and soon we walked over the fields as friends might walk in England. We came across French machine gunners, who looked at us curiously, asked for news of the situation, but did not seem very perturbed.

We eventually came to the village on the horizon (probably Solente). An officer of the engineers stood by the side of his horse at the cross-roads, smoking a cigarette. He asked me why I was retreating. The question seemed silly. 'We shall have to fight every inch of the way back again,' he said. 'These Frenchmen will never hold them.' I went on, too tired to answer.

Here I saw for the first time a new post stuck on the roadside. It had on it an arrow and 'Stragglers' Post' in bold letters. So I was a straggler. I felt very bitter and full of despair.

I followed the road indicated by the arrow. It was dotted with small parties of men, all dejected and weary. We trudged along till we came to the village of Carrepuits. Military police met us at the entrance, and told us to report to the Traffic Control in a house a few hundred yards away. It was now getting dusk. I went into the cottage indicated, and here found an officer, very harassed and bored. Men were collected, and separated into the divisions they belonged to, and then given orders to report to such and such a place. I found a party of about fifty men of my division, and was instructed to take them and report to a divisional headquarters situated in a certain street in Roye.

I've forgotten that walk: it was only about 2 miles, but our utter dejection induced a kind of unconsciousness in us. It would be between 10.00 and 11.00 when we got to Roye. I reported to a staff officer, who sent me off to the town major to get billets. The town major I found distracted, unable to say where I should find a billet. Apparently the town was packed with stragglers. We peered into two great gloomy marquees, floored densely with recumbent men. Meanwhile two other officers joined me with their men, and together we went off to search on our own. We found a magnificent house, quite empty, and here we lodged the men. Some kind of rations had been found. They soon had blazing wood fires going, and seemed happy in a way.

The town major had indicated a hut, where we officers might get rest, and perhaps some food. We went round, tired and aching though we were; we lifted the latch and found ourselves in a glowing room. A stove roared in one corner – and my teeth were chattering with cold, my clothes still being sodden – and a lamp hung from the roof. A large pan of coffee simmered on the stove, and the table was laden with bread, tinned foods, butter; food, food, food. I hadn't had a bite since early morning, and then not much.

I forget, if I ever knew, who or what the two occupants were, but they were not stragglers. Roye had been their station for some time. One of them was fat, very fat, with a tight, glossy skin. I don't remember the other. We explained that we would like a billet for the night – anything would do so long as it was warmth. They were sorry: they had no room. Could they spare us some rations? They were sorry: this was all they had got till tomorrow noon. We stood very dejected, sick at our reception. 'Come away!' I said. 'Before I go away,' cried one of my companions, 'I would just like to tell these blighters what I think of them.' He cursed them, and then we walked away, back to the men's billet. I looked in at my fellows; most of them were naked, drying their clothes at the fire. Some slept on the floor.

We went upstairs into an empty room. Two of us agreed to make a fire, while the other, the one who had given vent to his feelings, volunteered to go off in search of food. We split up wood we found in the house, and lit a fire. I took off my clothes to dry them, and sat on a bench in my shirt. If I had been asked then what I most desired, besides sleep I think I would have said: French bread, butter, honey, and hot milky coffee.

The forager soon turned up. God only knows where he got that food from: we did not ask him. But it was French bread, butter, honey, and hot milky coffee in a champagne bottle! We cried out with wonder: we almost wept. We shared the precious stuff out, eating and drinking with inexpressible zest.

As we supped we related our experiences. I forget their names; I don't think I ever knew them. Were they of the Border Regiment? I'm not sure; but they were Northerners. They had been trapped in a sunken road, with a Boche machine gun at either end, and Boche calling on them to surrender. I don't think either of them was more than 20 years old: they were fresh and boyish, and had been faced with this dilemma. They put it to the vote: there, with death literally staring them in the face, they solemnly called on the men to show hands as to whether they would surrender, or make a run for it. They had voted unanimously for the run. Half of them perished in the attempt. But here, a few hours afterwards, were the survivors, chatting over a blazing wood fire, passing a bottle of coffee round, very unperturbed, not in any way self-conscious. We stacked the fire high and stretched ourselves on the floor in front of it, and slept for a few hours.

IX

We were up at 6.00 the next morning, the 26th of March, and reporting to the Assistant Provost-Marshal, who was reorganising stragglers. We congregated in the Town Square, and I was amazed at the numbers there. The streets were thickly congested with infantrymen from several divisions, with French armoured cars, cavalry, and staff officers. We fell in by divisions, and presently marched off, a column a mile or two in length. Cavalry protected our flanks and rear from surprise.

At Villers-les-Roye I found B., the man who had been separated from me at Ramecourt Bridge. We were glad to be united again, and from there proceeded together. B. had had orders to go to a place called La Neuville, where the first-line transport awaited us. We were now passing through the battlefields of 1916, and everywhere was desolate and ruined. We marched on as far as Hangest-en-Santerre, where we met our battalion cookers loaded with a welcome meal. Just as we had devoured this, and were starting on our way again, we were met by a staff colonel, who, after inquiring who we were, ordered us to turn back and proceed to Folies, where our brigade was reorganising.

We could but mutely obey, but with dull despair and an aching bitterness. We had never thought since leaving Roye but that we were finally out of the melée. To turn back meant, we knew, that we might still be very much in it. We crossed country to Folies, about 2 miles away, in a blazing sun. There we found the details of the brigade, consisting mostly of returned leave men, already holding a line of trenches. We were told to reinforce them.

Here the second-in-command rejoined the battalion and assumed command. My endurance was broken, and I was ordered down to the transport lines. I pointed out that the men were as weary as I, and should on no account be ordered into action again. It was useless: no man could be spared. But there was not much more for them to bear. Good hot food came up to them again at dusk. The night was warm and restful.

On the morning of the 27th, the enemy had possession of Bouchoir, a village about a mile to the south-east. He began to advance during the morning, and a skirmishing fight went on during that day and the next; and during this time the battalion was withdrawn from the line without suffering any serious casualties.

X

But I had gone back with the transport officer on the 26th. I mounted the transport-sergeant's horse, and in a dazed sort of way galloped westward in the dusk. I arrived half-dead at La Neuville, and slept there for twelve hours or more. The next day we went to Braches, and thence on foot to Rouvrel. About here the country was yet unscathed by war, and very beautiful. On a bank by the roadside I took *Walden* out of my pocket, where it had been forgotten since the morning of the 21st, and there began to read it. At Rouvrel the rest of the battalion rejoined us the next day. On the 29th I set off on horseback with the transport to trek down the valley of the Somme.

When evening came and the hills of Moreuil were faint in the twilight, we were still travelling along the western road. No guns nor any clamour of war could be heard: a great silence filled the cup of misty hills. My weary horse drooped her head as she ambled along, and I, too, was sorrowful. To our north-east lay the squat towers of Amiens, a city in whose defence we had endured hardships until flesh had been defeated, and the brave heart broken. My mind held a vague wonder for her fate – a wonder devoid of hope. I could not believe in the avail of any effort. Then I listened to the rumbling cart, and the quiet voices of the men about me. The first stars were out when we reached Guignemicourt, and there we billeted for the night. In this manner we marched by easy stages down the valley of the Somme, halting finally at Salenelle, a village near Valery, and there we rested four days.

CHAPTER SIXTEEN

A BATTLE OF MONSTERS

By F. Mitchell

At the beginning of April, 1918, many of the tank units, which had been in practically continuous action since 21st March, were withdrawn and sent to the Tank Depot at Erin to refit. Here, after a brief spell of rest, they took over old tanks, overhauled and patched up for the occasion, and returned with them once more to the line, which had formed again as the German advance was checked.

'A' Company of the 1st Tank Battalion was hidden in the Bois l'Abbé, near Villers-Bretonneux. In this sector the Germans had advanced to within 7 miles of Amiens, and threatened the capture of that city. If they succeeded, they would cut the Amiens-Paris railway, which was even then being used solely at night, and the solitary railroad left for the British Army would be through Abbéville, only 10 miles from the coast.

To prevent this formidable disaster the French had placed their crack Moroccan division, the finest fighters in the French Army, at the danger spot.

In the Bois de Blangy, not far from the Bois l'Abbé, the Algerian and Moroccan troops had dug for themselves very deep and very narrow shelters. These were covered with branches of fir trees placed flat on the ground, so that it was exceedingly difficult to discover their presence, either from the air or from the ground level.

The first tanks entering the wood in the dark ran straight into the undergrowth, and were considerably alarmed to hear weird yells and shrieks coming from the ground. Terrified black faces popped up on all sides, and the wood suddenly swarmed with strange figures, who had bolted out of their holes like startled rabbits.

Next day, when the machines had been covered with tarpaulins, camouflage nets, and branches, the Moroccans were still not too trustful, and would creep up and gingerly touch the tanks with their fingers – as if to make sure that they were real – and then slink away again.

In the same wood were also detachments of the renowned Foreign Legion, including a company of Russians; and Australian troops, in their picturesque slouch hats, added to the variety of the scene; whilst away in front, for almost a quarter of a mile, stretched an unbroken line of French 75s (the famous quick-firing field gun) mingled with batteries of British 18-pounders.

On the 17th April the enemy shelled Bois l'Abbé with mustard gas, causing heavy casualties in the forward sections of tanks, whose crews returned with eyes swollen and weeping, and faces and bare knees heavily blistered.

As the German attack was daily expected, a new section of tanks, consisting of a male and two females, was sent to the Bois d'Aquenne, immediately behind Viller-Bretonneux. The wood was drenched with gas, and had been evacuated by the infantry. Dead horses, swollen to enormous size, and birds with bulging eyes and stiffened claws lay everywhere. In the tree-tops the half-stifled crows were hoarsely croaking. The gas hung about the bushes and undergrowth, and clung to the tarpaulins.

On the night of the 23rd April the shelling had made the spot almost unbearable. The crews had worn their masks during the greater part of the day, and their eyes were sore, their throats dry.

Then two enemy lanes appeared, flying slowly over the tree tops, and dropped Verey lights that fell right in the glade where the tanks were hidden. As the lights slowly flared up we flattened ourselves rigidly against the tree-trunks, not a man daring to move; but it was in vain, for the bulky outlines of the tanks showed up in vivid relief.

We were discovered!

An hour later, when clouds hid the moon, three huge toad-like forms, grunting and snorting, crept out of the wood, to a spot some 100 yards in the rear.

Just before dawn on 24th April, a tremendous deluge of shells swept down upon the wood, and I was aroused in the dark by someone shaking me violently.

'Gas, sir! Gas!'

I struggled up, half awake, inhaled a foul odour, and quickly slipped on my mask. My eyes were running, I could not see, my breath came with difficulty. I could hear the trees crashing to the ground near me. For a moment I was stricken with panic, and confused thoughts chased wildly through my mind; but, pulling myself together, I discovered to my great relief that I had omitted to attach my nose-clip!

My section commander and I and the orderly who had aroused us groped our way, hand in hand, to the open. It was pitch dark, save where, away on the edge of the wood, the rising sun showed blood red, and as we stumbled forward tree trunks, unseen in that infernal gloom, separated our joined hands, and bushes and brambles tripped us.

Suddenly a hoarse cry came from the orderly: 'My mouthpiece is broken, sir!'

'Run like mad for the open!' shouted the section commander.

There was a gasp, and then we heard the man crashing away through the undergrowth like a hunted beast.

Soon I found my tank, covered with its tarpaulin. The small oblong doors were open, but the interior was empty. In the wrappings of the tarpaulins, however, I felt something warm and fleshy, and found that it was one of the crew lying full length on the ground, wearing his mask but dazed by gas. The rest of my crew I discovered in a reserve line of trenches on the edge of the wood, and the crews of the other two tanks, as we found later on, were sheltering inside their machines, with doors and flaps shut tight.

Behind the trenches a battery of artillery was blazing away, the gunners in their gas masks feverishly loading and unloading like creatures of a nightmare.

The major in charge of the battery informed us that he had had no news from his FOO (Forward Observing Officer) for some time, the telephone wires having been blown up. If the Boche infantry came on, would our tanks immediately attack them, whilst his 18-pounders engaged them over open sights? Our captain agreed to this desperate measure, and grimly we waited.

Meanwhile, as the shelling grew in intensity, a few wounded men and some stragglers came into sight. Their report was depressing: Villers-Bretonneux had been captured, and with it many of our own men. The Boche had almost broken through.

By this time two of my crew had developed nasty gas symptoms, spitting, coughing, and getting purple in the face. They were led away to the rear, one sprawling limply in a wheelbarrow found in the wood. A little later an infantry brigadier appeared on the scene with two orderlies. He also was unaware of the exact position ahead, and, accompanied by Captain J.C. Brown, MC, and the runners, he went forward to investigate. In ten minutes one of the runners came back, limping badly, hit in the leg. In another ten minutes the second returned, his left arm torn by shrapnel. Twenty minutes after that, walking unhurt and serene through the barrage, came the brigadier and our captain.

The news was grave. We had suffered heavy losses and lost ground, and if our infantry were driven out of the switch-line between Cachy and Villers-Bretonneux, the Germans would obtain possession of the high ground dominating Amiens. They would then perhaps force us to evacuate that city and drive a wedge between the French and British armies.

A serious consultation was held, and the order came: 'Proceed to the Cachy switch-line and hold it at all costs.'

We put on our masks once more and plunged, like divers, into the gas-laden wood. As we struggled to crank up, one of the three men collapsed. We put him against a tree, gave him some tablets of ammonia to sniff, and then, as he did not seem to be coming round, we left him, for time was pressing. Out of a crew of seven there remained only four men, with red-rimmed, bulging eyes, while my driver, the second reserve driver, had had only a fortnight's driving experience. Fortunately one gearsman was loaned to me from another tank.

The three tanks, one male, armed with two 6-pounder guns and machine guns, and two females, armed with machine guns only, crawled out of the wood and set off over the open ground towards Cachy, Captain Brown coming in my tank.

Ahead loomed the German barrage, a menacing wall of fire in our path. There was no break in it anywhere. Should I go straight ahead and trust to luck? It seemed impossible that we could pass through that deadly area unhit. I decided to attempt a zig-zag course, as somehow it seemed safer.

Luck was with us. At top speed we went safely through the danger zone, and soon reached the Cachy lines; but there was no sign of our infantry.

Suddenly, out of the ground 10 yards away, an infantryman rose, waving his rifle furiously. We stopped. He ran forward and shouted through the flap: 'Look out! Jerry tanks about!' Swiftly he disappeared into the trench again, and Captain Brown immediately got out and ran across the heavily shelled ground to warn the female tanks.

I informed the crew, and a great thrill ran through us all. Opening a loophole, I looked out. There, some 300 yards away, a round, squat-looking monster was advancing; behind it came waves of infantry, and farther away to the left and right crawled two more of these armed tortoises.

So we had met our rivals at last! For the first time in history tank was encountering tank!

The 6-pounder gunners, crouching on the floor, their backs against the engine cover, loaded their guns expectantly.

We still kept on a zig-zag course, threading the gaps between the lines of hastily dug trenches, and coming near the small protecting belt of wire we turned left, and the right gunner, peering through his narrow slit, made a sighting shot. The shell burst some distance beyond the leading enemy tank. No reply came. A second shot boomed out, landing just to the right, but again there was no reply. More shots followed.

Suddenly a hurricane of hail pattered against our steel wall, filling the interior with myriads of sparks and flying splinters! Something rattled against the steel helmet of the driver sitting next to me, and my face was stung with minute fragments of steel. The crew flung themselves flat on the floor. The driver ducked his head and drove straight on.

Above the roar of our engine sounded the staccato rat-tat-tat-tat of machine guns, and another furious jet of bullets sprayed our steel side, the splinters clanging against the engine cover. The Jerry tank had treated us to a broadside of armour-piercing bullets!

Taking advantage of a dip in the ground, we got beyond range, and then turning we manoeuvred to get the left gunner on to the moving target. Owing to our gas casualties the gunner was working single-handed, and his right eye being swollen with gas, he aimed with the left. Moreover, as the ground was heavily scarred with shell holes, we kept going up and down like a ship in a heavy sea, which made accurate shooting difficult. His first shot fell some 15 yards in front, the next went beyond, and then I saw the shells bursting all around the tank. He fired shot after shot in rapid succession every time it came into view.

Nearing the village of Cachy, I noticed to my astonishment that the two females were slowly limping away to the rear. Almost immediately on their arrival they had both been hit by shells which tore great holes in their sides, leaving them defenceless against machine gun bullets, and as their Lewis guns were useless against the heavy armour-plate of the enemy they could do nothing but withdraw.

Now the battle was to us, with our infantry in their trenches tensely watching the duel, like spectators in the pit of a theatre. For a moment they became uncomfortably more than spectators. As we turned and twisted to dodge the enemy's shells I looked down to find that we were going straight into a trench full of British soldiers, who were huddled together and yelling at the tops of their voices to attract our attention. A quick signal to the gearsman seated in the rear of the tank and we turned swiftly, avoiding catastrophe by a second.

Then came our first casualty. Another raking broadside from the German tank, and the rear Lewis gunner was wounded in both legs by an armour-piercing bullet which tore through our steel plate. We had no time to put on more than a temporary dressing, and he lay on the floor, bleeding and groaning, whilst the 6-pounder boomed over his head and the empty shell cases clattered all round him.

The roar of our engine, the nerve-racking rat-tat-tat of our machine guns blazing at the Boche infantry, and the thunderous boom of the 6-pounders, all bottled up in that narrow space, filled our ears with tumult, while the fumes of petrol and cordite half stifled us. We turned again and proceeded at a slower pace. The left gunner, registering carefully, began to hit the ground right in front of the Jerry tank. I took a risk and stopped the tank for a moment. The pause was justified; a well-aimed shot hit the enemy's conning tower, bringing him to a stand-still. Another roar and yet another white puff at the front of the tank denoted a second hit! Peering with swollen eyes through his narrow slit, the gunner shouted words of triumph that were drowned by the roar of the engine. Then once more he aimed with great deliberation and hit for the third time. Through a loophole I saw the tank heel over to one side; then a door opened, and out ran the crew. We had knocked the monster out.

Quickly I signed to the machine gunner, and he poured volley after volley into the retreating figures.

My nearest enemy being now out of action, I turned to look at the other two, who were coming forward slowly, while our 6-pounder gunners spread havoc in the ranks of the advancing German infantry with round after round of case-shot, which scattered like the charge of a shotgun.

Now, I thought, we shall not last very long. The two great tanks were creeping relentlessly forward; if they both concentrated their fire on us at once we would be finished. We fired rapidly at the nearest tank, and to my intense joy and amazement I saw it slowly back away. Its companion also did not appear to relish a fight, for it turned and followed its mate, and in a few minutes they had both disappeared, leaving our tank the sole possessor of the field.

This situation, however gratifying, soon displayed numerous disadvantages. We were now the only thing above ground, and naturally the German artillery made savage efforts to wipe us off the map. Up and down we went, followed by a trail of bursting shells. I was afraid that at any minute a shell would penetrate the roof and set the petrol alight, making the tank a roaring furnace before we could escape.

Then I saw an aeroplane flying overhead not more than 100 feet up. A great black cross was on each underwing, and as it crossed over us I could see clearly the figures of the pilot and observer. Something round and black dropped from it. For a fraction of a second I watched it, horrified; the front of the tank suddenly bounded up into the air, and the whole machine seemed to stand on end.

Everything shook, rattled, jarred with an earthquaking shock. We fell back with a mighty crash, and then continued on our journey unhurt. Our steel walls had held nobly, but how much more would they endure?

A few minutes later, as we were turning, the driver failed to notice that we were on the edge of a steep shell hole, and down we went with a crash, so suddenly that one of the gunners was thrown forward on top of me. In order to right the tank the driver jerked open the throttle to its fullest extent. We snorted up the opposite lip of the crater at full speed, but when just about to clamber over the edge the engine stopped. Our nose was pointing heavenwards, a lovely stationary target for the Boche artillery.

A deadly silence ensued ...

After the intolerable racket of the past few hours it seemed to us uncanny. Now we could hear the whining of shells, and the vicious crump as they exploded near at hand. Fear entered our hearts; we were inclined at such a steep angle that we found it impossible to crank up the engine again. Every second we expected to get a shell through the top. Almost lying on their sides, the crew strained and heaved at the starting handle, but to no effect.

Our nerves were on edge; there was but one thing left, to put the tank in reverse gear, release the rear brake, and run backwards down the shell hole under our own weight. Back we slid, and happily the engine began to splutter, then, carefully nursing the throttle, the driver changed gear and we climbed out unhurt.

What sweet music was the roar of the engine in our ears now!

But the day was not yet over. As I peeped through my flap I noticed that the German infantry were forming up some distance away, preparing for an attack. Then my heart bounded with joy, for away on the right I saw seven small whippets, the newest and fastest type of tank, unleashed at last and racing into action. They came on at 6 to 8 miles an hour, heading straight for the Germans, who scattered in all directions, fleeing terror-stricken from this whirlwind of death. The whippets plunged into the midst of them, ran over them, spitting fire into their retreating ranks.

Their work was soon over. Twenty-one men in seven small tanks overran some 1,200 of the enemy and killed at least 400, nipping an attack in the bud. Three of the seven came back, their tracks dripping with blood; the other four were left burning out there in front, and their crews could not hope to be made prisoners after such slaughter. One broke down not far from Cachy, and I saw a man in overalls get out and, with a machine gun under his arm, run to another whippet, which stopped to pick him up.

We continued to cruise to and fro in front of the Cachy switch-line, and presently a fourth German tank appeared, about 800 yards away. The left gunner opened fire immediately, and a few minutes later the reply came swift and sharp, three shells hitting the ground alongside of us. Pursuing the same tactics as before, we increased our speed, and then turned, but the Jerry tank had disappeared; there was to be no second duel.

Later on, when turning again, we heard a tremendous crack, and the tank continued to go round in a circle. 'What the blazes are you doing?' I roared at the driver in exasperation. He looked at me in bewilderment and made another effort, but still we turned round and round. Peeping out, I saw one caterpillar track doubled high in the air. We had been hit by the Boche artillery at last, two of the track plates being blown clean away!

I decided to quit. The engine stopped. Defiantly we blazed away our last few rounds at the slopes near Villers-Bretonneux, and then crept gingerly out of the tank, the wounded man riding on the back of a comrade.

We were making for the nearest trench when – rat-tat-tat-tat – the air became alive with bullets. We flopped to the ground, waiting breathlessly whilst the bullets threw up the dirt a few feet away. When the shooting ceased we got up again and ran forward. By a miracle nothing touched us, and we reached the parapet of a trench. Our faces were black with grime and smoke, and our eyes bloodshot. The astonished infantrymen gazed at us open-mouthed, as if we were apparitions from a ghostly land. 'Get your bayonets out of the way,' we yelled, and tumbled down into the trench.

It was now almost one o'clock, and we had been in action since 8.30am, but, so intense had been the fighting, so fierce the unexpected duel, that it scarcely seemed half an hour since we had quitted the gas-laden wood.

We stayed in the narrow trench for a couple of hours, and as the enemy made no further attack, and the officer in charge of the infantry no longer required my services, I decided to return to Company Headquarters.

By this time I had procured a stretcher for the wounded man, and climbing over the parapet we made for home. To our great amazement machine guns immediately opened on us from the wood on our right, practically in the rear of the trench we were leaving. We fell to earth automatically. Breathless minutes passed. Then I gave the signal to go forward again, and in some mysterious manner we escaped untouched, even by the heavy shelling.

About 100 yards back we met a team of horses wildly dragging an 18-pounder across the open. The youthful officer on horseback addressed me excitedly.

'I say, old man, I've been sent forward to knock out a German tank. Is that the blighter over there?' He pointed in the direction of my derelict.

'No,' I replied, 'you are a bit late; the German tank is already knocked out, and ...'

'What,' he interrupted me, 'already knocked out? Good enough!' and without another word he turned, gave a sharp command, and rode swiftly back, the gun team galloping furiously after him.

I felt immensely relieved to think that he had not been sent up earlier in the day, or my tank might have been heavily shelled from the rear! As it was, we all reached Company Headquarters in safety, and handed over the wounded gunner to a field dressing-station.

For his part in the tank duel, my sergeant, a courageous and cool-headed Scot name McKenzie, was awarded a well-earned Military Medal. The official report contains the following interesting details:

'Although his eyes were affected by the enemy gas, and his face badly cut by armour-piercing bullets, in spite of his suffering this non-commissioned officer continued to serve his quick-firing gun for four hours, while his own tank, No. 4066, was engaged with large enemy tanks, one of which was eventually put out of action. Throughout, this NCO, by his conduct and coolness, set a splendid example to all the men in his crew.'

A Military Cross was awarded to me.

CHAPTER SEVENTEEN

THE ADVANCE – 1918

By Mark Severn

On the morning of the 4th of April a white-faced Shadbolt walked slowly up the hill from Bertrancourt into the village of Beaussart. His recollections of the last ten days were hazy. He dimly remembered lying on a stretcher in the top bunk of a hospital train, the groans of a badly wounded man below him, the swinging and the jolting of the train, the stuffy atmosphere, the smell of blood. When he came to again it was dark; he was lying on a station platform; men were rushing to and fro, lights kept flashing, the smoke of the snorting engines eddied under the vast glass roof. He shivered in the cold night air. At the end of an eternity of time he was lifted into an ambulance. He awoke to clean sheets and sunshine. A voice said: 'He's all right, nurse, only a bang on the head, concussion.' For a week he struggled to leave the hospital. What was happening to his beloved battery? Where were they? He must get back to them. Pictures of a dead Cherub, of shattered gun-pits, of Hugh, Tipple, Queenie and the remainder of his men marching back as prisoners, kept flashing through his mind. At the Base no one knew anything. The wildest rumours were current. Papers from England two days old, and six days behind with their news, brought the only reliable intelligence. At last the obstinate doctor let Shadbolt go. 'Of course, I know you're quite mad, and, in any case, the RTO won't allow anyone on the train but staff and drafts from England, but you can try.' He went down to the station. A friendly military policeman informed him that the only train left for Amiens at 2.00pm. No one was allowed to travel but Staff officers. He turned into a hotel for lunch. The Base Commandant and a number of his staff were at the next table. At five minutes to two he crept out into the passage. Hanging on the wall, amongst others, were five hats with red bands. One fitted. Hiding his own hat under his trench coat he ran down to the station. The train was just moving out. He waved a piece of official-looking paper at the astonished RTO and jumped on board. 'Your kit is in the last carriage at the back, sir,' said a grinning MP at the window – 20 francs changed hands.

It was pitch dark when they got to Amiens. The enemy were shelling the station, and the train stopped half a mile outside. Shadbolt humped his valise down the line. The town was silent and empty. At last he found a bed. The next morning he jumped a lorry which took him to Beauquesne. There was no news there of the Brigade, but an ASC officer told him that he was in the Corps Area, and offered to drive him to Doullens. In the evening he found Corps Heavies.

The Staff Captain told him the Brigade were in action near Bertrancourt, and that some supply lorries were leaving for that village at six the next morning.

He met Merredew where the railway lines run across the road on the western outskirts of Beaussart.

'Damn you, Hugh! Why do you put the guns bang in the open, near a railway station of all places?'

Hugh grinned. 'I thought the sleepers would come in handy for platforms; besides it's just as safe here as anywhere else.' A salvo of whizz-bangs emphasised his statement. Shadbolt ducked.

'Come on, Major. Let's go and have some breakfast.'

It was not until the evening that the full story of the retreat was told. Shadbolt's batman, who in private life was butler to a duke, was also in charge of the mess. Gunner Prout bore himself with dignity and distinction befitting a duke's personal retainer. His appearance was so episcopal and his whole personality so portentous and solemn that he was always known as *Mr* Prout in the battery. When Shadbolt offended the canons of good taste by wearing grey flannel trousers in the evenings, Mr Prout's rebuke was a marvel of tact and delicacy. On such occasions he always referred to his Grace, and intimated that his Grace did such and such, but never this or that. His Grace was a model of gentlemanly behaviour, a pattern which gunner officers might do well to follow, but could not hope to emulate.

'What a pity we haven't got any of that loot from the canteen left, I should like to drink the Major's health in something better than this washy beer,' said Tipple. 'Yes,' went on the Cherub, 'you missed something at Bapaume, Major. You ought to have seen Tipple scoffing down a bottle of Grand Marnier for breakfast!'

'Pardon me, sir,' interrupted Mr Prout, 'but, anticipating the speedy return of the Commanding Officer, I took the liberty of concealing a case of the Lanson '06, and two bottles of the best brandy.'

Shadbolt found himself 1.5 miles from his old battery position of July, 1916. The zone of fire was almost the same. Again the Germans held Serre, again he walked up to the same OPs and looked out on the same trenches and strong points. How many lives had been lost during the last two years? How much blood poured out in vain?

Whilst the bulk of the heavy artillery was engaged in the serious fighting which now took place in Flanders, Colonel Carp's Brigade remained in this sector until the battles of August and September finally broke down the enemy's resistance, and all the British Armies moved forward in their last great advance. The batteries had the good fortune to be almost continuously in support of the New Zealanders, than whom there were no finer troops in the whole of the Third Army. These big, cheerful men used to wander into the mess at Beaussart for a friendly talk over a drink, and the gunner officers returned their visits to the company messes in the line.

One evening, one of their officers announced that he had located an enemy trench mortar which could be observed from a short sap leading out into No Man's Land. Shadbolt promised to come and shoot it up the next morning. He arrived at company headquarters at 7.00am, and set off with the New Zealander to find the sap. At last the latter announced: 'This is about the spot but it has been shelled a bit since I was last here, and we shall have to crawl on our stomachs about 20 yards, to get into the sap.' They crawled. Eventually they slid down into a little trench. 'Here is the sap,' said the infantry officer, 'at least I think it is. I will just make sure.' He put his head cautiously over the top. Not 10 yards away were three Germans cooking breakfast. They had crawled almost into an enemy listening-post.

A night or two later Queenie was working out tables for a concentration in the OP dug-out when a large Belgian hare lopped down the steps, sat up on her hind legs, took one look at him, and ran back into the trench. Soon afterwards a terrified linesman almost fell into the dug-out. 'What's the matter, Randall?' said Queenie. 'Oh, sir!' the man exclaimed, 'I have just been chased down the trench by the biggest rat I've ever seen in my life!'

Aeroplane shoots on hostile batteries took place daily. Much wire-cutting and destruction of machine gun nests were also carried out for the infantry. On one occasion the Brigadier of a neighbouring Infantry Brigade sent an infuriated memo to the Colonel complaining of the short shooting of his howitzers. General Currie-Savage had the reputation of being able to consume four subalterns before breakfast and to partake of that meal afterwards with digestion un-impaired. It was with no little trepidation therefore that the Cherub, who had been at the OP on the day in question, set forth to make what explanation he could. Arriving at the Great Man's dug-out he walked trembling down the steps. The General, clad only in a shirt, was sitting on the edge of his bed, shaving. He produced a fuse, which he declared had arrived from a westerly direction. The Cherub pointed out the German marking on its nose and base. The General was not accustomed to being contradicted, but it is impossible for the fiercest subaltern-eater to roar properly without his trousers. They subsequently had breakfast together and the Cherub, wearing the complacent smile of a lion-tamer, devoured eggs and bacon before the astonished staff.

A month later a battery of 18-pounders came into action near 2XX and the officers of the two units decided to mess together in the large farmhouse which Shadbolt had commandeered at the end of the village. For many weeks these two units were almost the only inhabitants, as Beaussart had attained an unenviable reputation in the neighbourhood. True, the village was shelled daily and nightly by the enemy, but always at regular hours and in definite areas. The deep-mined dug-outs constructed on the battery, and the cellars under the men's billets prevented the heavy casualties that might otherwise have occurred. Shadbolt used to wake to the sound of flocks of scurrying shells whistling over the roof of his dug-out. Through the little window at the back, the whole village seemed to be going up in reddish-grey smoke. Another summer's day had begun in 'bright, breezy, bracing, bloody Beaussart?' Five minutes later all was quiet again. Mr Prout would announce that the Major's bath was ready, and he would step into the tin-bath on the lawn behind the house and revel in nakedness and sunshine, and the early morning song of the birds. At midday everyone would go to ground again for ten minutes, and again about ten o'clock at night. It was not always easy to remember the evening curfew as the mess had now got possession of a piano in addition to the gramophone. The field battery would be asking the heavies in a rousing chorus whether they knew: 'The Muffin Man who lives in Armentières,' when the first crash outside would send the whole laughing crowd tumbling into the signallers' cellar down below.

The Colonel also did his best to add to the gaiety of nations by displaying a latent genius in the invention of code names. Everything had its code name, batteries, OPs, targets, ammunition dumps; even all the correspondence was thus labelled. Instead of referring to his memo No. H/Q24672 of the 16th inst. he would simply write: 're Clara.' All lists of SOS targets, hostile batteries, night firing programmes, and aeroplanes shoots were labelled with the names of well-known actresses or film-stars. A telegram from Brigade which read: 'Are you engaging Gladys Cooper?' meant: 'Are you firing Night-Firing Programme Number So-and-So?' Amendments were suitably and ingeniously named. An elderly Battery Commander, rather deficient in humour, was wakened out of his first sleep one night and the following cryptic message thrust into his hand: 'Have you got Twins?' This was an amendment to 'Violet Loraine', a night programme, which included certain well-known road junctions and communication trenches.

It was during this period, between April and August, 1918, that the German big gun known as 'Big Bertha' bombarded Paris. The gun was in action near St Quentin, and so great was the range, approximately 80 miles, that the enemy Battery Commander had to allow for the rotation of the earth when making out his calculations before shooting. The actual size of the shell was not very large, probably about the same as the 5.9 inch, and the material damage effected was negligible. The object aimed at was to lower the morale of the citizens of Paris, and, through them, that of the whole French people. With a similar end in view, the Germans had constructed a further 400 of these guns, their intention being to line the coast near Calais should they be successful in their offensive in Flanders, and shell London.

The incalculable value of morale, both of armies and of peoples, was fully appreciated at this stage by all the belligerents. The spirit of man, under the conditions that exist in war, is affected unfavourably by a number of factors, among which may be mentioned fear, need of food, lack of sleep, weight of responsibility and the continuous endurance of shell-fire. At the other end of the scale, discipline, patriotism and a confidence and belief in inevitable justice assisted the individual to rise superior to the infectious elements of depression and defeat. The heavy losses suffered during the retreat, the perpetual fighting against overwhelming odds, and the endless marching before a pursuing enemy, had for the time being seriously affected the morale of the British Army. But they were not a beaten army. It was astonishing to see how quickly the flagging infantry recovered after a few hours of rest and sleep. The indomitable spirit of these gallant men was never more clearly shown than in the dark days of March and early April.

Meanwhile, as the summer wore on, the failure of the enemy arracks in Flanders, in Champagne, near Montdidier and at Rheims, and their consequent enormous losses in manpower, was beginning to have an effect not only on their Generals and soldiers, but on the long-deceived German people. The balance of moral ascendancy commenced slowly to swing from east to west. Moreover the German Great General Staff, in addition to serious errors of strategy, had made the fatal mistake of underrating the recuperative powers of their opponents. On August 8th, the British Fourth Army, on a front of about 14 miles between Albert and Billers Bretonneux, launched an attack which achieved a complete and startling success. Three divisions of cavalry and 450 tanks went through the enemy lines, the French armies on the British right joined in, and the Germans were swept completely off their feet. It is doubtful whether any offensive during the war came as so great a surprise to the enemy, who never really recovered from the overwhelming nature of the disaster. A fortnight later the Third Army widened the front of attack to the north, captured Bapaume, and added enormously to the difficulties and embarrassments of the enemy. On August 26th the battle was again extended to the north. The pressure brought to bear by the First Army on the Sensèe and the Scarpe concluded in the successful storming of the Drocourt-Quéant line, and the enemy fell back, still stubbornly fighting, to his main line of resistance, the strongly fortified zone of defences known as the Hindenburg Line. The culminating point of this great counter-offensive was now reached, and at the end of September four simultaneous and convergent attacks were delivered by the Allies. In Flanders, the Passchendaele Ridge, the scene of such bitter fighting the year before, was crossed in one day by the Belgians and the Second British Army. In the Argonne, the French and American forces pressed the Germans steadily back in the direction of Mezières, and on the 29th of the month the First, Third and Fourth British Armies attacked and captured the last enemy stronghold, the supposedly impregnable Hindenburg Line. The enemy had now no alternative but to withdraw his forces along the whole front, and to make such use of semi-prepared and natural positions as would enable him to carry out his retirement in good order. The obstacles of the Selle and Sambre rivers proved insufficient however to check the advance of our armies. Flushed with victory, and eager to transform the retirement of their enemies into a rout, our troops moved triumphantly onwards. The unexpected rapidity of their advance caused the enemy to fall back in widespread disorder and confusion, and the destruction of the whole German Army was only averted by the signing of the Armistice on November 11th. Thus ended the Battles of the Hundred Days.

In all these battles and advances the heavy and siege artillery took a prominent and important part. On September 28th the greatest amount of ammunition ever fired in one day throughout the war was expended. The actual figure inclusive of expenditure from field guns, was 944,000 rounds. Even the 9.2s were firing at express speed – three rounds per gun every two minutes – till their barrels were red hot and the strain on the equipment caused Battery Commanders to moderate their rates. After the breach of the Hindenburg Line, owing to the limitations of the roads and the difficulties of ammunition supply, all of these great pieces could not immediately be moved forward. Their crews were therefore set to work to salve the captured German guns that lay scattered over the blasted battlefields, whilst volunteer arties, under enthusiastic officers, pushed forward with the infantry, with the object of locating any German batteries that might be over-run in the course of the attack, and using them against the enemy. On October 23rd near Pommereuil, a village about 2 miles east of Le Cateau, one of these parties discovered a battery of enemy field guns still warm from firing at our troops. The guns were turned round, some necessary repairs were swiftly effected by the 9.2-inch artificer, and in a very short time the 200 rounds of his own metal were being fired into the retreating enemy.

Meanwhile the 60-pounders and the 6-inch howitzers were pushed forward into the very forefront of the battle. On several occasions 2XX was in action less than 1,000 yards from the front line. Casualties were sometimes heavy, the strain of continuous movement without rest from firing and fighting was tremendous, but, buoyed up with the hope of victory, the men worked joyfully on. After much digging of gun-pits and laying of platforms, after heaving heavy shells all night, after a long day's firing, after suffering from bursts of enemy shell-fire, they would read the laconic statement in the night's orders: 'The battery will move at dawn.' Grumbling cheerfully, the tired men heave and strain on the ropes. The guns are brought back to the road, the platforms dug up, the shells are reloaded on to the lorries, and everything made ready for another long march into the enemy's country.

On one such night Shadbolt was returning from the front where he had been observing the fire of the battery during the day's battle. Three signallers trailed wearily behind him. That day they had seen the barrage crash down on the enemy defences, and lift and move forward like a pillar of cloud before the waves of our advancing infantry. They had seen the tanks, like the chariots of old, rolling relentlessly onward, their steel sides spitting out fire and death. They had seen the cavalry, troops, squadrons and regiments; field guns, rattling up at the trot, their limbers swaying and bumping over the rough ground; more infantry following, marching, marching, battalion after battalion; batteries of 60-pounders, the heavy Clydesdales plodding patiently forward, the drivers nodding in their saddles, the big guns rumbling behind. Shadbolt was very tired. As he walked slowly and heavily over the shell-shattered fields he noted, half-unconsciously, an overturned limber with its team of dead horses, the twisted coils of rusty wire, a stranded tank, the grotesque attitudes of the dead as they lay in the moonlight. Suddenly he seemed to see an even mightier army than they had seen that day. Infantry, cavalry, and artillery, the armies of 1915, of the Somme, the armies of Arras, of Messines and the Salient, they moved towards him with shining faces, and the roar of their coming was like the sound of the sea when the tide is on the turn. These were the men who had died that victory might in the end be ours. The Army of the Dead marched forward with the Living in the last Valley of Decision.

'Look out, sir, you was walking straight into that big crater.' Shadbolt shook himself awake. They had passed the overturned limber; in front lay the wounded mammoth, moon-splashed, immovable, and to the left the long stream of traffic on the narrow road rolled endlessly eastward. They trudged on.

Ten days before the end, the battery was in action before Le Quesnoy. Merredew had left to command a battery in the north. The guns were in a little field, sloping down to a stream on the other side of which was a large mill. The only road to the front ran over the bridge past the mill. All day long the columns of men, guns, and transport passed over this bridge, and all day long the enemy shelled it with a high-velocity gun. In the afternoon when the gunners had ceased firing they lay back on the grass and speculated which of the endless teams of horses and mules, limbers and guns would get safely across the bridge. The sappers were working hard at repairs under this steady shell-fire. A gallant party of military police and others were clearing away the dead horses and men that littered the road both sides of the stream. A gun team would come trotting down the hill towards the bridge and 100 yards from it, break into a gallop. 'Hooray! They are safely across. Here come the next lot! Bang! That's got them. No, it hasn't!! as horses and men, less one driver, emerge from the smoke, and gallop up the road into safety the other side. At dusk the enemy ceased fire, and the mill being the only available billet, the men moved into its vast, underground store-room, whilst Shadbolt and the officers occupied an upstairs room, where there were some beds. Soon after midnight that accursed gun began again. Whee-oo! Whoosh! Bang! The shells sailed over the mill-house and crashed on to the road beyond. An argument began between Queenie and the Cherub as to whether a retirement to the cellar would not be sound policy. CRASH! and Shadbolt woke up, soaked to the skin, his bedclothes in ribbons – unhurt! The shell had come through the roof and burst in the attic above, upsetting a bucket of water and ripping a great hole in the ceiling. At this critical moment Mr Prout appeared, dignified and urbane even at that hour. 'Excuse me, sir, but before retiring to rest I deemed it advisable to put the officers' kits in the cellar. I have laid out your valise and placed your flannel trousers and a clean shirt under the pillow.'

The next day they moved forward again and supported the New Zealanders in the assault on Le Quesnoy. The brigade car was the first to enter the town, where the Colonel, to his intense embarrassment, was soundly kissed by a grateful old woman. He was so unnerved that on his return to headquarters he poured himself out a tumblerful of neat gin and started to drink, thinking it was water. His staff watched him with amusement. Expressions of astonishment, anger, defiance, and gratification chased each other in succession across his face as without a word, he emptied the tumbler.

Alone 2XX went forward into the Forest of Mormal. It was here, on the 8th of November, that news was received that Merredew had been killed four days earlier at Moen on the Scheldt.

Very early on the last morning Shadbolt was watching the men dragging the heavy howitzers into a little clearing in the wood. The day was grey and overcast and the raindrops from a recent shower were dripping sadly off the trees. Above them a few pigeons, disturbed by the movements and cries of the men, circled and wheeled. A despatch rider rode up and handed him a message form. 'Hostilities will cease at 11.00am today. AAA. No firing will take place after this hour.' He sat down on the stump of a tree. In any case, the order did not affect them. The enemy was already out of range, and they could move no further.

This, then, was the end. Visions of the early days, their hopes and ambitions, swam before his eyes. He saw again his prehistoric howitzer in the orchard at Festubert, and Alington's long legs moved towards him through the trees. He was back with the Australians in their dug-out below Pozières. He saw the long slope of the hill at Heninel, covered with guns, ammunition dumps, tents and dug-outs. Ypres, the Salient, Trois Tours, St Julien – the names made unforgettable pictures in his mind. Happy days at Beugny and Beaussart, they were gone and the bad ones with them. Hugh was gone, and Tyler and little Rawson; Sergeant Powell, that brave old man; Elliot and James and Johnson – the names of his dead gunners strung themselves before him. This was the very end. What good had it all been? To serve what purpose had they all died? For the moment he could find no answer. His brain was too numb with memories.

'Mr Straker.'

'Sir.'

'You can fall the men out for breakfast. The war is over.'

'Very good, sir.'

Overhead the pigeons circled and wheeled.

Index

Albert, 113–14, 116, 119–22, 124, 191
Ammunition, 17, 19, 29, 31–2, 37, 47–9, 51–2, 68, 72, 94, 116, 123, 125, 127, 134, 161, 163, 165–6, 168, 171, 173, 190–1, 194
Artillery, 1, 3–4, 7, 14, 18–23, 25, 47–8, 50, 54, 59, 64, 69–70, 74, 81, 83, 85–7, 89, 93–5, 97, 99–105, 107, 115, 117, 125, 127, 129, 131, 136, 145, 148, 162–6, 169–70, 173–4, 180, 183–5, 188, 191–2

Battery, 3, 19, 21–2, 30, 47–57, 59, 89, 99, 121–3, 151, 174, 180–1, 187–93
Bomb(s)/bombing, 4, 22, 69, 71, 74, 86–7, 91, 95, 109, 114, 134, 143, 167
Bombardment, 28–9, 33, 51, 53, 74, 76, 78, 89, 97–8, 104, 111, 125, 135, 144, 160, 162

Dardanelles, 37, 42–5, 146
Dug-out(s), 35, 49, 54–5, 62–3, 68, 71–3, 82–3, 86, 88–91, 93–5, 97, 99, 102, 106, 114, 120, 124, 138, 143, 145, 166, 189

England, 17–18, 25, 47, 52, 69, 79, 85, 100, 110, 116, 124, 133, 135, 146, 153, 156, 174
English, 19–20, 26, 31, 41–3, 45–6, 82, 109, 115, 119, 165, 174

Festubert, 47–50, 52, 194
Flanders, 30, 47, 55, 60, 80, 82, 103, 110, 188, 191
Foreign Legion, 37, 39, 179
France, 20, 41, 47–8, 52, 54, 56–7, 74, 76–7, 103, 108–10, 158
Front-line, 26, 34, 63, 109, 119, 161–2

Gallipoli, 37, 42, 76–7
Gas, 28–9, 68–9, 77, 92, 100, 102–4, 112, 114, 117, 140, 147, 179–82, 185–6
German(s), 3, 8–9, 13, 16, 20–2, 25–7, 29–31, 35, 48, 50–6, 68–70, 73, 76, 78–82, 86, 89, 91, 93, 98–9, 101–6, 113–17, 120–3, 125–6, 129–31, 134–6, 144–5, 149, 157, 164–5, 167–8, 173, 179–81, 183–5, 188–92
Germany, 74, 76

Grenade(s), 63, 67–8, 70, 79, 81, 86, 97, 101–103, 124, 127, 130, 163

Infantry, 1, 3, 6, 12, 15–16, 28, 31, 35, 47, 49, 51, 54–5, 59–60, 66, 74, 81, 85, 87, 89, 91, 93–6, 101–3, 105, 114–16, 119–20, 146, 151–2, 158, 169–70, 173, 177, 180–5, 189–90, 192

Kut, 58–60, 64–5

Machine gun, 14, 25–6, 30–1, 34–5, 40, 48, 51–2, 69–74, 79, 81, 85–92, 94, 96, 101, 103–6, 117, 125–6, 129, 134, 141, 158, 162–4, 166–8, 171–6, 181–5, 189
Mud, 24–5, 30, 47, 51, 54, 56, 67, 71, 73, 81, 88, 100, 105–6, 114, 120, 127–8, 130–1, 133–4, 136, 138, 142–4, 147

Passchendaele, 127, 191

Rifle(s), 1, 7, 10, 14, 22, 25–6, 28, 31, 34–5, 37–40, 42, 48–51, 53, 63–4, 67, 70, 77–8, 81–2, 84–5, 87, 90–1, 95, 97, 102–3, 114–18, 124, 126–31, 133–5, 140, 145, 150, 156, 158, 162–4, 166, 171, 173–5, 181

Salonika, 146, 149, 153–4, 157
Sap-Head, 141–2, 144–5
Shelling, 1, 30, 33, 42–3, 45, 51, 54, 73–4, 83–4, 89, 92, 94, 109, 114, 116–17, 121, 124, 136–7, 142, 162, 164, 180–1, 185, 187
Shrapnel, 23, 28, 30–1, 33, 52, 69–70, 86–7, 90, 96, 98, 100–1, 106, 115–16, 122, 130, 172, 175, 181

Tank(s), 86, 169, 179–86, 191–2
Trench(es), 1–2, 15–16, 24–7, 29, 31–5, 38, 44, 46, 50–3, 55–7, 59, 61–71, 73–4, 78–81, 84–5, 87, 89–90, 92–5, 97–8, 100–6, 109, 113–16, 119–22, 124–8, 141–2, 144–5, 152, 160, 164–8, 171–4, 177, 180, 182, 185, 187–90

V Beach, 42–3